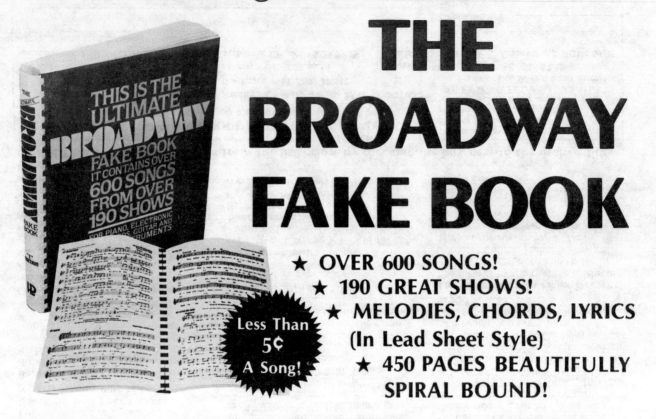

# Has it been years since you've touched a piano?

**Y**ou always promised yourself you would get back to the piano someday. The best way to do just that is to preview the greatest magazine ever played...the masterpiece of a magazine that begins where the old *Etude* left off...the magazine that brings you the complete scores of up to 10 of the world's best-loved classics in every issue.

## A PIANIST'S DELIGHT

KEYBOARD CLASSICS comes to you every other month with the finest compositions in 500 years of musical history. The best Baroque. The most Romantic. The jazziest of Jazz.

You'll play the best music of Scarlatti, Grieg, Liszt, Beethoven, Tchaikovsky, Brahms, Bach, Chopin, Mendelssohn, Schubert, Rachmaninoff, Mozart, Paderewsky, Schumann, Franck and Bizet.

You get the classiest and jazziest of Billy Taylor, Chick Corea, Erik Satie, Aaron Copland, Virgil Thompson, Charles Ives, Ned Rorem, Prokofieff, Stravinsky, Bernstein. You get the fun of Gottschalk, Debussy and P.D.Q. Bach!

## You'll love...
## Keyboard Classics
### THE MAGAZINE YOU CAN PLAY

## ADVICE YOU CAN'T GET ANYWHERE ELSE

Six times a year in KEYBOARD CLASSICS you'll find useful, practical how-to articles by our editors and respected outside experts. For instance: Liszt's Secret Weapon: Gymnastics...How To Bring A Glow To Every Tone...Sight Reading: A KEYBOARD CLASSICS Workshop...The Art Of Fingering...Pedal Technique.

You'll get major advice and musical insights from some of the greatest pianists who have ever lived...The Artistry Of Artur Rubinstein...Franz Liszt On Gypsy Music...John Steinway On Caring For Your Piano...My Lessons With Josef Hoffman...Vladimir Horowitz...Andre Watts...Claudio Arrau...and more!

Since the golden days of *Etude* there hasn't been a magazine for classical pianists, teachers and students, quite like this!

## MONEY BACK IF NOT DELIGHTED

If, after you receive your first issue of *Keyboard Classics,* you are not completely thrilled and delighted, and if you don't agree that it is the *marvelous* musical

## RARE DISCOVERIES

Not only do you get the best-loved pieces of the piano repertoire, but you'll also enjoy many little known gems of the masters...charming duets that two of you can play...rare and undiscovered masterpieces *never before published.* If we find it in an attic in Vienna, you'll find it in Keyboard Classics! (A recent issue has a lovely waltz in a never-before-published arrangement by Victor Borge!)

treat we say it is, simply tell us to cancel your subscription and that will end the matter. We will gladly refund you the subscription price on all unmailed issues. But we know that *if you love the piano, you'll love Keyboard Classics.*

*Save even more.* Subscribe now for two years at a substantial savings of $6.00 off the cover price. It's the best musical bargain you'll ever find!

# WHAT IS A 'FAKE' MUSIC BOOK?

(For Starters, It Has Over 1000 Songs In It!)

**IT'S THE ONE BOOK EVERY MUSICIAN, PROFESSIONAL OR AMATEUR, MUST OWN.**

**IT'S WHAT PRO MUSICIANS CALL THE BIBLE.**

Here are just some of the **1010** songs you get...

I Write The Songs ★ Feelings ★ Alley Cat ★ Ain't Misbehavin'
Deep Purple ★ Paper Roses ★ Tomorrow (from ''Annie'')
Don't It Make My Brown Eyes Blue ★ Moonlight Serenade
Stardust ★ Just The Way You Are ★ We've Only Just Begun
Release Me ★ I Left My Heart In San Francisco ★ It's
Impossible ★ Annie (from ''Annie'') ★ Alice Blue Gown
Charmaine ★ Blue Moon ★ Roses Are Red My Love ★ Don't
Blame Me ★ City of New Orleans ★ Peg O' My Heart ★ Who
Can I Turn To ★ The Star Spangled Banner ★ Bye Bye Love
Make Believe ★ Somewhere My Love ★ Be Honest With Me
Don't Be Cruel ★ Ruby ★ And I Love You So ★ The Shadow
Of Your Smile ★ Over The Rainbow ★ A Bicycle Built For Two
Ebb Tide ★ All Shook Up My Blue Heaven ★ Toot Toot Tootsie
Gimme A Little Kiss ★ Lovely To Look At ★ Sweet and Lovely
The Whiffenpoof Song ★ Laura ★ Nobody Does It Better
The Impossible Dream

It contains every kind of song for every kind of occasion. Hit songs of today such as **Don't It Make My Brown Eyes Blue** . . . great standards like **I'll See You In My Dreams** . . . show tunes like **Tomorrow!** . . . songs of the Roaring 20's such as **Five Foot Two!** . . . Irish songs, folk songs, Italian songs, Hawaiian songs, great classical themes, sacred songs, rock n' roll songs, Christmas songs, movie songs, latin songs, patriotic songs, waltzes, marches, you name it! *It is the one songbook meant to fill every request.*
**CHOCK FULL OF HITS** It has four pounds, almost 500 pages, of *solid music* . . . with all the lyrics, melodies, and chord names. It contains a complete alphabetical listing *plus* a cross-reference listing by song category for the immediate location of any song. It is handsomely spiral bound so that it lies perfectly flat on your music stand, and has a durable leatherette textured cover. It was built to last through years of use.
**A MUSICIAN'S DREAM COME TRUE** Until recently, such books, if you could find them, were sold ''under the table.'' And musicians would pay a great amount. But now we can *legally* bring you what those same musicians are calling the *greatest* fake book of them all . . . **The Legit Professional Fake Book.**
**MONEY BACK GUARANTEE TOO!** If you do not agree that this book is everything we say it is and more . . . if you are not completely thrilled and delighted for any reason whatsoever, simply return it to us within 30 days, (it will take you a *full* 30 days just to get through it!), and we will send you a *complete* refund. When you think of all this music, 1010 great songs, *at less than 3¢ a song*, songs which sell for up to $2.00 each in stores, you realize what a great bargain this book is for just $25. It is a book which you will use and cherish over and over again in years to come, whether it's party time, or Christmas time, or just by yourself time at the piano.
**A GREAT GIFT IDEA!** If you are not a musician yourself, don't you know someone who would really love to have this book? It is truly a gift for all seasons.

**FREE! Mystery Gift**
if you order within 30 days

# If You Read Music...
# You'll Love Our Magazine

Get the New Pocket Music Dictionary Absolutely FREE... Just for Trying Our Magazine!

# The Only Magazine You Can Play!

*We call it SHEET MUSIC MAGAZINE*. And that's exactly what it is! Each and every issue is filled with the most popular sheet music ever published, including *Pop, Great Standards, Jazz, Show Tunes, Folk, Country, Tin Pan Alley, Movie Songs, Classics, Ragtime, Blues,* and more.

When you sit down at your piano, organ, guitar, or any musical instrument, *we want to be your music book!* And when you want to improve your own musical ability, we want our staff of writers to *show you how.* And in every issue they do just that! There are Keyboard Clinics, Guitar Workshops, Composers' Workshops, Sight-reading, Playing By Ear, Theory And Harmony, Rhythm Workshops, and so much, much more.

A single year's subscription brings you dozens and dozens of great songs. And when you consider the price of sheet music these days, about $3.00 per song, and realize that Sheet Music Magazine provides the exact same thing for less than *18¢ a song,* you can understand why it has more subscribers than any other music magazine in the

world today. A one-year subscription for $13.97 brings you over $200 worth of music!

And now you can choose between a *Piano Edition* and an *Organ Edition.* Each edition is specifically arranged for *your* instrument, and includes feature articles of special interest to *you.* Also, you can choose an *easy-to-play* version of the piano edition as well as the organ edition. The *easy-to-play* editions are especially good for you beginners and new students, young or adult, who don't think you are quite ready for the standard and special arrangements found in our stan-

dard editions. (If you are undecided as to which version would be right for you, we suggest you try the *Easy Edition.* You can change at any time, at no cost whatsoever.) Check your preference on the subscription application.

Let us send you your first issue with these wonderful songs .. *After The Lovin'* .. *The Way We Were* .. *Nadia's Theme* .. *If* .. *Mona Lisa* .. *Theme from "The Love Boat"* .. *Didn't We* .. *You'll Never Know* .. *I'll Never Love This Way Again* .. *You've Lost That Lovin' Feeling.*

# KEYBOARD TRICKS OF THE TRADE

## A Sequel To
## "The Do-It-Yourself Handbook
## For Keyboard Playing"

### Compiled & Edited by
Edward J. Shanaphy
Stuart Isacoff

**From the Pages of Sheet Music Magazine and Keyboard Classics Magazine**

### Contributors

Raphael Crystal

Debbie Culbertson

Robert Dumm

Michael Esterowitz

Walter Gieseking & Karl Leimer

Ronald Herder

Bill Horn

Bill Irwin

Stuart Isacoff

Dave Kopp

Mark Laub

Samuel Sanders

Ed Shanaphy

Lou Stein

Paulette Weiss

Anatole Zemlinsky

ISBN # 0-943748-05-4

# Table Of Contents

## CHORDS, THEORY & HARMONY

## KEYBOARD STYLES

# ORGAN TECHNIQUE AND STYLES

# IMPROVISATION

# TECHNIQUE

# RHYTHM

# SPECIAL FEATURES

# Chords, Theory & Harmony

# Guide To Music Notation

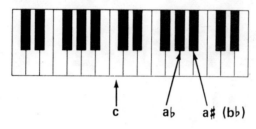

c     ab   a♯ (bb)

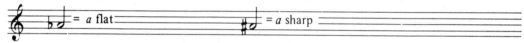

♭ = *a* flat     ♯ = *a* sharp

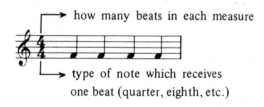

how many beats in each measure

type of note which receives
one beat (quarter, eighth, etc.)

| Name | Rest Symbol | Note Value |
|---|---|---|
| Whole | | |
| Half | | |
| Quarter | | |
| Eighth | | |
| Sixteenth | | |
| Thirty-second | | |
| Sixty-fourth | | |

A note with a dot next to it has its normal duration increased by half again its value.

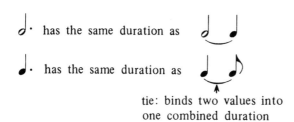

tie: binds two values into
one combined duration

Repeat the material enclosed by these signs:

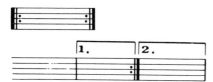

After playing the first ending, go to the beginning;
the second time around use ending number two.

phrase mark divides music into phrases

Stress Marks

Dynamics

**pp**    very softly

**p**    softly

**mp**    moderately soft

**mf**    moderately loud

**f**    loud

**ff**    very loud

crescendo

decrescendo

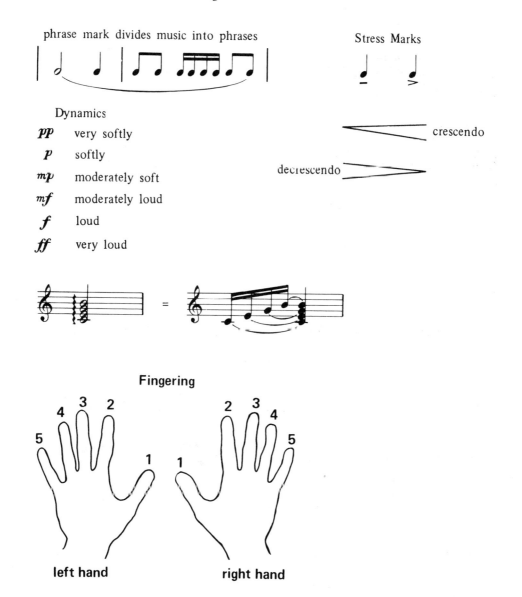

**Fingering**

**left hand**    **right hand**

# Harmony at the Keyboard

## Defining Our Terms

With this issue we begin a new series of articles dealing with keyboard harmony. We will be discussing subjects like playing by ear, harmonizing a melody, transposition, modulation, and so on.

But first it seems like a good idea to define some basic terms, and in the process review some fundamental concepts. This article will serve as an introduction to those that follow.

**MELODY.** A melody is a succession of individual notes with a definite rhythm. A melody is something you can hum or sing, and in a popular song it usually has words. Here is the melody of the first four bars of *Yankee Doodle*.

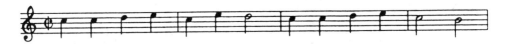

**KEY.** A melody is played or sung in a specific key. Our previous example showed *Yankee Doodle* in the key of C major. This means that the melody makes use, primarily, of the notes of the C major scale. Also, the melody usually begins, and almost always ends, on the first note of the scale.

A given melody can be played in any key. Our next example shows the scale of G major (a), and the first four bars of *Yankee Doodle* in the key of G major (b).

**KEY SIGNATURE.** When *Yankee Doodle* moved to the key of G major an F sharp was required. In every major key except for C one or more accidentals (i.e. flats or sharps) are necessary. The key signature lists the accidentals that are used in a particular key. Here are the signatures for the most common major keys.

**HARMONY.** Of course a melody is usually not heard by itself. It is ordinarily accompanied by other notes, creating a fuller, more satisfying sound. The combining of notes is known as **har-mony,** and when we speak of harmonizing a melody we mean the addition of these accompanying tones. This is a harmonized version of the next four bars of *Yankee Doodle.*

**CHORDS.** Just as a melody is made up of individual notes, the harmony is composed of individual chords. A chord is a group of notes played (or sung) simultaneously. In our previous example the melody and accompanying chords were intermingled. But we can simplify the arrangement so that the chords appear in the left hand, while the right hand plays only the melody.

**CHORD SYMBOLS.** Notice that we labelled the chords in the previous example with a series of symbols: C, F, G7, and C. The letters indicate the notes upon which the chords are built; they are referred to as the "roots" of the chords. When the letter stands alone a "major" chord is meant. The numeral "7" indicates a "dominant seventh" chord.

Our next example shows the most commonly used chords in the key of C major, together with their symbols. C and F are major chords. D, E, and A are minor chords, indicated by the lower case "m". G is a dominant seventh chord. (The chord on the seventh note of the scale, B, is rarely used.)

If you play through our last example several times you will begin to hear that each type of chord — major, minor, or dominant seventh — has a distinctive sound. In a later column we will explain exactly how these chords are constructed. We will also deal with more complicated chords.

What is the final goal of these articles? We hope they will enable you to vary and improvise on existing sheet music, invent your own arrangements, play fluently in many keys, and find your way around the keyboard with ease and grace. ♩  **RC**

# Harmony at the Keyboard

## Constructing Simple Chords

A chord is a group of notes played or sung simultaneously. In popular music the chords are usually represented by symbols that appear over the vocal line. If the pianist wants to vary the written keyboard part, or make up a completely new one, he or she will use those symbols as a basis. Here are the melody and chord symbols for the first four bars of "The Twelve Days of Christmas."

The letters refer to the chord "roots," the notes on which the chords will be constructed. Ordinarily those notes appear at the bottoms of the chords, so the bass part will look something like this:

Above those roots the chords are built up in "thirds." A third is an interval that spans three letter names. For example, the interval C-E is a third because it includes the letter names C, D, and E.

There are two kinds of thirds: major and minor. They can be defined in terms of the "half-step" —the distance between two adjacent notes on the piano. The major third consists of four half-steps and the minor third consists of three. C-E is a major third, since it includes the half-steps C-C#, C#-D, D-D#, and D#-E. The minor third D-F consists of the half-steps D-D#, D#-E, and E-F.

Let us look back at the chord symbols for "The Twelve Days of Christmas." The first chord is represented by the letter "C". When a chord symbol consists only of a letter name, a "major" chord is indicated. The major chord is made up of a major third and, above that, a minor third; thus, the C major chord includes the intervals C-E (major third, four half-steps) and E-G (minor third, three half-steps).

The abbreviation "min" after a chord root, or simply a lower-case "m", stands for a "minor" chord. Here the lower interval is a minor third, and the upper is a major third; thus, the A minor chord includes the intervals A-C (minor third) and C-E (major third).

The numeral "7" after a chord root stands for a "dominant seventh" chord. This is a four-note structure, consisting of a major third, a minor third, and then another minor third. The G7 chord is made up of the intervals G-B (major third), B-D (minor third), and D-F (minor third).

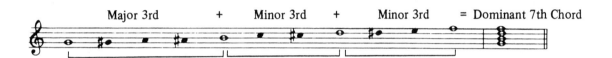

With these chord-types in mind we can now translate the chord symbols of "The Twelve Days of Christmas" into notes. Let us put the chords in the left hand, underneath the melody.

This represents the simplest kind of chordal accompaniment; however, the same chord structures can be arranged in much more interesting, musically sophisticated forms.

If you would like to gain facility in constructing chords, try building major and minor thirds on all twelve tones of the chromatic scale. Then go on to construct major, minor, and dominant seventh chords on each tone. Do this on paper and also at the keyboard. At first you will have to laboriously count out the half-steps—four to a major third, three to a minor third—but soon you will become familiar with these intervals and you will be able to pick them out immediately. Eventually the chords themselves will become second nature to you.

RC

# Harmony at the Keyboard

## The Three Primary Chords

How do you go about harmonizing a melody? It helps to know that in any key there are three chords that are especially important. Those are the chords built on the first, fourth, and fifth notes of the scale. Our first example shows the scale of C major. The roots of the three primary chords — which we have labeled I, IV, and V — and C, F, and G.

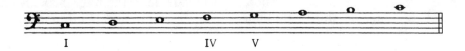

In major keys the chords built on I and IV are major chords. The chord on V can be either major or a dominant seventh. The next example shows the three primary chords in C major: C major, F major, and G7.

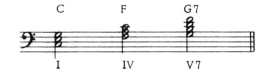

Those three chords will suffice for the harmonization of many simple tunes. In many others they serve as the backbone of the harmony. Let us look at the first four bars of the traditional student song *Gaudeamus Igitur,* in C major. Play through this melody and try to imagine how you might harmonize it using the C, F, and G7 chords.

It isn't possible to lay down hard and fast rules for harmonizing a melody. In the last analysis your ear must be your guide. But ordinarily the main notes of the tune will be present in the chords that accompany them. For example, in the first bar we find the notes C and G. These notes are both present in the C major chord. In the second bar we find the note A; of our three primary chords that note is present only in the F major chord. In the third bar the important notes are B and D (the C functions as a "passing tone" between them). Those two notes are present in the G7 chord. Finally, in the fourth bar we encounter the notes C and E, which form part of the C major chord. This completes our harmonization of these four bars. We will put the chords into the left-hand part.

Another way of arranging this passage would be to play only chord roots with the left hand, and put the chord tones into the right, underneath the melody. (Notice that in the first bar the C and G are already present in the melody, so only the E must be added to complete the chord. In the third bar the B and D are present, so only the F and G must be added.)

14

Because the I, IV, and V7 chords are so important, it is very worthwhile to become familiar with their positions on the keyboard. Our final example shows three basic forms of the I-IV-V7-I progression, with chord tones in the right hand and roots in the left. If you practice this exercise in all major keys you will be taking an important first step in developing the ability to harmonize melodies at the keyboard.

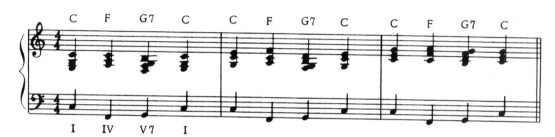

**RC**

# Harmony at the Keyboard

## Harmonizing A Melody

In the previous issue we began to discuss the harmonization of melodies. We saw that in any key there are three primary chords, built on the first, fourth, and fifth notes of the scale. In a major key I and IV are major, while V may be major or a dominant seventh.

Let us work out the harmonization for the familiar tune *Auld Lang Syne* in the key of F major.

In the key of F major the three primary chords are F, B flat, and C7. All three of these are needed in the first four bars of the tune. In the first bar the notes F and A suggest an F chord. And, in fact, the "I" chord is usually present at the beginning of a melody. In the second bar the main note is G, which forms part of the C7 chord. In the third bar the melody spells out the F chord. And the D in bar four is part of the B—flat chord.

The second half of the tune is a bit more problematical. In bar five the melody spells out an F chord. Bar six is the same as the second bar, and C7 is again a good harmonization. The last three notes of the tune, beginning with the second half of bar seven, suggest the progression B flat-C7-F. But what harmony is right for the first half of the seventh bar?

Let us consider the alternatives. The F at the beginning of bar seven could, of course, be accompanied by an F-major chord ("a" in our next example). But this seems a little dull, and we really don't want to arrive at the F major until the eighth bar. The note F also forms part of the B-flat major chord (b), but it would be better to reserve this chord for the second half of bar seven. So we must look beyond the primary chords. The note F is also part of the D-minor chord (c), and if you try this harmony in the seventh bar, you will find that it sounds just right.

Now we can complete the harmonization of the second half of *Auld Lang Syne*, with a D-minor chord in the seventh bar. This chord is built on the sixth note of the scale. Because it is a minor chord it introduces a new, interesting sound. Another improvement would be to use an inversion of the F chord, with A in the bass, at the start of bar five.

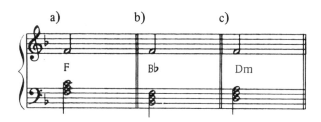

There is a system to be followed here. Begin the harmonization of a tune with the expectation that the three primary chords will play an important part. The tune often starts with the "I" chord, and almost always ends with it. When you come to a problem spot, try various chords that contain the main melody note. Once you hit on the best solution you will usually know immediately: your ear will tell you that it is right.

**RC**

# basic training

## Variations on a Triad: Suspended 4ths and Added 6ths

In early classical music, a triad was often made more colorful by delaying the arrival of one of its notes — usually the 3rd of the chord — in this way:

In this example, we do not hear the complete F major triad (F-A-C) until the "suspended" B finally resolves downward to the A.

Jazz harmony adapted this suspension to its own purposes, simply by keeping the suspended B and ignoring the resolution note A. The result is a "chord of the suspended 4th" or, in jazz shorthand, "F^sus 4" ("4" refers to the interval between the root of the triad and the suspended note):

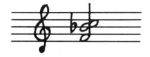

All "sus 4" chords have the same construction: a root, and both a perfect 4th and perfect 5th above the root.

Since the absent 3rd would have given the chord its major or minor feeling, the "sus 4" chord is neither major nor minor; it is simply a colorful, mildly dissonant variation of the "normal" triad.

The chart below contains all "sus 4" chords:

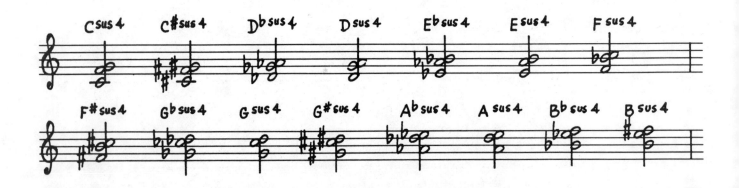

The "chord of the added 6th," or "6th chord," is a triad with a 6th added above the root. The 6th is always a *major* 6th unless otherwise marked. The notation " 6" or "-6" indicates the addition of a *minor* 6th above the root.

The chart below contains all 6th chords commonly found in sheet music. Chords in parentheses are "enharmonic" spellings: that is, they sound the same as the previous chord but are notated differently.

RH ♩

# Harmony at the Keyboard

## Constructing Seventh Chords

Now we will go on to build chords consisting of four notes. These are called "seventh chords" because there is an interval of a seventh between the lowest and highest notes.

Seventh chords are a basic staple in popular music. Our first example shows the melody and chord symbols for the first four bars of Stephen Foster's "Old Folks at Home." Notice that four different kinds of seventh chords are called for.

As you will recall, chords are built up in thirds, and there are two kinds of thirds—major and minor. The major third consists of four half-steps (the half-step is the smallest interval on the piano) and the minor third consists of three.

The second chord in "Old Folks at Home" is a "minor seventh" chord, symbolized as "min7" or simply "m7" (with a lowercase "m"). This chord consists of a minor triad (made up of a minor third and a major third) and, on top of that, another minor third. Thus the Gmin7 chord includes the notes G, B flat, D, and F.

When the numeral "7" stands alone after a chord root, a "dominant seventh" chord is indicated. This consists of a major triad (major third and minor third) and, above that, a minor third. Thus the C7 chord is made up of the notes C, E, G, and B flat.

The symbol "maj7" stands for a "major seventh" chord, consisting of a major triad (major third and minor third) and, on top of that, a major third. The Fmaj7 chord includes the notes F, A, C, and E.

Finally, the symbol "dim7" stands for a "diminished seventh" chord. (The symbol "07" is sometimes used instead.) This chord is a bit different from the seventh chords we have encountered so far, because it is not built on a major or minor triad. Rather, it consists of three superposed minor thirds, and it has a slightly dissonant sound. The F sharp dim7 chord is made up of the notes F sharp, A, C, and E flat.

min. 3rd + min. 3rd + min. 3rd = diminished seventh chord

We can now construct all the chords for the first four bars of "Old Folks at Home." (The symbol "C/G" in the third bar stands for a C chord with a G in the bass; this is an example of inversion.

Our previous example is not a very satisfactory arrangement, even though all the chords are correct. This is because the chords are in too low a register, where they tend to sound muddy. A more euphonious solution would be to put the chord tones into the right hand and play only the bass notes with the left. The notes of the chords are exactly the same; they have simply been shifted to a higher position on the keyboard.

**RC**

# basic training

## A Chart of 7th Chords

The chart on these two pages contains eight types of 7th chords, in all keys.

These include *the major 7th; the major 7th with a raised 5th (+5); the dominant 7th; the dominant 7th with a flatted 5th (-5); the minor 7th; the minor/major 7th; the half-diminished 7th;* and *the diminished 7th,* sometimes renotated for easier reading.

Although a few seldom-found chords are included, the chart omits chords that are either very rare or unusually awkward in notation.

Below each chord type is a breakdown of its intervals, *always calculated above the root.* The dominant 7th, for instance, contains a root, major 3rd (M3) above the root, a perfect 5th (P5) above the root, and a minor 7th (m7) above the root.

| NAME: | MAJ 7th | MAJ 7th +5 | DOM 7th | DOM 7th -5 | MIN 7th | MIN/MAJ 7th | HALF-DIM 7th | DIM 7th | (alternate notation) |
|---|---|---|---|---|---|---|---|---|---|
| 7th: | M7 | M7 | m7 | m7 | m7 | M7 | m7 | dim 7 | |
| 5th: | P5 | aug 5 | P5 | dim 5 | P5 | P5 | dim 5 | dim 5 | |
| 3rd: | M3 | M3 | M3 | M3 | m3 | m3 | m3 | m3 | |
| Root: | root | root | root | root | root | root | root | root | |

cmaj 7 · cmaj 7(+5) · c7 · c7(−5) · Cm7 · Cmmaj 7 · cø7 · c°7

c#maj 7 · c#maj 7(+5) · c#7 · c#7(−5) · C#m7 · C#mmaj 7 · C#ø7 · c#°7

Dbmaj 7 · Dbmaj 7(+5) · Db7 · Db7(−5) · Dbm7 · Dbmmaj 7 · Dbø7 · Db°7

Dmaj 7 · Dmaj 7(+5) · D7 · D7(−5) · Dm7 · Dmmaj 7 · Dø7 · D°7

Ebmaj 7 · Ebmaj 7(+5) · Eb7 · Eb7(−5) · Ebm7 · Ebmmaj 7 · Ebø7 · Eb°7

Emaj 7 · Emaj 7(+5) · E7 · E7(−5) · Em7 · Emmaj 7 · Eø7 · E°7

Fmaj 7 · Fmaj 7(+5) · F7 · F7(−5) · Fm7 · Fmmaj 7 · Fø7 · F°7

22

# basic training
## A Dictionary of 9th Chords

The eight kinds of 9th chords listed in this chart are identified and analyzed as extensions of the various 7th chords discussed in previous Basic Training articles. In each case, they consist of either a major or minor 3rd added above the basic 7th chord. In addition, the chart lists all of the intervals contained in each kind of 9th chord, calculated from the root of the chord.

1. *Dominant 7th chord + major 9th:* The most widely used 9th chord. Mildly dissonant. Used as rich substitute for any Dominant 7ths.

2. *Dominant 7th chord + minor 9th:* Useful and colorful, but infrequently found in sheet music. Interesting substitute for Dominant 7th or for Diminished 7th chord (the 9th chord minus its root).

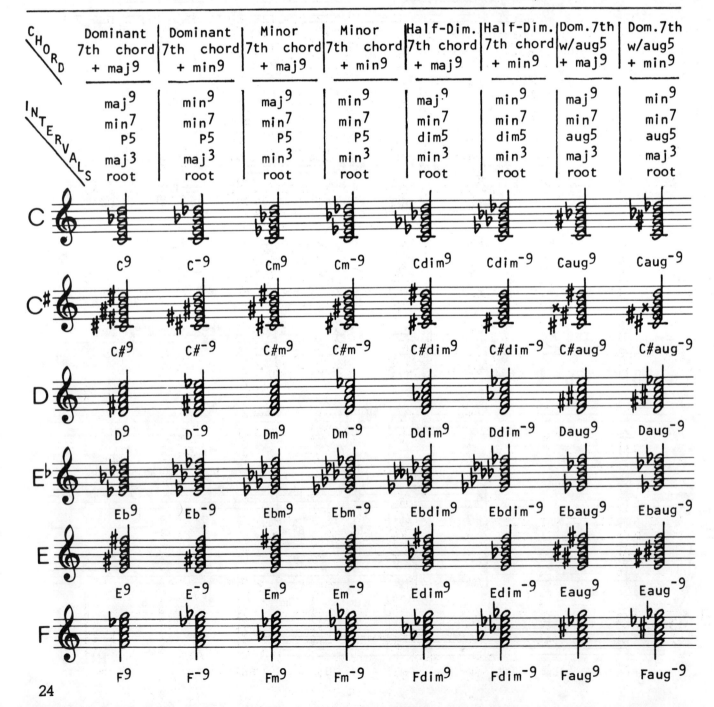

| CHORD | Dominant 7th chord + maj9 | Dominant 7th chord + min9 | Minor 7th chord + maj9 | Minor 7th chord + min9 | Half-Dim. 7th chord + maj9 | Half-Dim. 7th chord + min9 | Dom.7th w/aug5 + maj9 | Dom.7th w/aug5 + min9 |
|---|---|---|---|---|---|---|---|---|
| INTERVALS | maj9 | min9 | maj9 | min9 | maj9 | min9 | maj9 | min9 |
| | min7 | min7 | min7 | min7 | min7 | min7 | min7 | min7 |
| | P5 | P5 | P5 | P5 | dim5 | dim5 | aug5 | aug5 |
| | maj3 | maj3 | min3 | min3 | min3 | min3 | maj3 | maj3 |
| | root | root | root | root | root | root | root | root |
| C | c9 | c−9 | Cm9 | Cm−9 | Cdim9 | Cdim−9 | Caug9 | Caug−9 |
| C# | C#9 | C#−9 | C#m9 | C#m−9 | C#dim9 | C#dim−9 | C#aug9 | C#aug−9 |
| D | D9 | D−9 | Dm9 | Dm−9 | Ddim9 | Ddim−9 | Daug9 | Daug−9 |
| Eb | Eb9 | Eb−9 | Ebm9 | Ebm−9 | Ebdim9 | Ebdim−9 | Ebaug9 | Ebaug−9 |
| E | E9 | E−9 | Em9 | Em−9 | Edim9 | Edim−9 | Eaug9 | Eaug−9 |
| F | F9 | F−9 | Fm9 | Fm−9 | Fdim9 | Fdim−9 | Faug9 | Faug−9 |

3. *Minor 7th chord + major 9th:* Lush harmony. Good substitute for Minor 7th chord, occasionally for Major 7th chord (the 9th chord minus its root).

4. *Minor 7th chord + minor 9th:* An intriguing color, especially in the Blues, as substitute for the Minor 7th chord.

5. *Half-Diminished 7th chord + major 9th:* Rare and interesting dissonance. A substitute for any Half-Diminished 7th chord where added harmonic "bite" is appropriate.

6. *Half-Diminished 7th chord + minor 9th:* Good substitute for the plain Half-Diminished 7th chord, especially where the minor 9th fits a more blues-y mood.

7. *Dominant 7th chord with augmented 5th + major 9th:* Despite its complicated label, this chord is nothing more than an augmented triad with an added minor 7th and major 9th. It is very rare, and best used with discretion because of its exotic quality.

8. *Dominant 7th chord with augment 5th + minor 9th:* Another chord built on an augmented triad, with an added minor 7th and a *minor* 9th. An intense dissonance, best used sparingly for special effect.

RH 𝅘𝅥

# Encyclopedia of Keyboard Chords

# Chord Chart

| Root | TRIADS |  |  | SEVENTHS |  |  |  | SIXTHS |  | NINTHS |
|---|---|---|---|---|---|---|---|---|---|---|
|  | Major | Minor | Augmented | Dominant | Minor | Major | Diminished | Major | Minor | Dominant |
| C | C | Cm | C+ | C7 | Cm7 | Cma7 | Cdim7 | C6 | Cm6 | C9 |
| C♯ | C♯ | C♯m | C♯+ | C♯7 | C♯m7 | C♯ma7 | C♯dim7 | C♯6 | C♯m6 | C♯9 |
| D♭ | D♭ | D♭m | D♭+ | D♭7 | D♭m7 | D♭ma7 | D♭dim7 | D♭6 | D♭m6 | D♭9 |
| D | D | Dm | D+ | D7 | Dm7 | Dma7 | Ddim7 | D6 | Dm6 | D9 |
| E♭ | E♭ | E♭m | E♭+ | E♭7 | E♭m7 | E♭ma7 | E♭dim7 | E♭6 | E♭m6 | E♭9 |
| E | E | Em | E+ | E7 | Em7 | Ema7 | Edim7 | E6 | Em6 | E9 |
| F | F | Fm | F+ | F7 | Fm7 | Fma7 | Fdim7 | F6 | Fm6 | F9 |
| F♯ | F♯ | F♯m | F♯+ | F♯7 | F♯m7 | F♯ma7 | F♯dim7 | F♯6 | F♯m6 | F♯9 |
| G | G | Gm | G+ | G7 | Gm7 | Gma7 | Gdim7 | G6 | Gm6 | G9 |
| A♭ | A♭ | A♭m | A♭+ | A♭7 | A♭m7 | A♭ma7 | A♭dim7 | A♭6 | A♭m6 | A♭9 |
| A | A | Am | A+ | A7 | Am7 | Ama7 | Adim7 | A6 | Am6 | A9 |
| B♭ | B♭ | B♭m | B♭+ | B♭7 | B♭m7 | B♭ma7 | B♭dim7 | B♭6 | B♭m6 | B♭9 |
| B | B | Bm | B+ | B7 | Bm7 | Bma7 | Bdim7 | B6 | Bm6 | B9 |

# Chord Roots

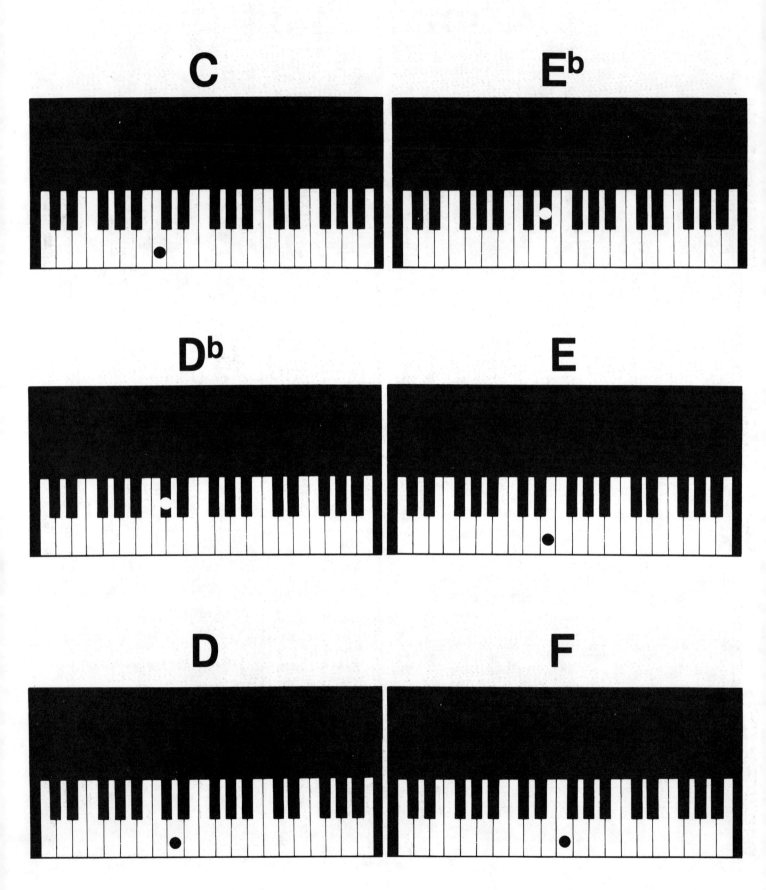

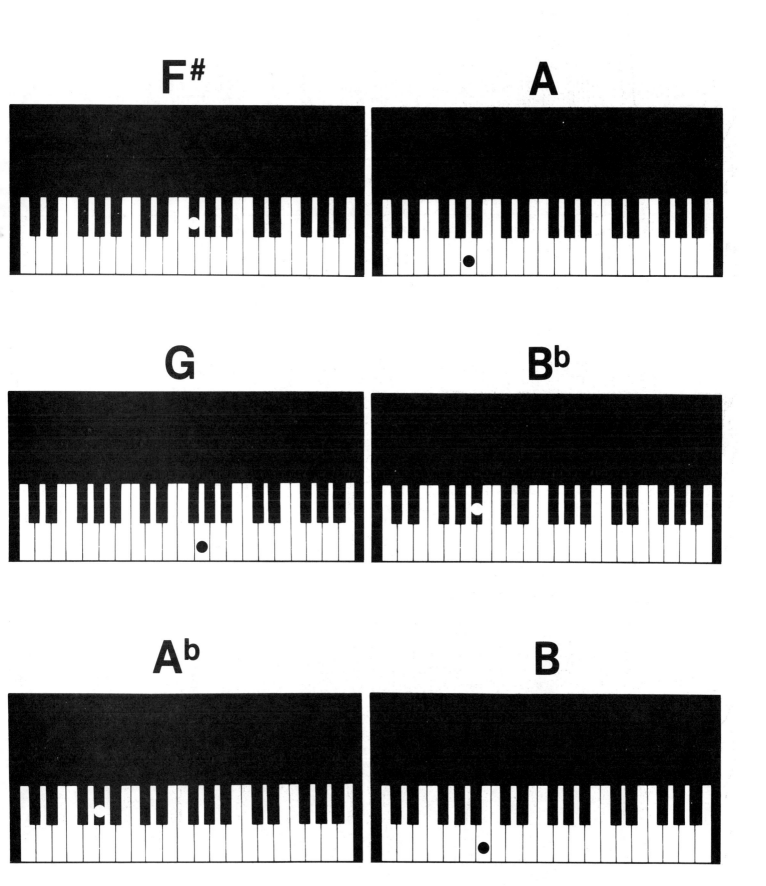

# Major Chords

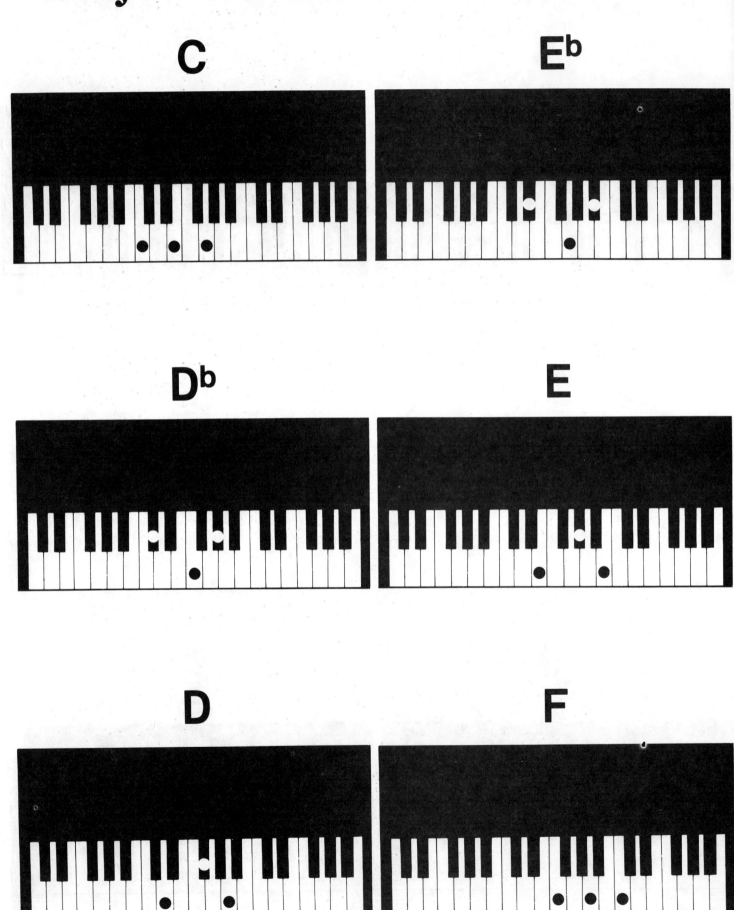

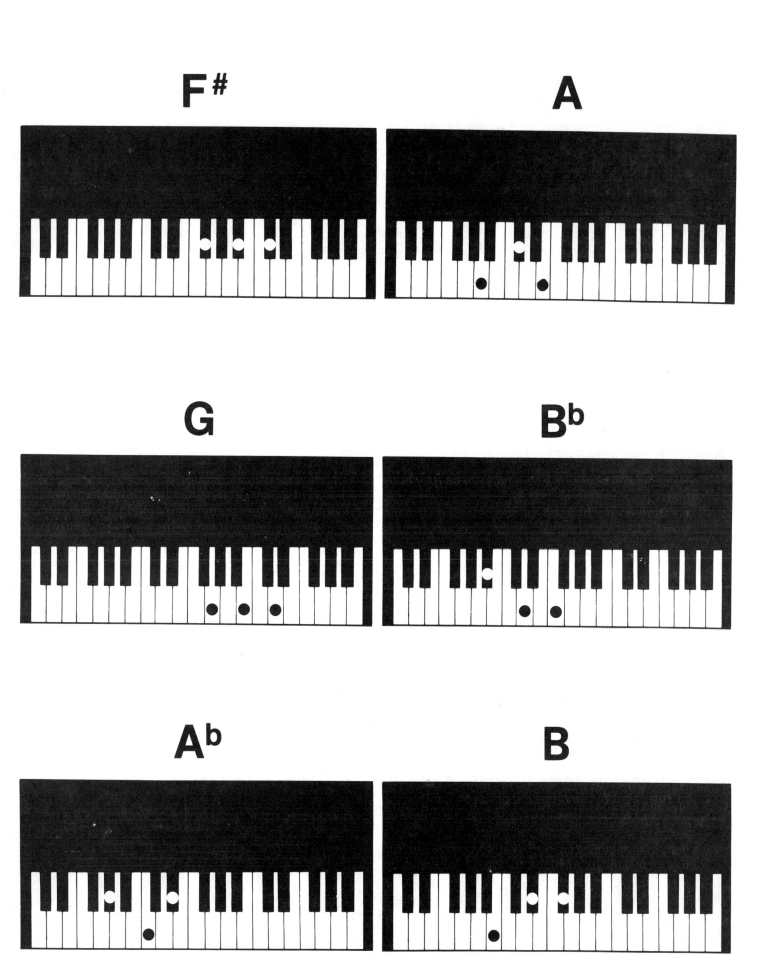

F#

A

G

Bb

Ab

B

31

# Minor Chords

## Cm
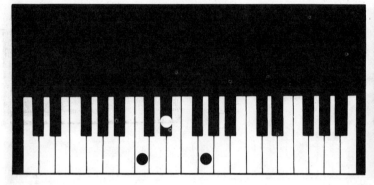

## E♭m
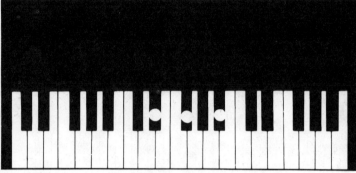

## D♭m
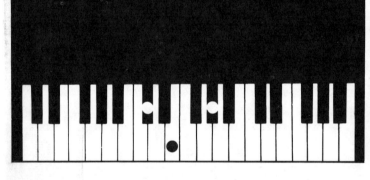

## Em
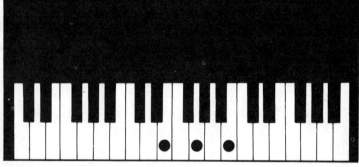

## Dm
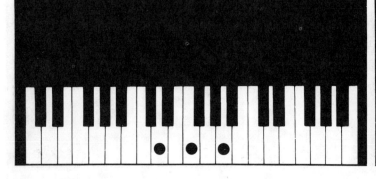

## Fm
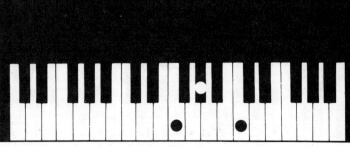

# F#m

# Am

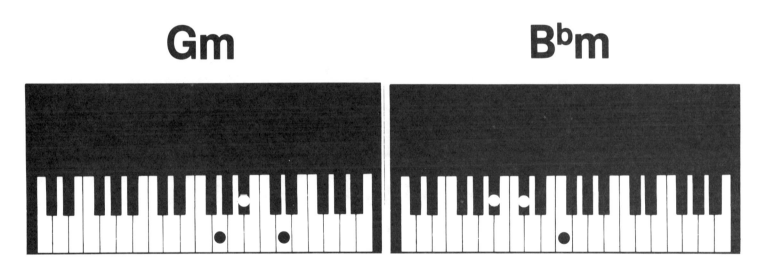

# Gm

# B♭m

# A♭m

# Bm

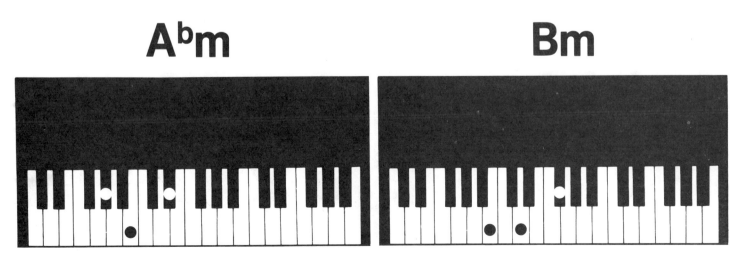

# Suspended Chords

## Csus

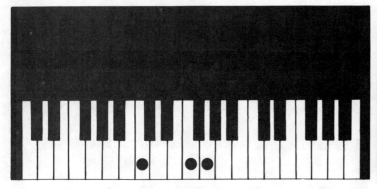

## E♭sus

## D♭sus

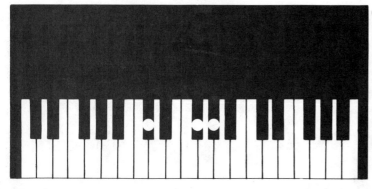

## Esus

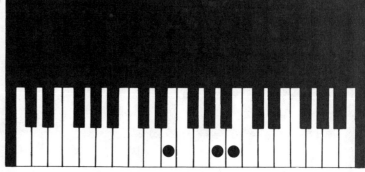

## Dsus

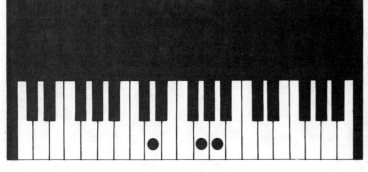

## Fsus

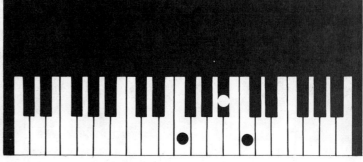

34

# F#sus

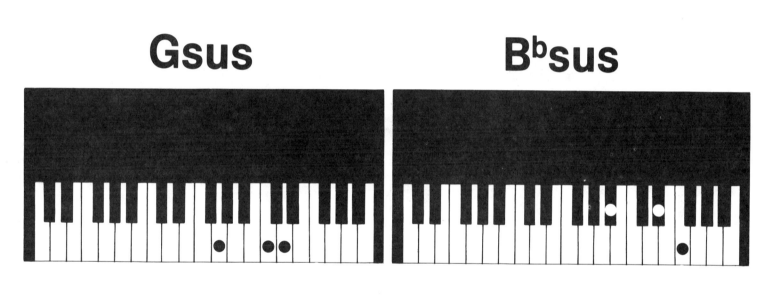

# Asus

# Gsus

# B♭sus

# A♭sus

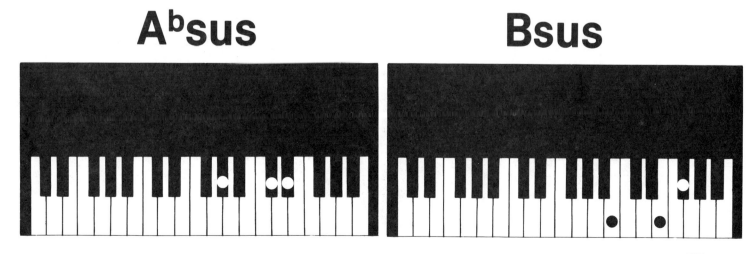

# Bsus

# Diminished Chords

## Cdim

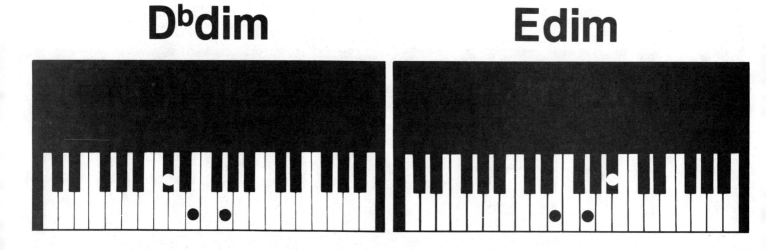

## E♭dim

## D♭dim

## Edim

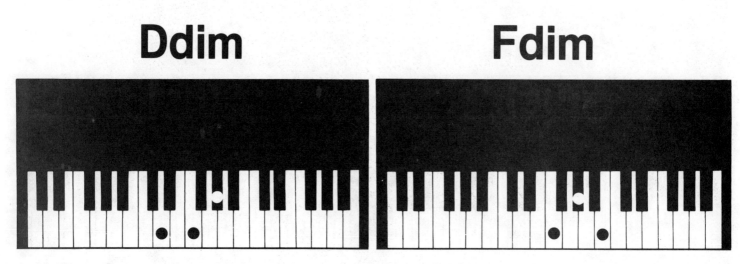

## Ddim

## Fdim

# F#dim

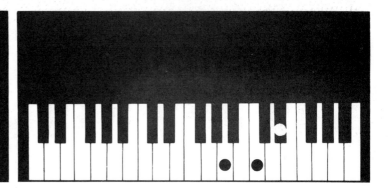

# Adim

# Gdim

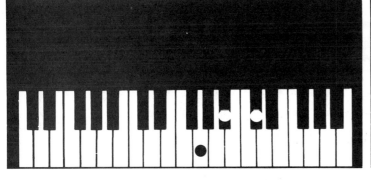

# Bbdim

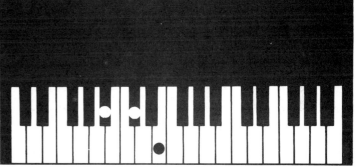

# Abdim

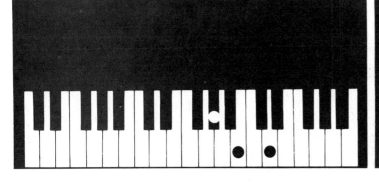

# Bdim

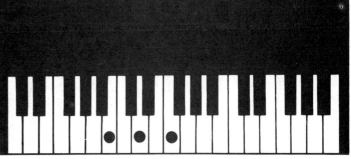

# Augmented Chords

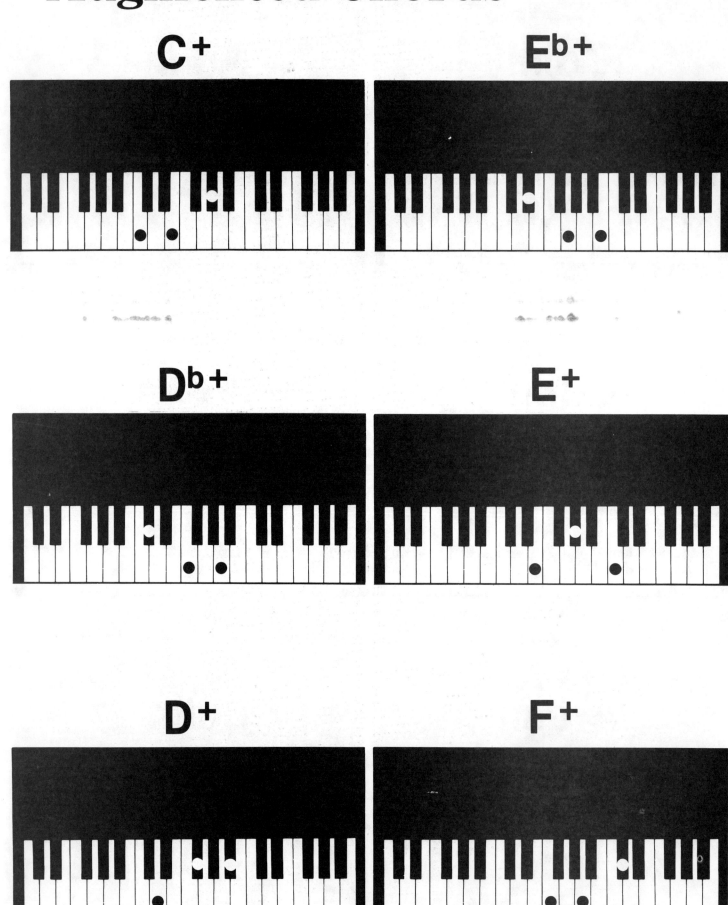

C+

E♭+

D♭+

E+

D+

F+

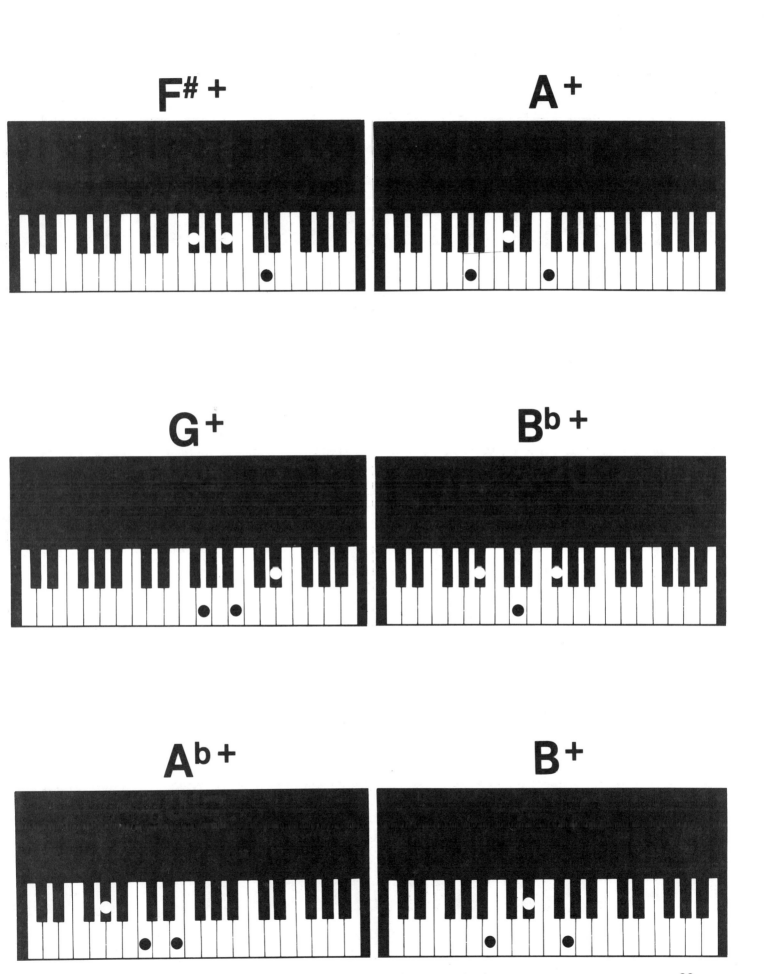

39

# Sixth Chords

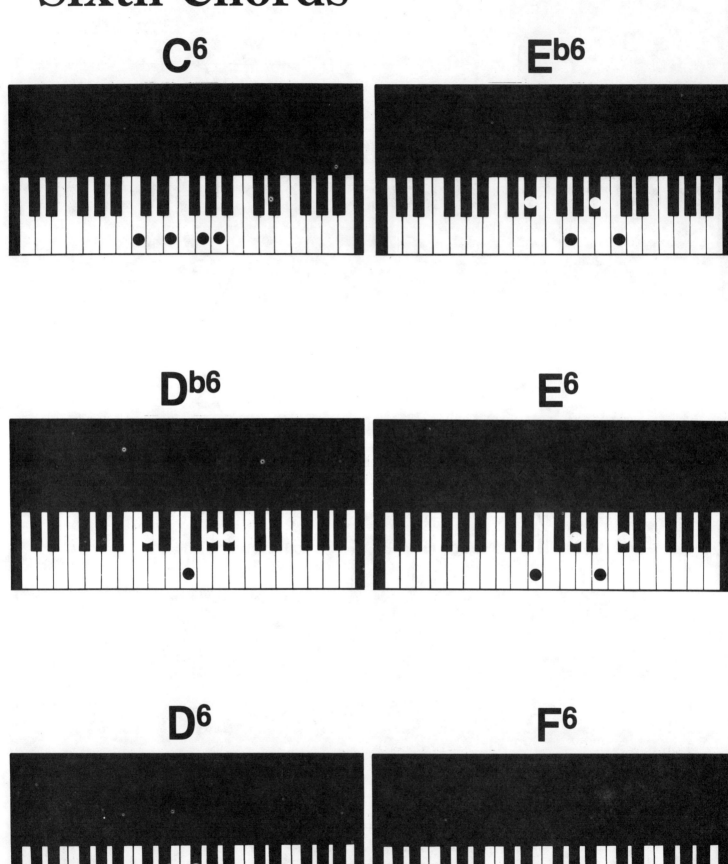

C⁶

Eᵇ⁶

Dᵇ⁶

E⁶

D⁶

F⁶

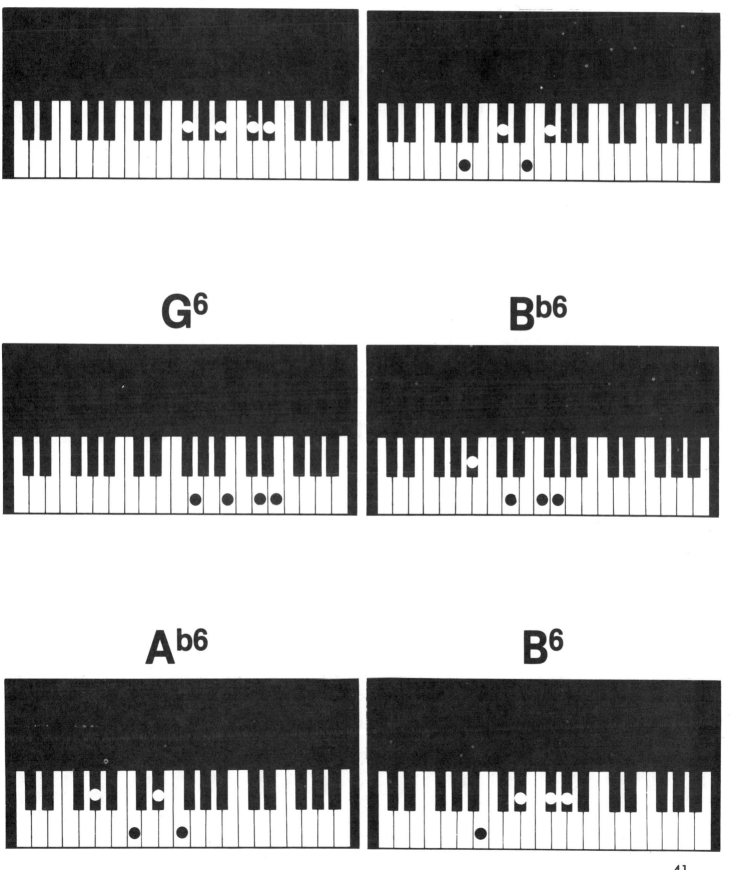

# Minor Sixth Chords

## Cm⁶

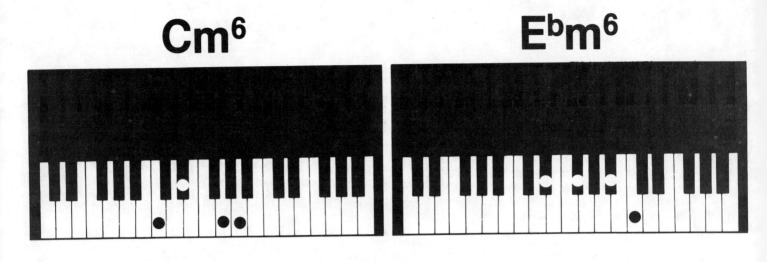

## E♭m⁶

## D♭m⁶

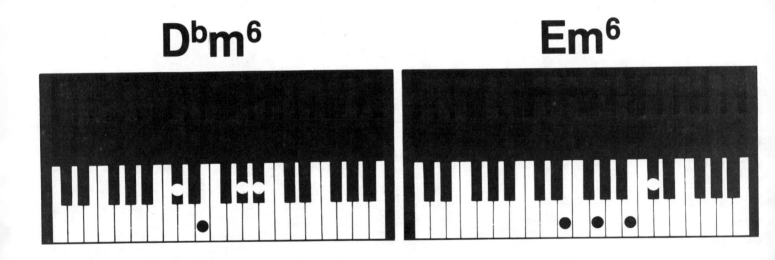

## Em⁶

## Dm⁶

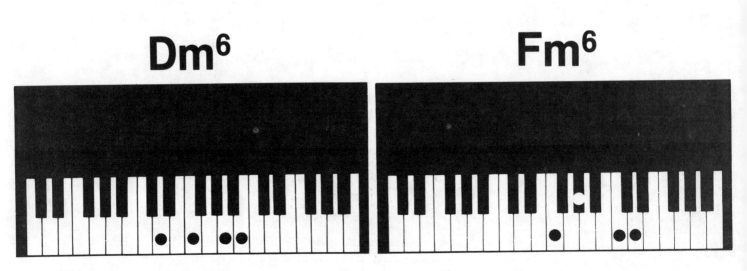

## Fm⁶

## F#m⁶

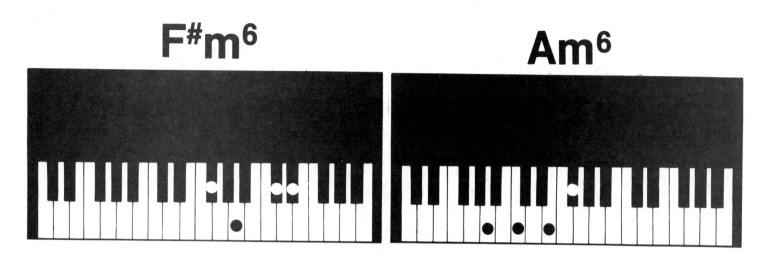

## Am⁶

## Gm⁶

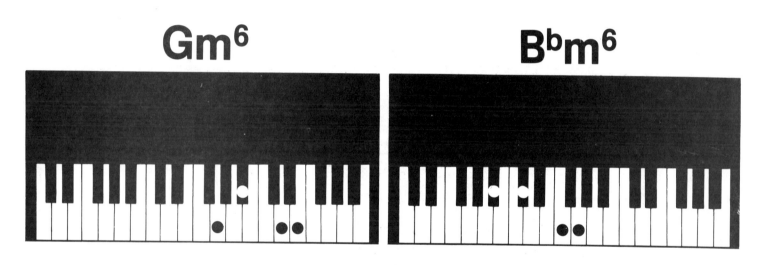

## B♭m⁶

## A♭m⁶

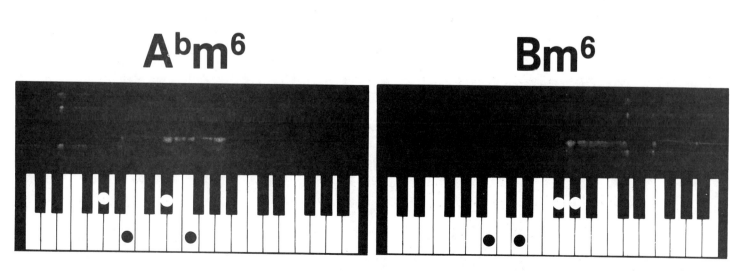

## Bm⁶

# Major Seventh Chords

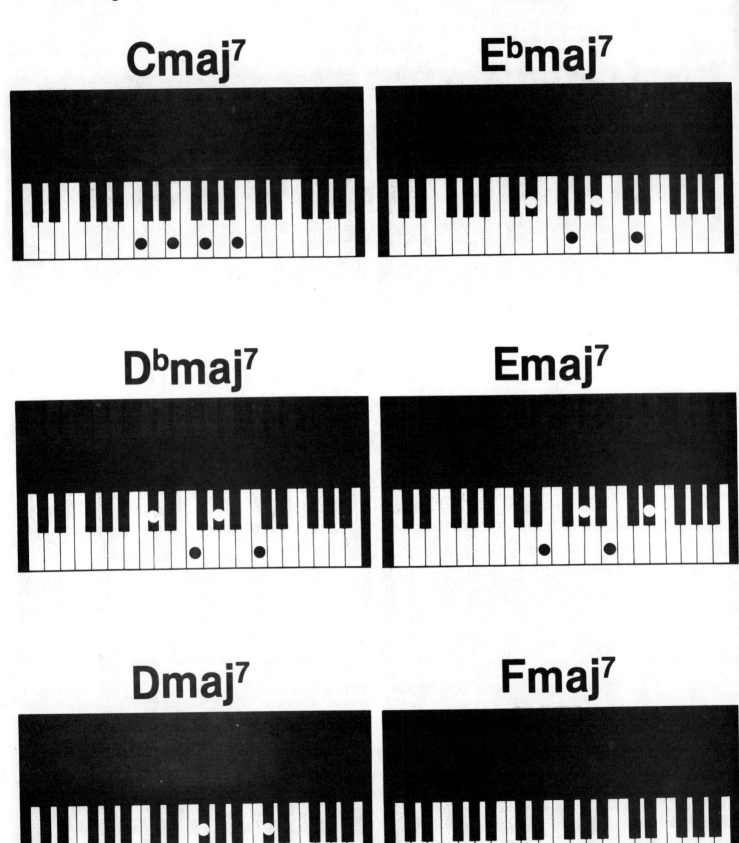

**Cmaj⁷**

**Eᵇmaj⁷**

**Dᵇmaj⁷**

**Emaj⁷**

**Dmaj⁷**

**Fmaj⁷**

# F#maj⁷

# Amaj⁷

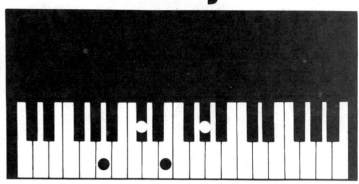

# Gmaj⁷

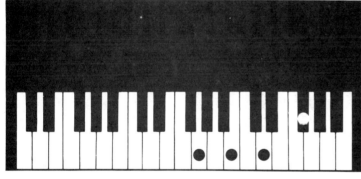

# B♭maj⁷

# A♭maj⁷

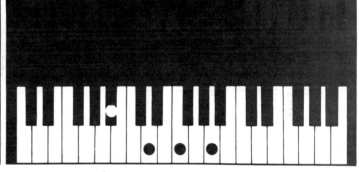

# Bmaj⁷

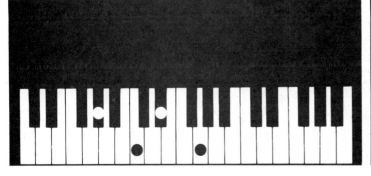

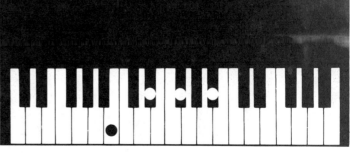

# Dominant Seventh Chords

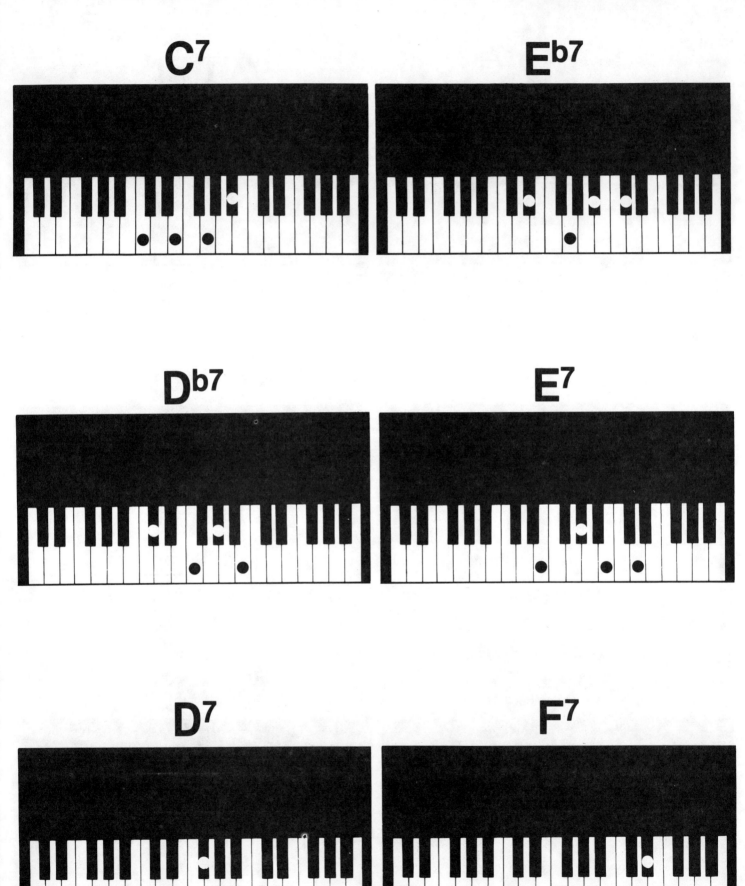

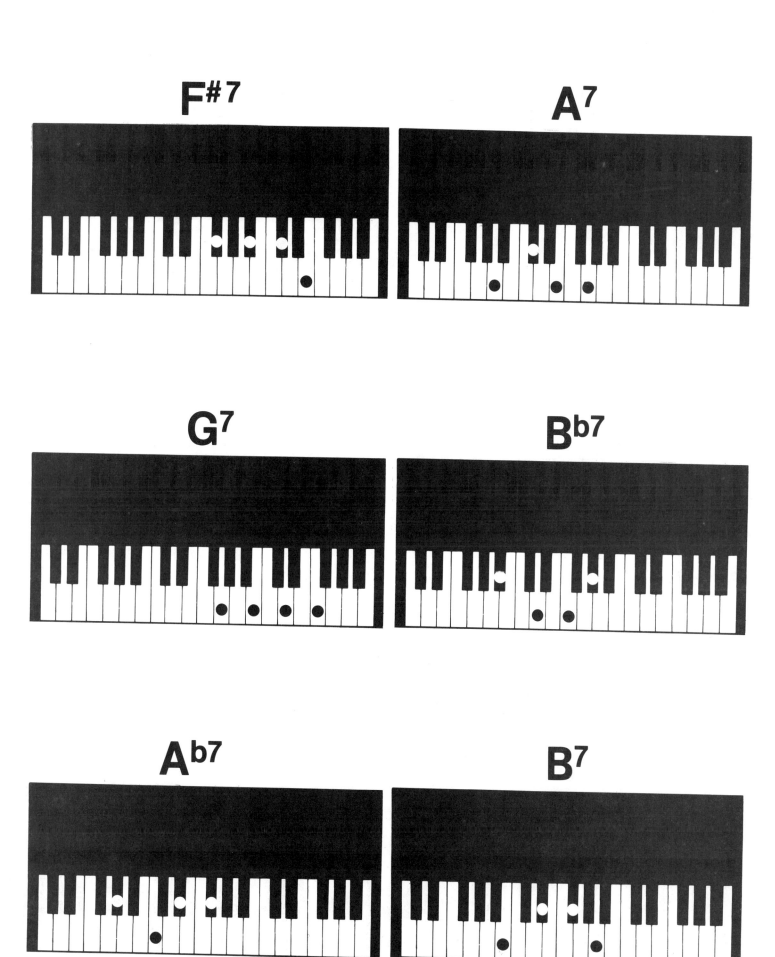

47

# Minor Seventh Chords

## Cm⁷

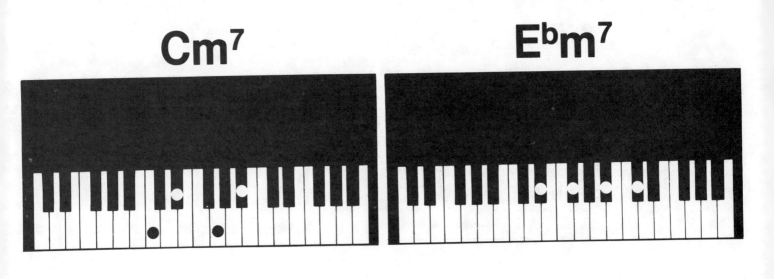

## E♭m⁷

## D♭m⁷

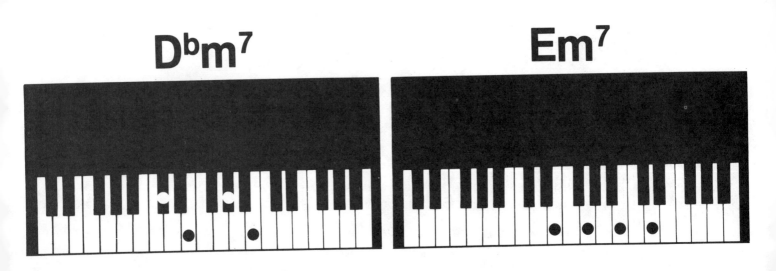

## Em⁷

## Dm⁷

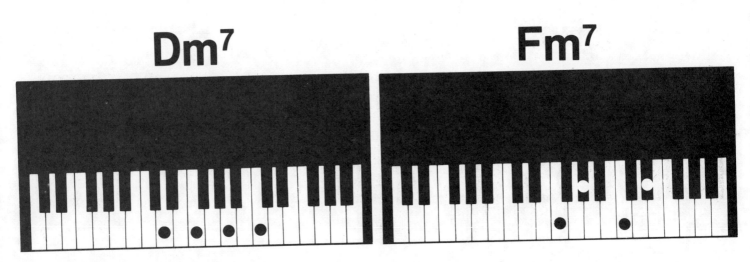

## Fm⁷

## F#m⁷

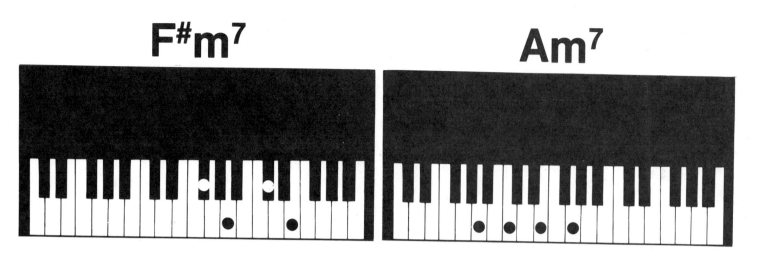

## Am⁷

## Gm⁷

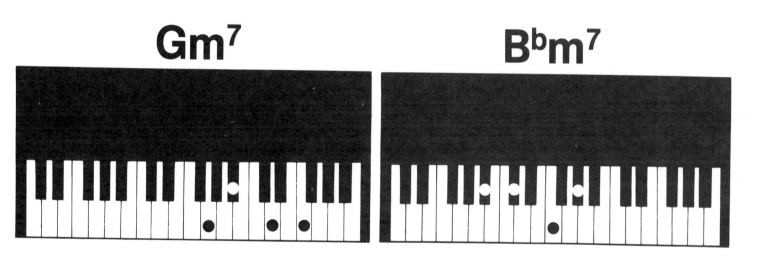

## B♭m⁷

## A♭m⁷

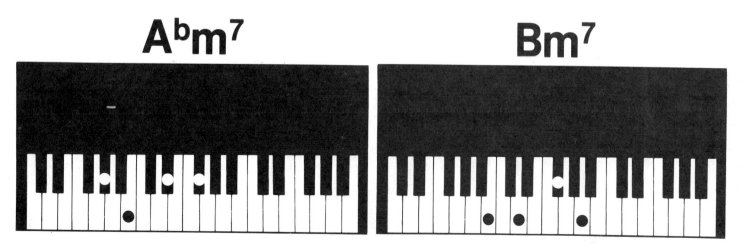

## Bm⁷

49

# Diminished Seventh Chords

## Cdim⁷

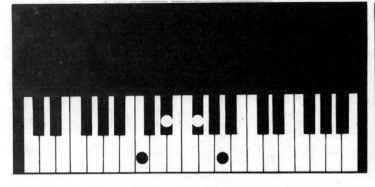

## E♭dim⁷

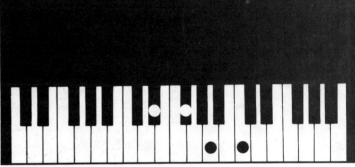

## D♭dim⁷

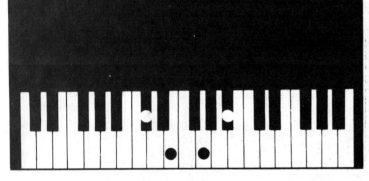

## Edim⁷

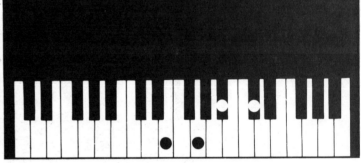

## Ddim⁷

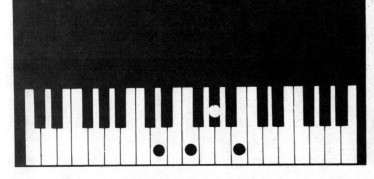

## Fdim⁷

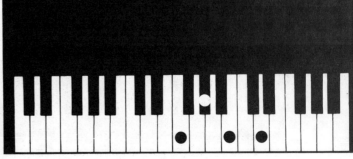

# F#dim⁷

# Adim⁷

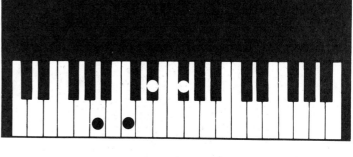

# Gdim⁷

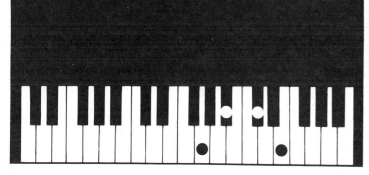

# B♭dim⁷

# A♭dim⁷

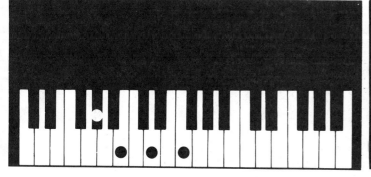

# Bdim⁷

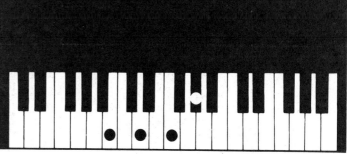

# Half-Diminished Chords

### C∅7

### E♭∅7

### D♭∅7

### E∅7

### D∅7

### F∅7

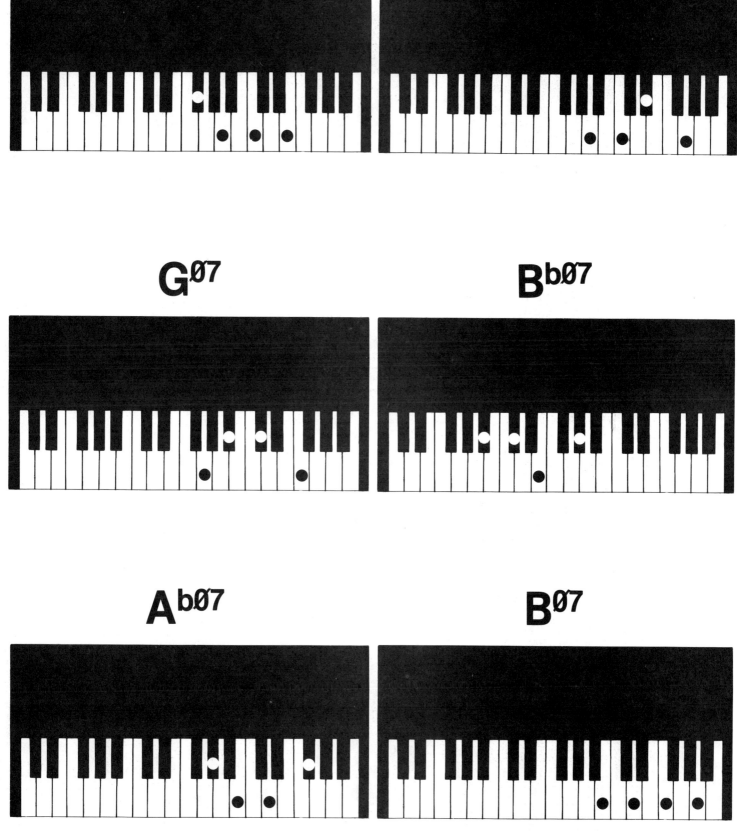

# Major Ninth Chords

## Cmaj⁹

## E♭maj⁹

## D♭maj⁹

## Emaj⁹

## Dmaj⁹

## Fmaj⁹

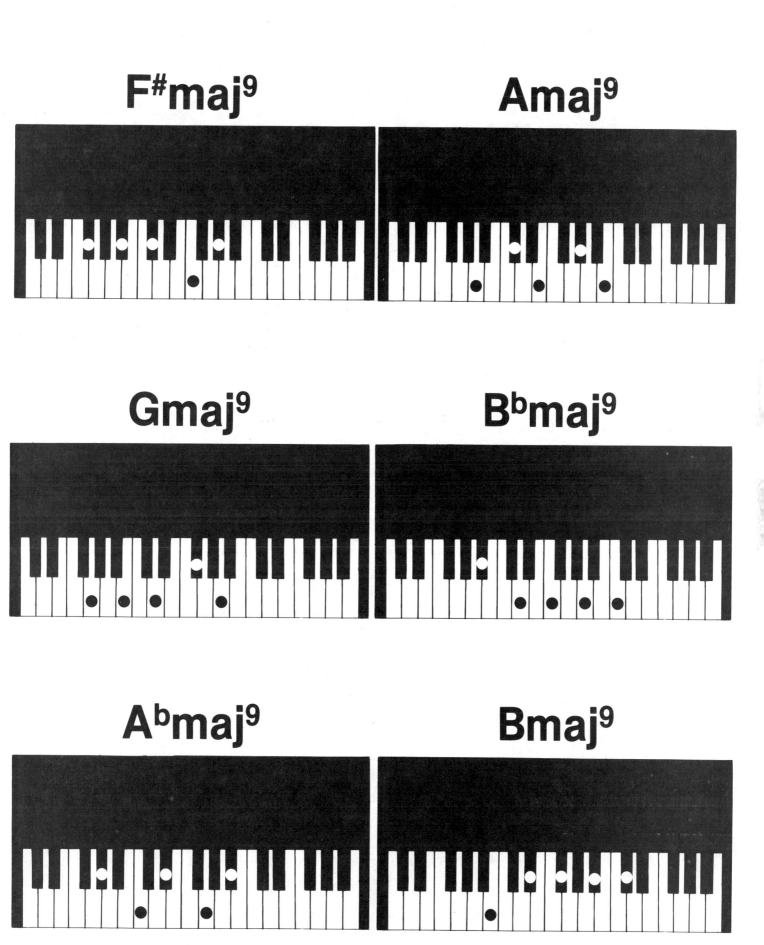

# Dominant Ninth Chords

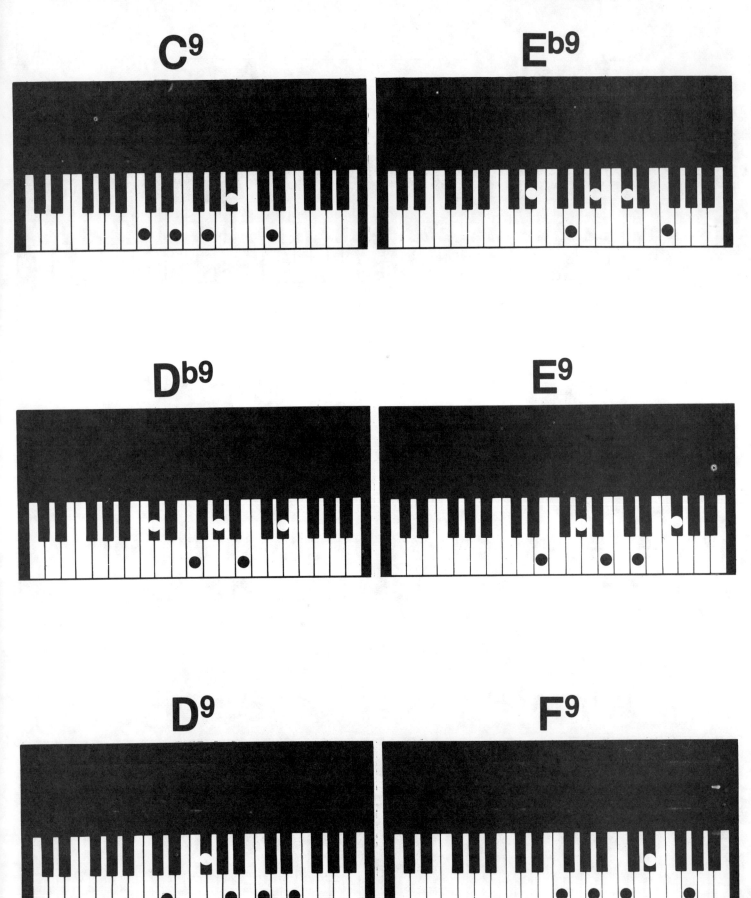

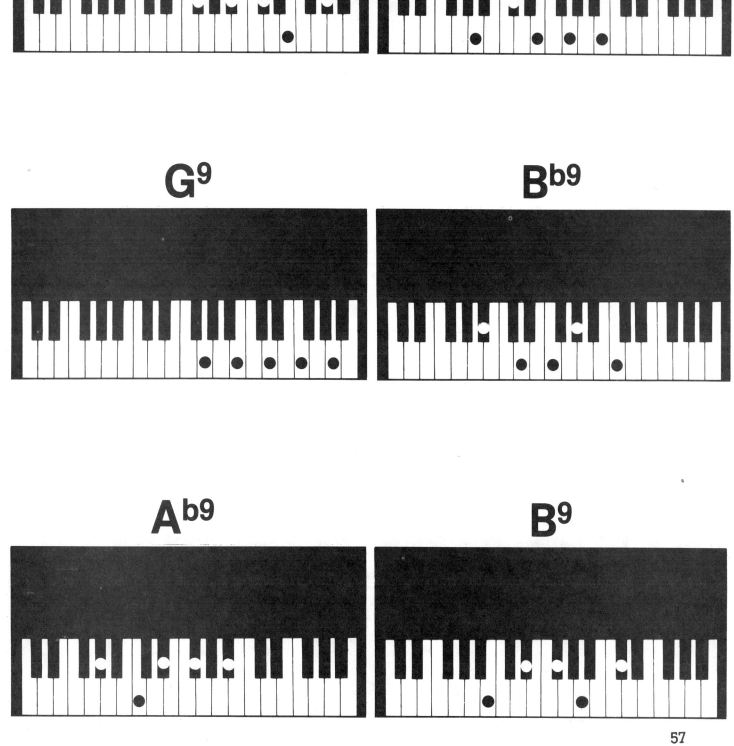

# Augmented Ninth Chords

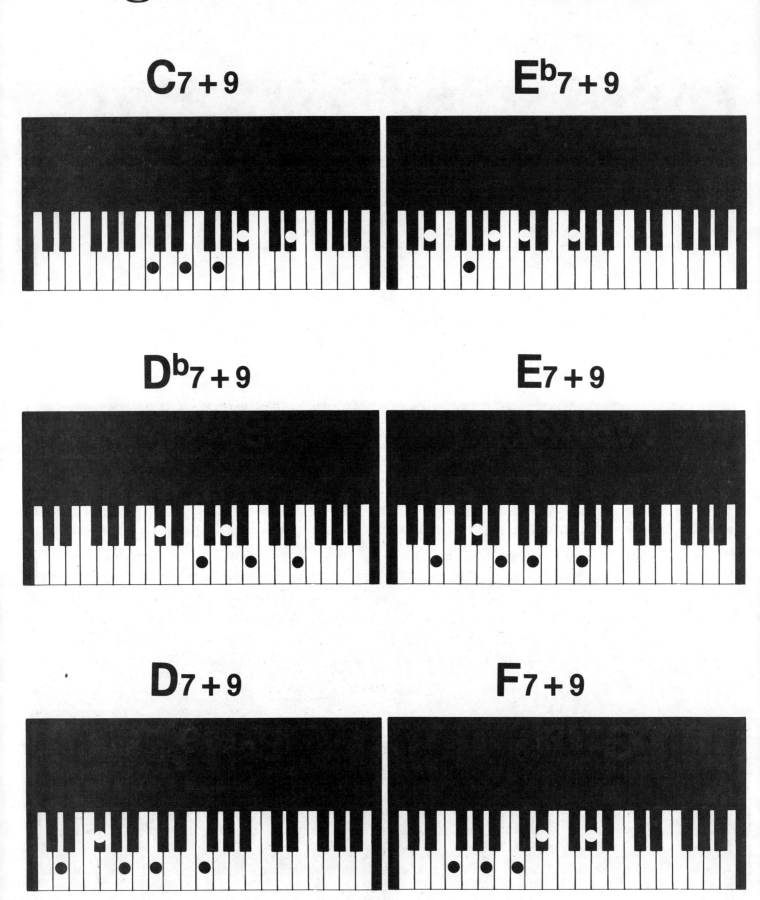

$C_{7+9}$

$E^b_{7+9}$

$D^b_{7+9}$

$E_{7+9}$

$D_{7+9}$

$F_{7+9}$

## F#7+9

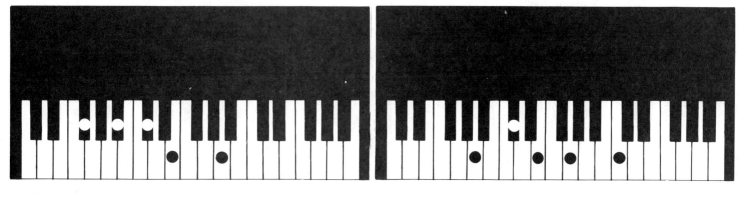

## A7+9

## G7+9

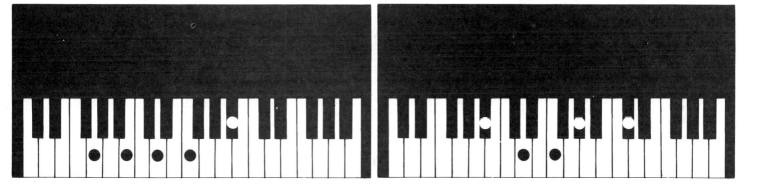

## Bb7+9

## Ab7+9

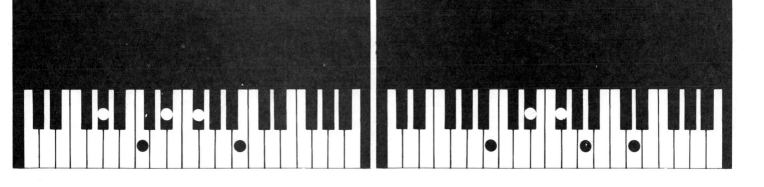

## B7+9

# Augmented Eleventh Chords

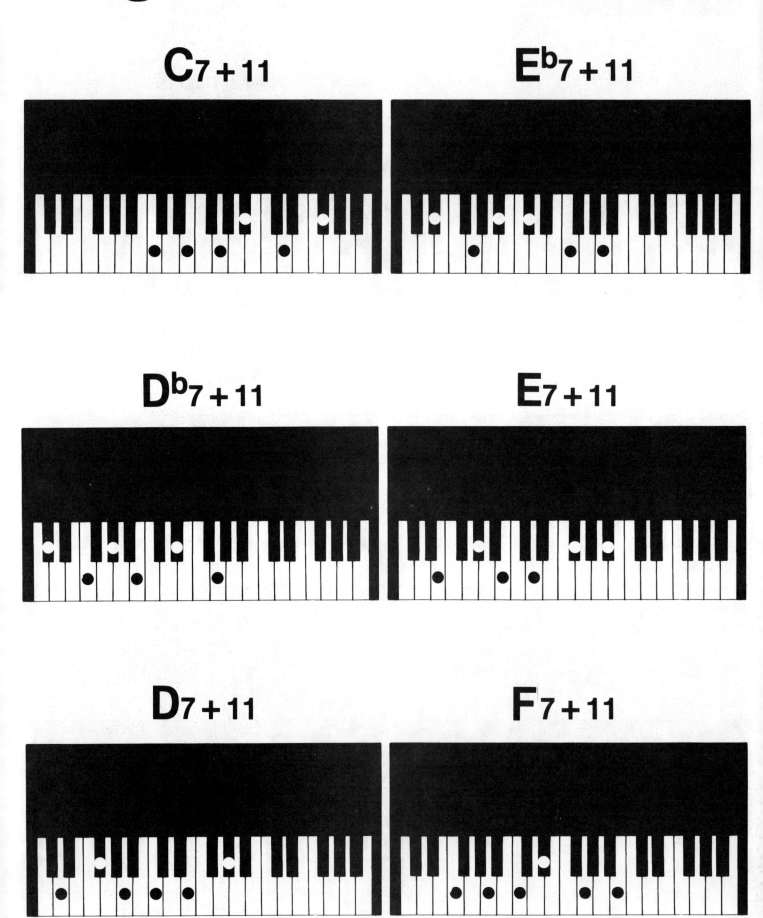

C7+11

Eb7+11

Db7+11

E7+11

D7+11

F7+11

## F#7 + 11

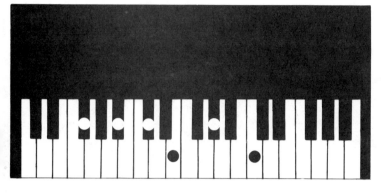

## A7 + 11

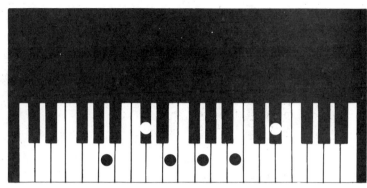

## G7 + 11

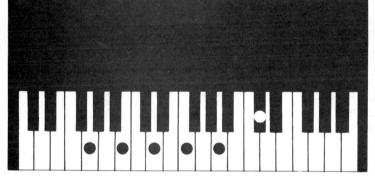

## Bb7 + 11

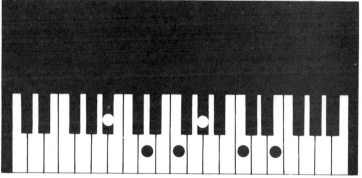

## Ab7 + 11

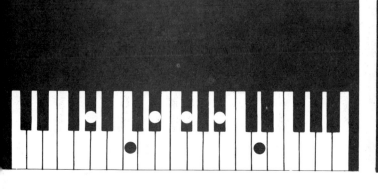

## B7 + 11

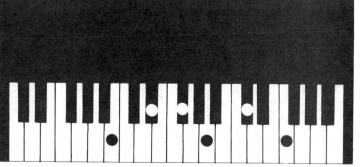

# Thirteenth Chords

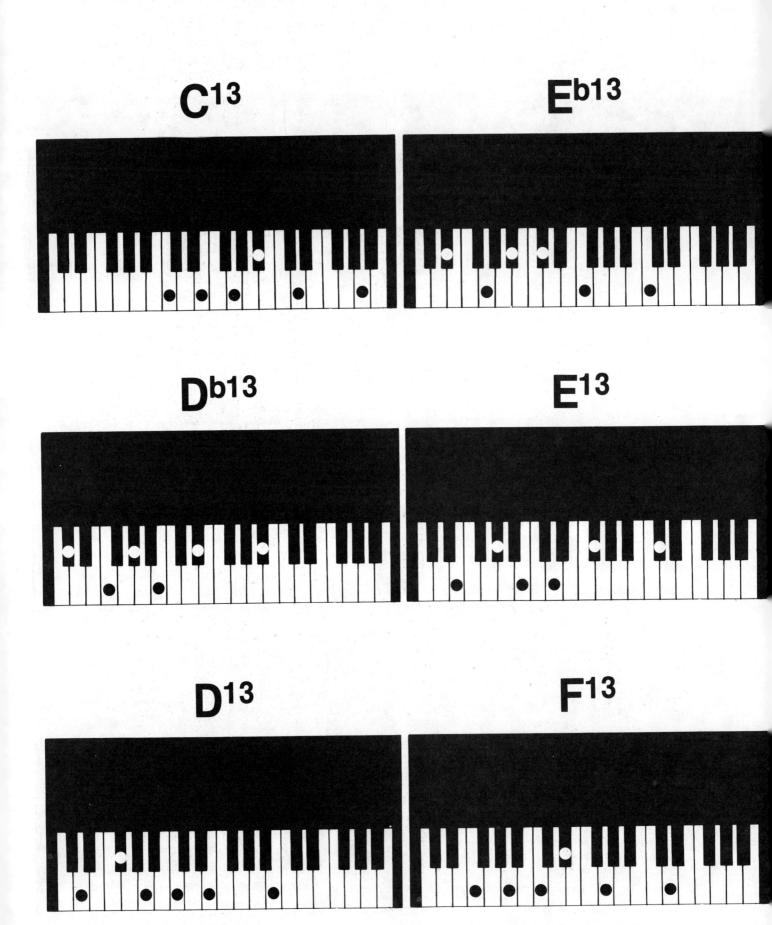

# F#13

# A13

# G13

# Bb13

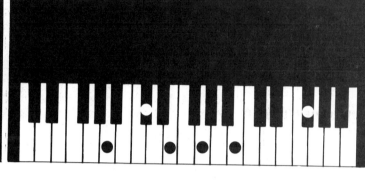

# Ab13

# B13

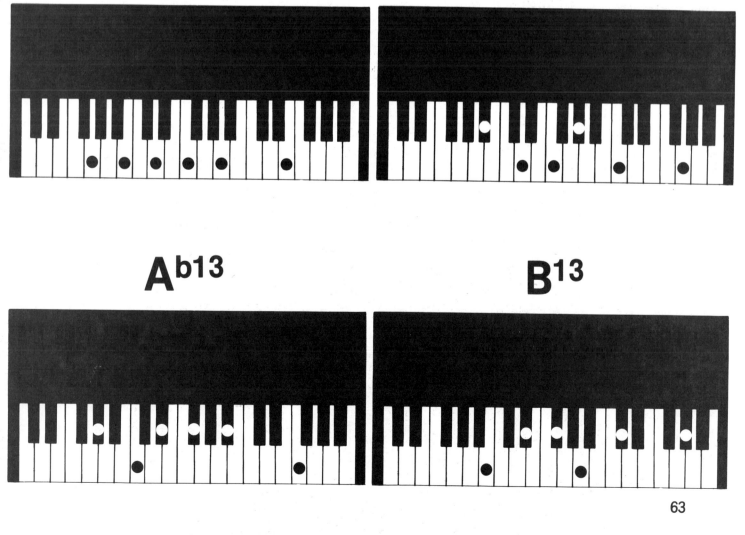

63

# Harmony at the Keyboard

## Chord Inversions

A chord, as we have seen, is built upon a note called the "root." So far we have placed these roots at the bottoms of the chords, but they do not necessarily have to be in this position. When another note of the chord is in the bass the chord is said to be "inverted."

The C major chord, for example, has C as its root and consists of the notes C, E, and G. When the C is in the bass the chord is in "root position." We can invert the chord so that E or G is the bottom note. These chords are written as "C/E" and "C/G", a form known as "slash chords." Our first example shows the C major chord in root position and in its two inversions.

Inversions figure prominently in the harmony of many tunes. The next example shows the melody and chord symbols for the first four bars of *My Country, 'Tis of Thee*. Notice that almost half the chords are inverted.

We can begin to harmonize this melody by constructing all of the chords in their root position. Only three kinds of chords are called for: major, minor, and dominant seventh. (We discussed the construction of these types of chords in the October '83 issue.)

In playing through the above example you probably noticed that, although each chord is correct, the harmonization as a whole doesn't sound right.

That is because the inversions are missing. If we now invert the appropriate chords the accompaniment will fall into place.

Another kind of arrangement places the chord tones in the right hand, underneath the melody, and gives the left hand only a bass line. This bass line consists of the chord roots and, in the case of inversions, the other notes of the chords. In the first bar, for example, the C chord is supported by its root, C, while the D minor chord is supported by its third, the note F.

In printed sheet music the symbol "C(E bass)" is often used instead of "C/E." The meaning is exactly the same. It is extremely important to "read" and play these inversions when they occur. One of the most common mistakes that inexperienced musicians make is to put every chord in root position. This can play havoc with the accompaniment, and also make it sound as if an "amateur" is playing. Inversions, when they are called for, are an essential part of harmony at the keyboard.

RC

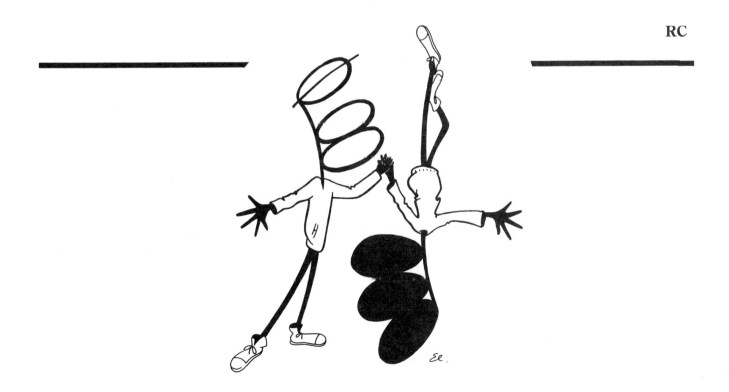

# "VOICING" YOUR CHORDS

The chords formed by the major scale are easy enough to locate and play, but the trick of making them sound full and professionally polished requires study and practice. Here are the chords of the C major scale: C Major, D Minor, E minor, F Major, G Major, A Minor, B Diminished.

If we add sevenths onto our basic triads, we arrive at the most commonly used chord qualities: Major Seventh, Minor Seventh, Dominant Seventh, and Half-Diminished Seventh.

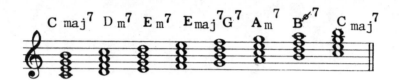

We can create any chord type by remembering the distance (the interval) between each of its tones. A major chord, for example, is built by the interval of 2 whole steps, followed by 1½ steps; the minor chord consists of 1½ steps followed by 2 whole steps; a diminished chord uses two intervals of 1½ steps each.

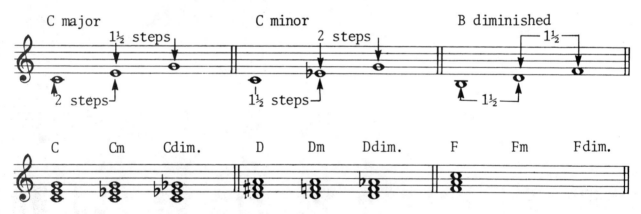

In the above example, fill in the correct notes for the Fm and F^dim. chords.

The major seventh interval is 5½ steps wide.

The dominant seventh interval is 5 steps wide.

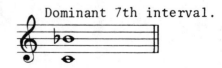

Dominant 7th interval.

The chord formed on step VII of the major scale is called "half-diminished." It is a diminished chord with a dominant seventh on top. A "diminished seventh" chord lowers the dominant seventh tone by ½ step.

The VII is called "half-diminished". Its symbol is ø.

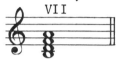

A "diminished 7th" chord lowers the dominant 7th another ½ step.

Although these very specific intervals determine the type of chord you are playing, the *order* the notes appear in on the keyboard is not rigidly determined. If we were to play all chords in the "close" position used in the preceding examples, the sound would be boring and at times ugly. Once the correct notes for a chord have been decided, there is great leeway in arranging those notes between the hands.

The art of "voicing" allows a musician to produce just the kind of sound he or she wants.

We can begin our look at this art with a very practical and standard voicing: the root and fifth of the chord in the left hand, and the third, seventh, and third again in the right. Here is a series of major seventh chords, using this voicing, in the circle of fifths.

The symbol for a major 7th chord is △ or Maj. 7.

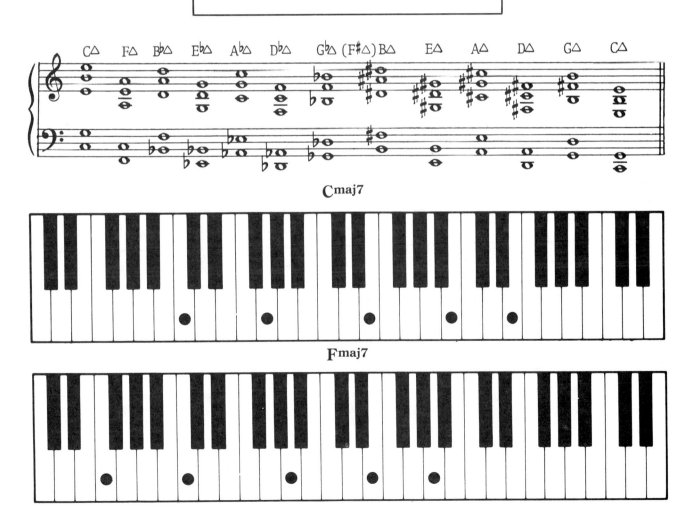

67

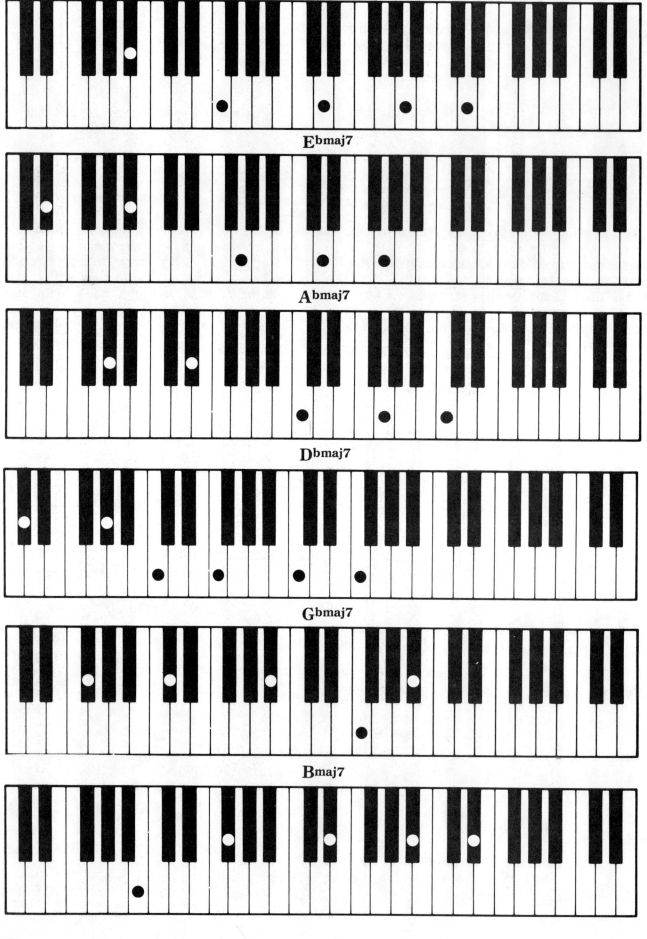

Bbmaj7

Ebmaj7

Abmaj7

Dbmaj7

Gbmaj7

Bmaj7

68

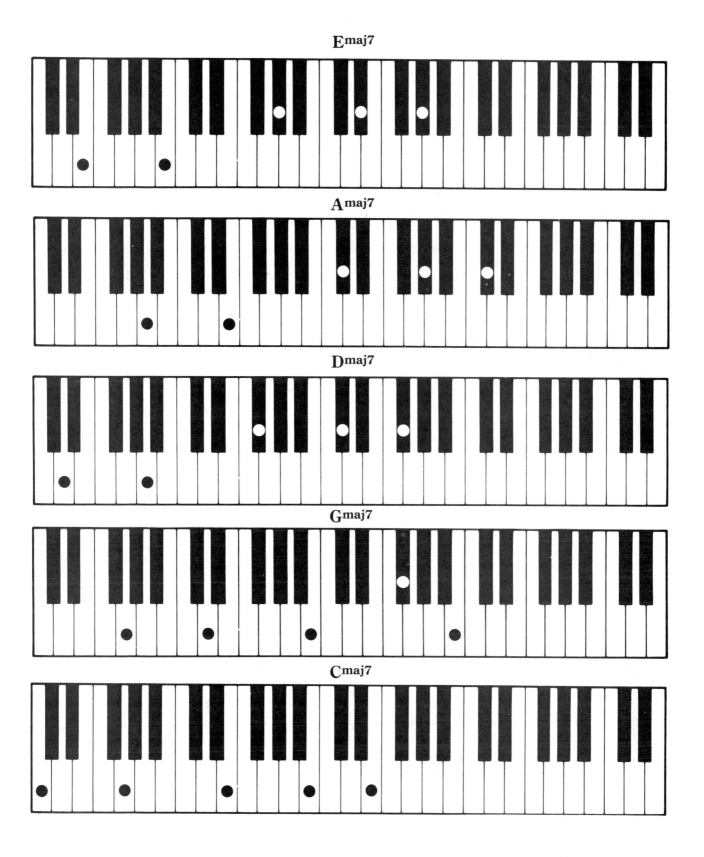

The same voicing can be used with dominant
seventh chords.

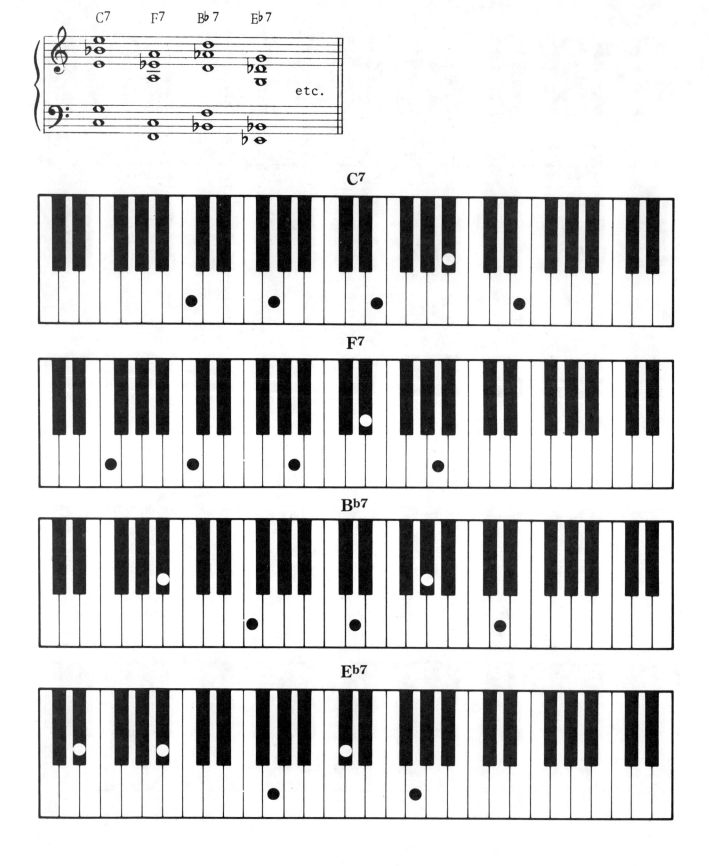

Here it is with minor seventh chords.

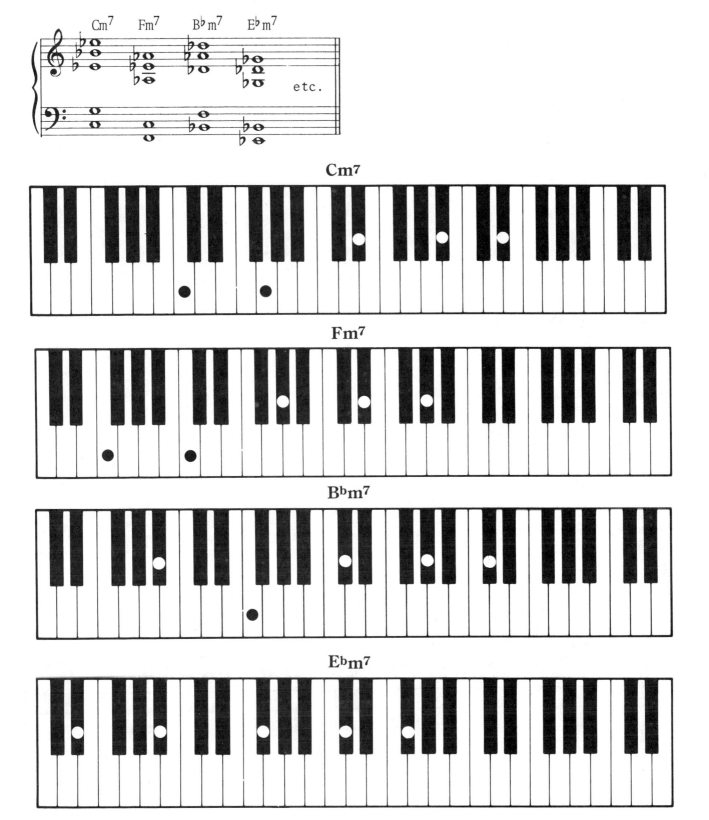

**Cm⁷**

**Fm⁷**

**B♭m⁷**

**E♭m⁷**

One key to good voicing is the technique of making changes from one chord to another as smoothly as possible; often, this involves holding "common tones": those notes shared by both chords. Here is an example using the circle of fifths.

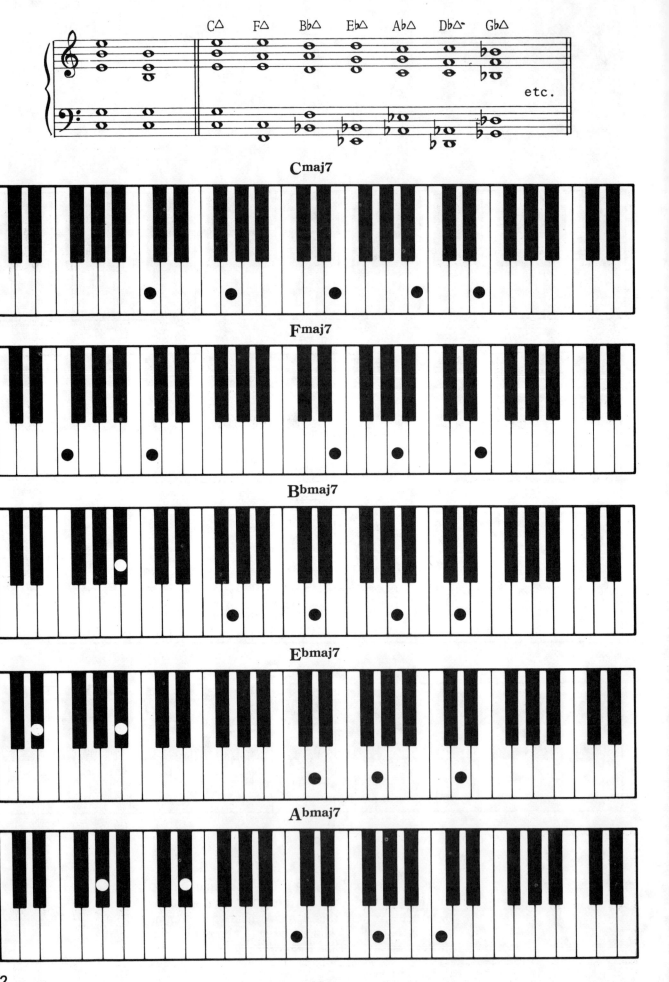

Cmaj7

Fmaj7

B♭maj7

E♭maj7

A♭maj7

**Dbmaj7**

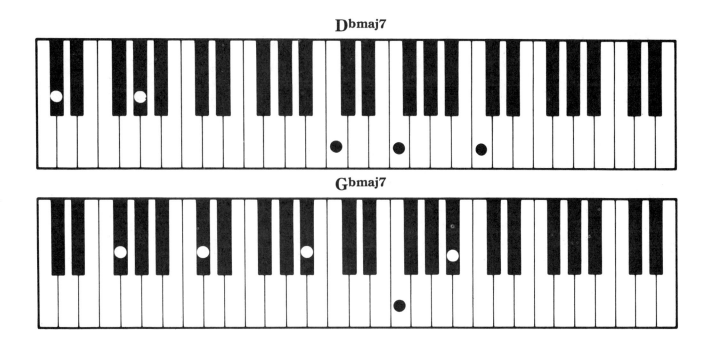

**Gbmaj7**

Here is another example, remaining within the key of C.

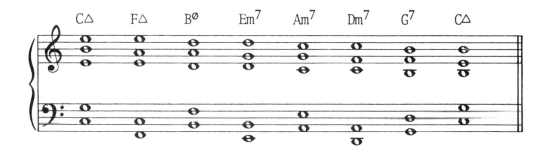

**Cmaj7**

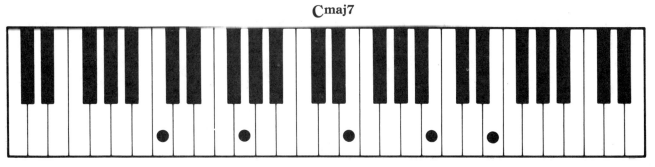

Fmaj7

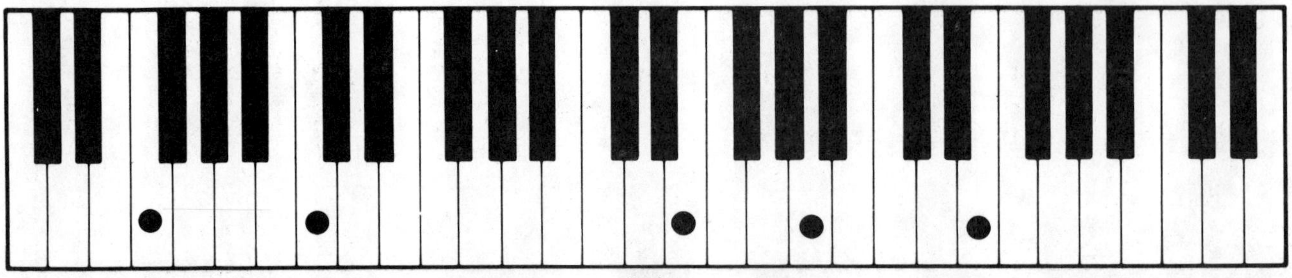

B°

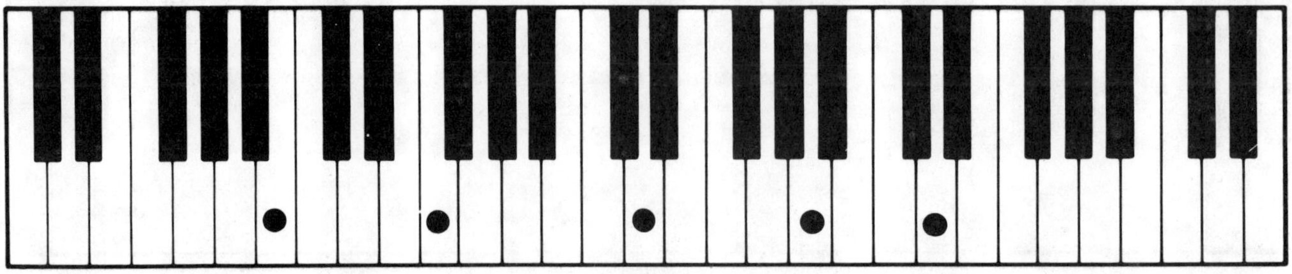

Em7

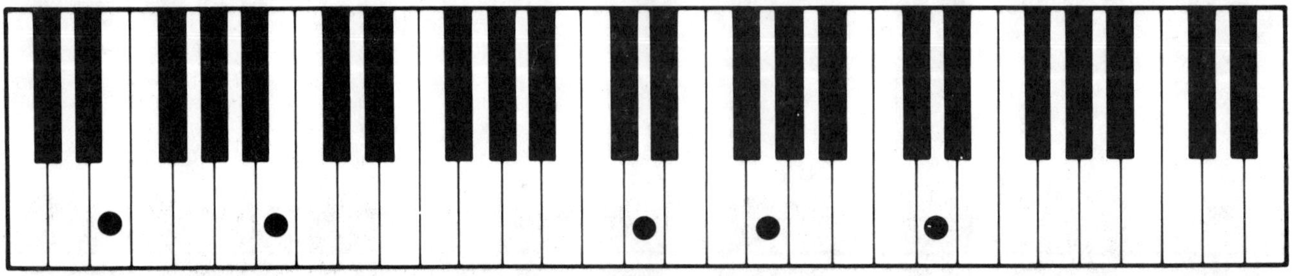

Am7

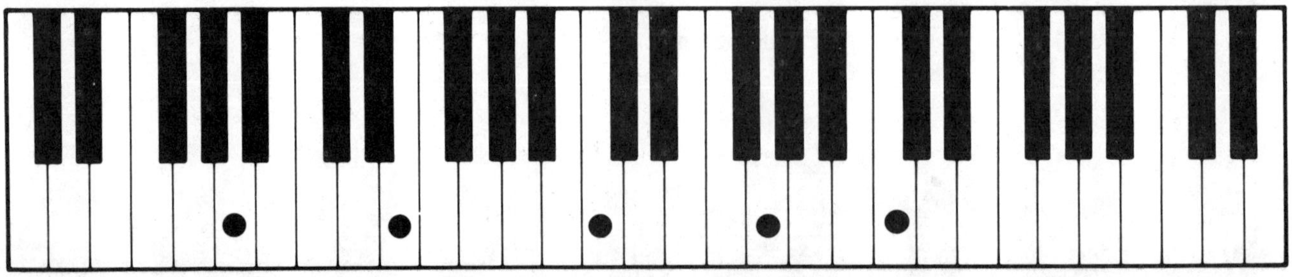

Dm7

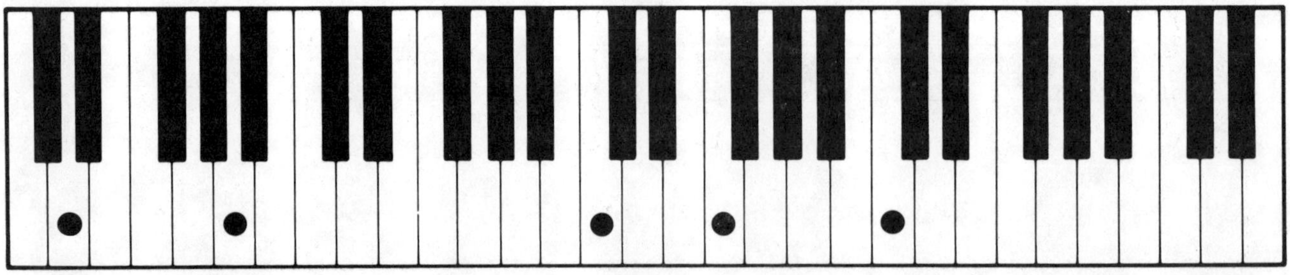

G7

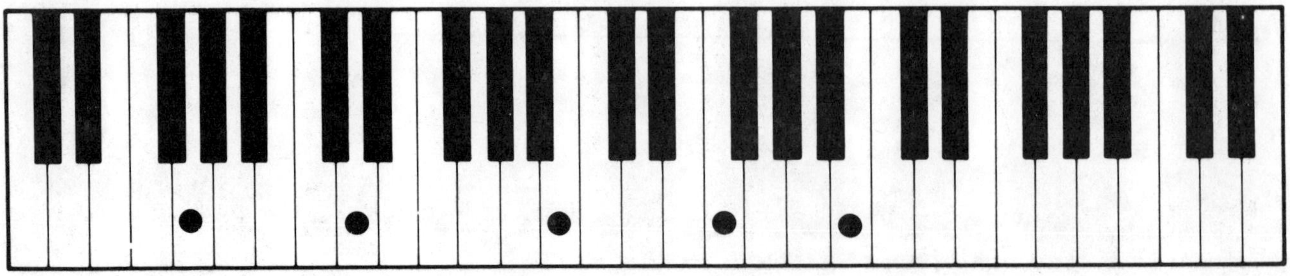

74

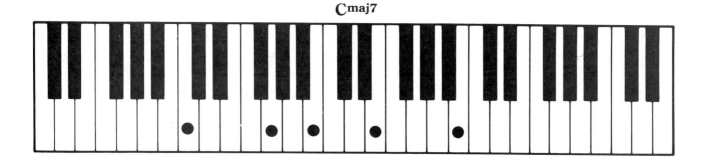

Cmaj7

Up until now we've been using a fairly "open" voicing. The notes of a chord can be arranged in much closer proximity to one another, however.

Here's another type of voicing, which also makes use of the common tone technique.

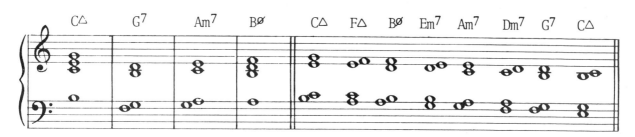

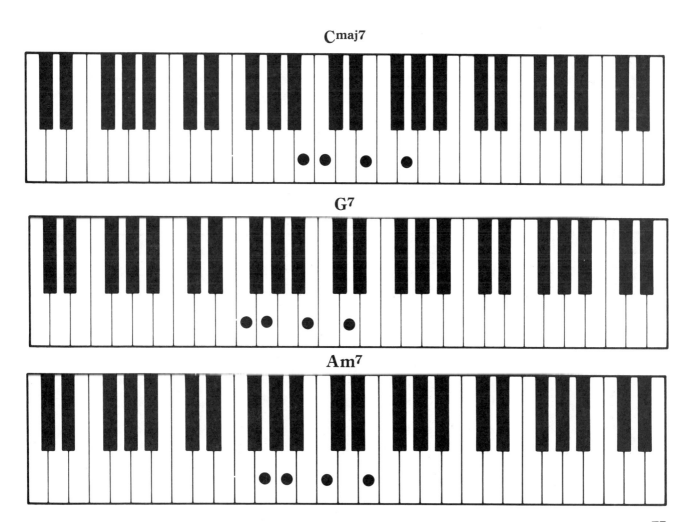

Cmaj7

G7

Am7

### B♭

### Cmaj7

### Fmaj7

### Bø

### Em7

### Am7

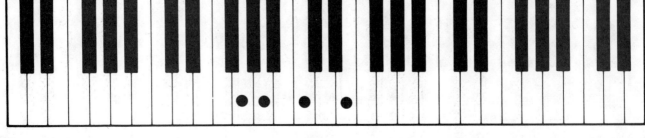

**Dm⁷**

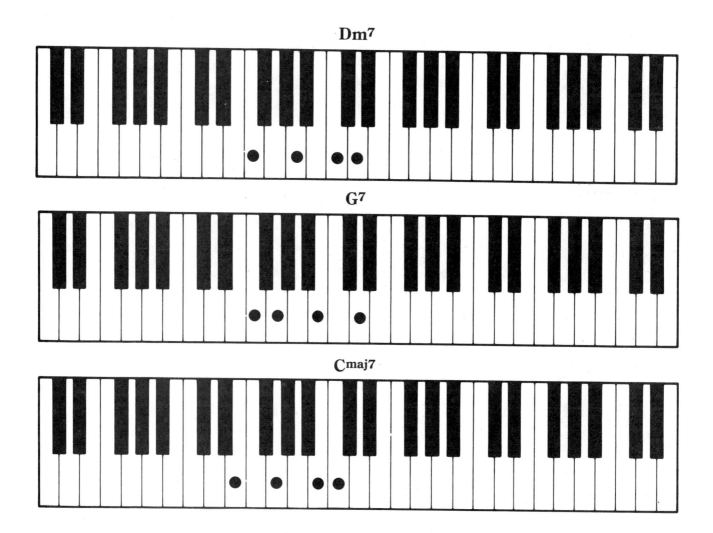

**G⁷**

**Cmaj7**

Any progression can be made to move in numerous ways on the keyboard. Turning again to an open voicing, we can play the circle of fifths so that the bass line descends. Here we are not using the same voicing for each chord, but constructing the right hand configurations so that they sound uncluttered and effective above the bass notes.

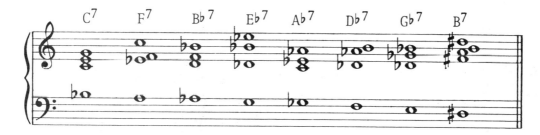

**C⁷**

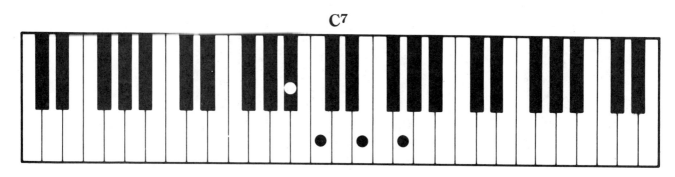

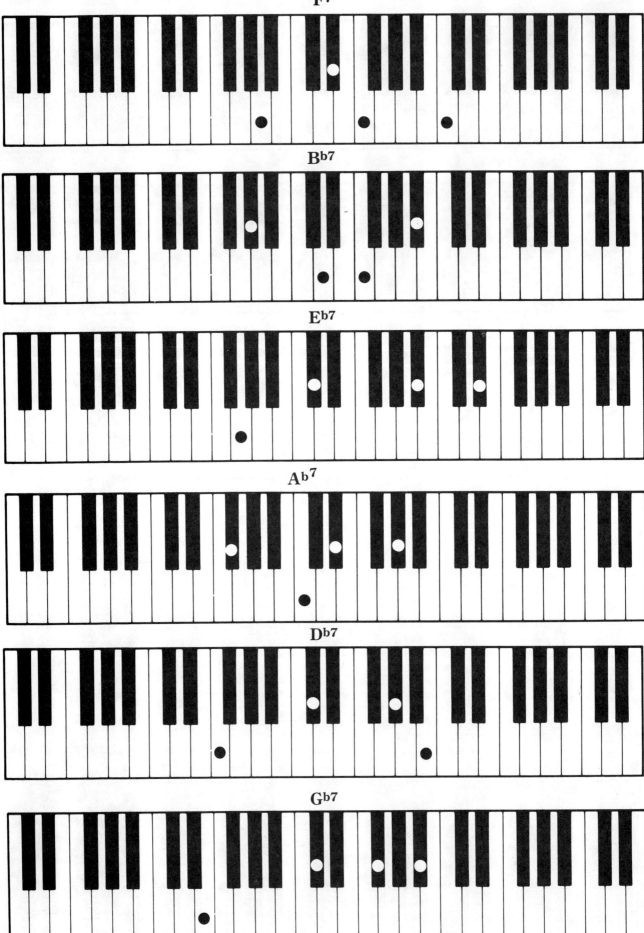

**B⁷**

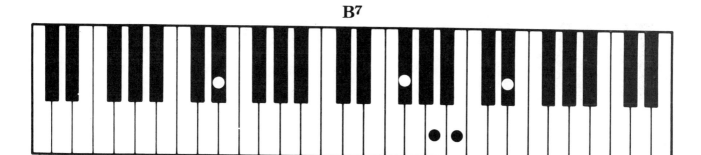

We can also keep our common tones in the bass!

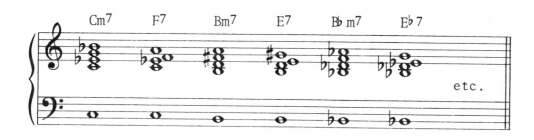

**Cm⁷**

**F⁷**

**Bm⁷**

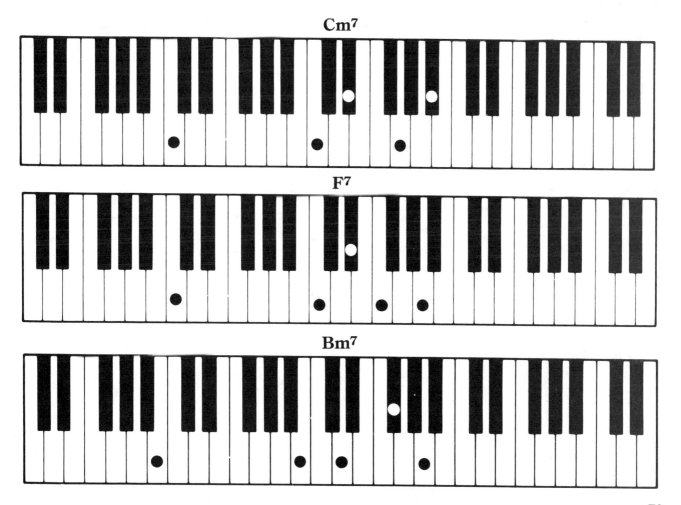

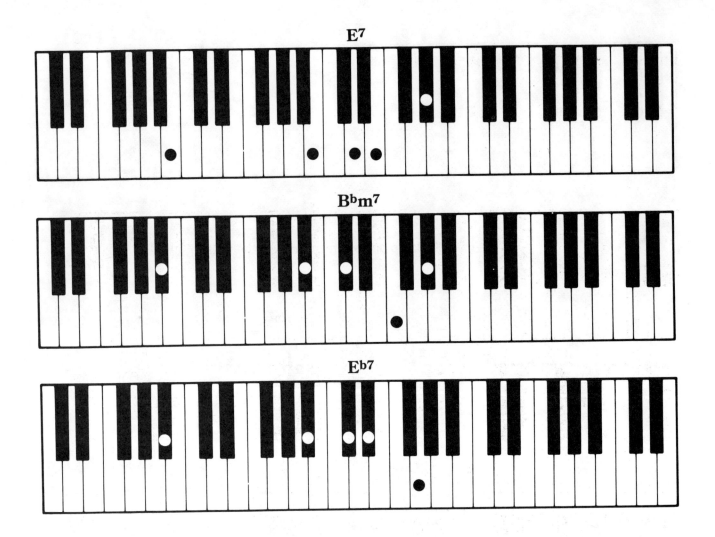

# From Close To Open

There is a simple way in which band arrangers change the instrumental sound of an ensemble from very dense to spacious, and we can apply their method to keyboard arranging. Let's look at our "close" or dense voicing, in a circle of fifths pattern within the key of C.

If we take the note second from the bottom and drop it down an octave, we will change the voicing to a semi-open sound.

We can take the top note of the voicing and drop it down to the bottom as well. We now have an open voicing.

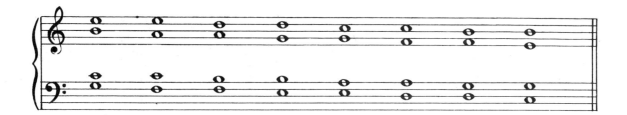

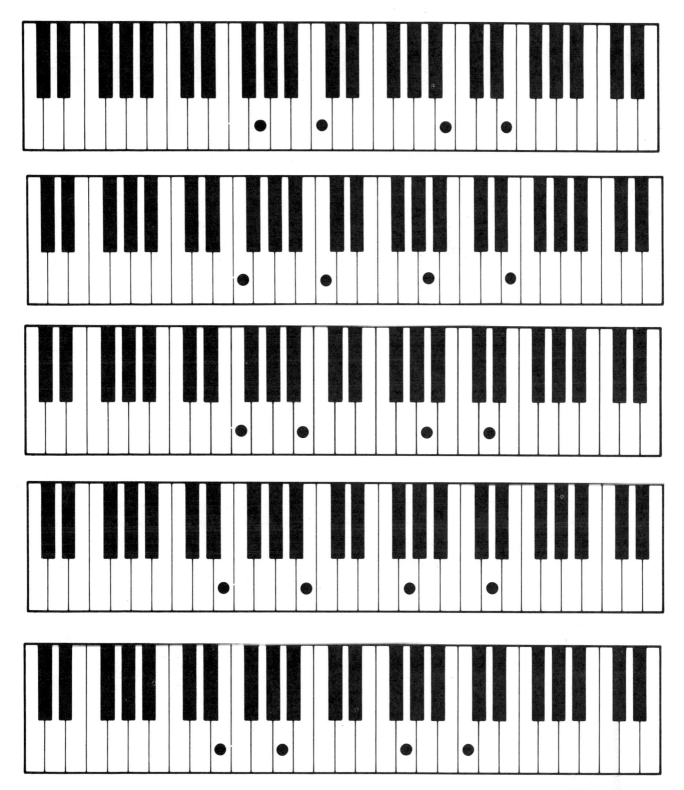

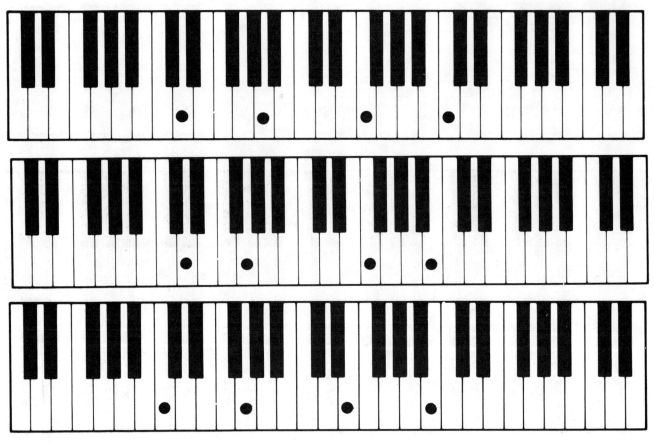

If we like, we can arrange the notes of these chords so that they expand outward — creating a more and more open sound as we play!

**Cmaj7**

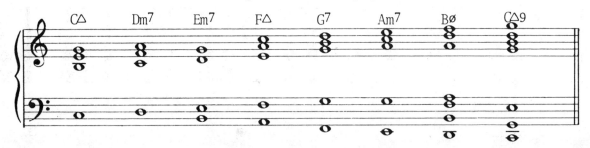

**Dm7**

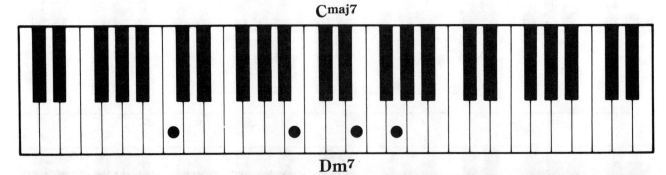

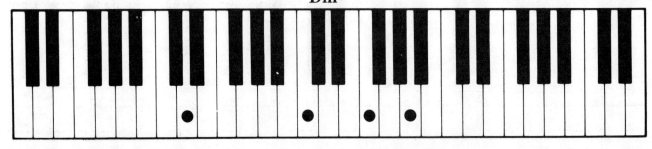

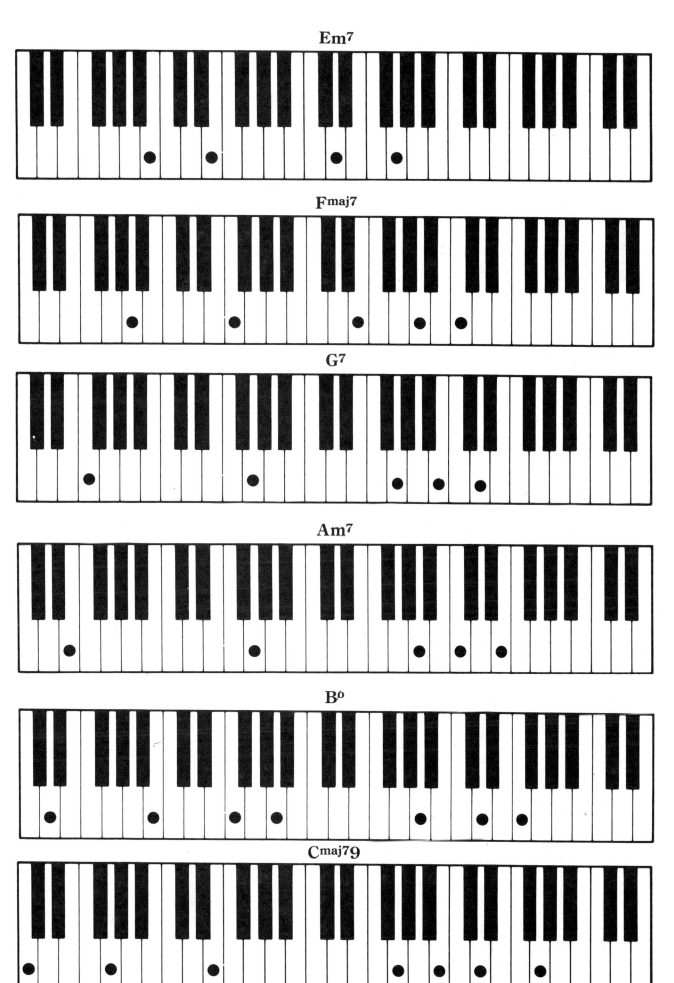

This is the complete opposite to the "locked hand" or block chord style made famous by George Shearing, in which the top and bottom notes are the same, and the spacing between tones remains very tight.

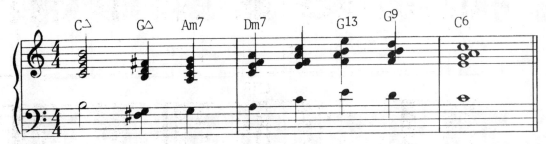

# Altered Chords

Today's music uses many different kinds of chord qualities. Complex chords are sometimes referred to as "altered" chords, because the player is often asked to sharp or flat chord members, or alter the usual chord in some way.

Here is a list of most of the sophisticated chords you'll find in contemporary arrangements.

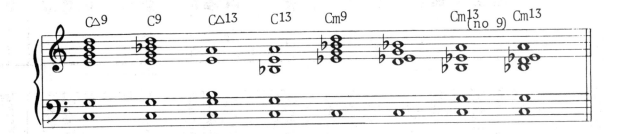

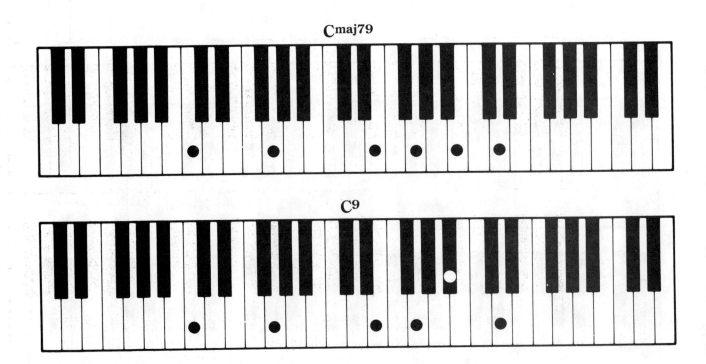

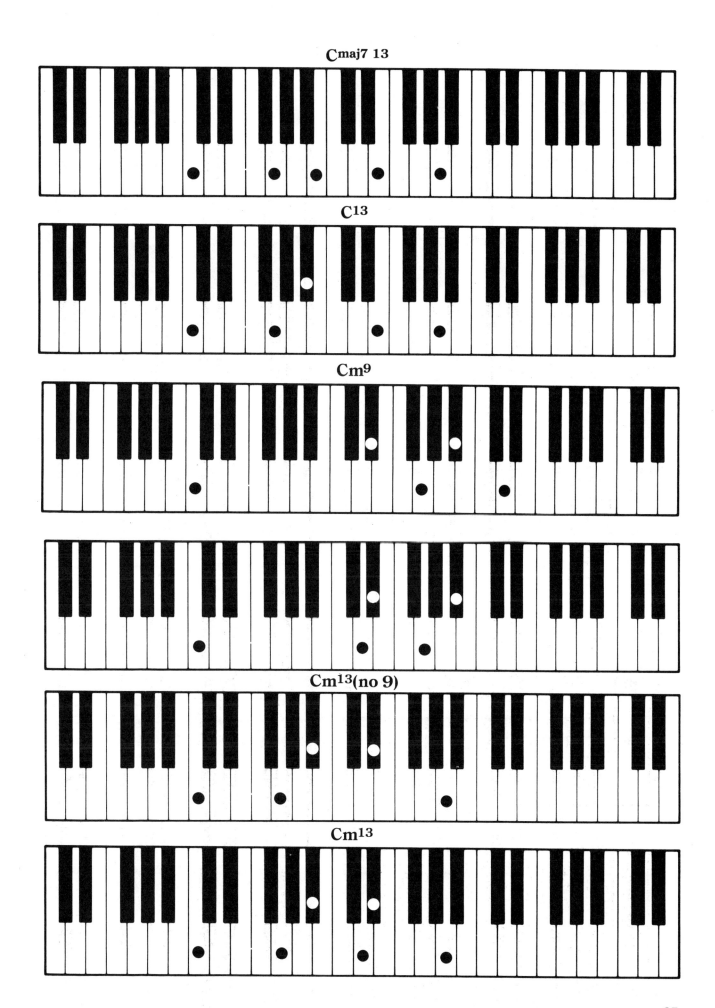

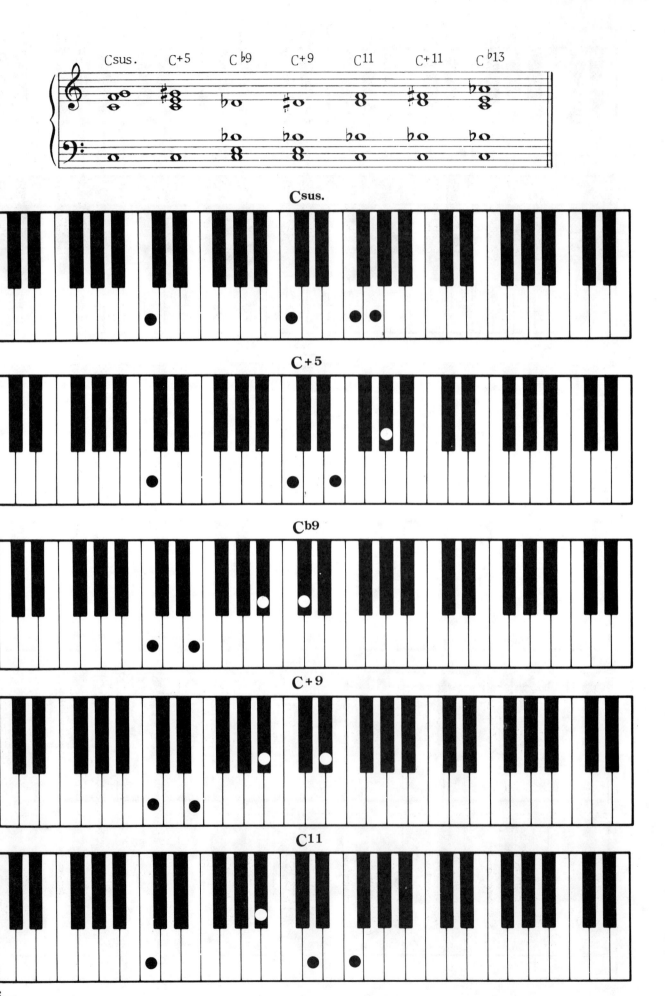

**C + 11**

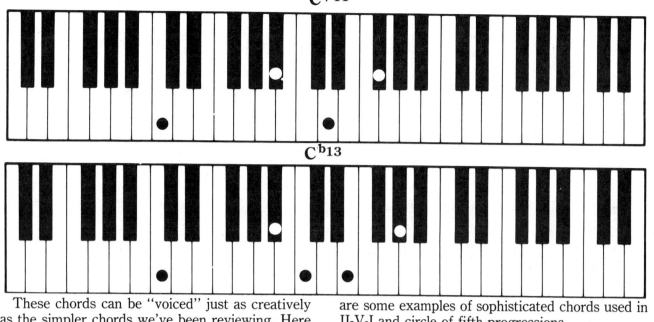

**C<sup>b</sup>13**

These chords can be "voiced" just as creatively as the simpler chords we've been reviewing. Here are some examples of sophisticated chords used in II-V-I and circle of fifth progressions.

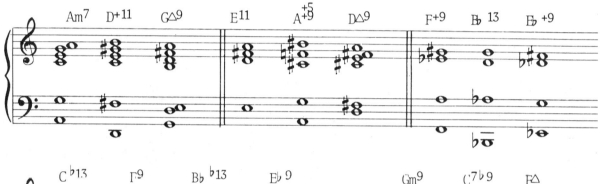

**Am⁷**

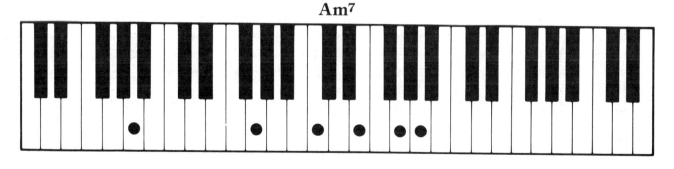

**D + 11**

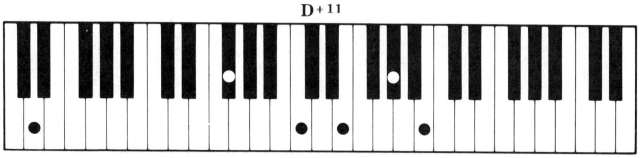

Gmaj79

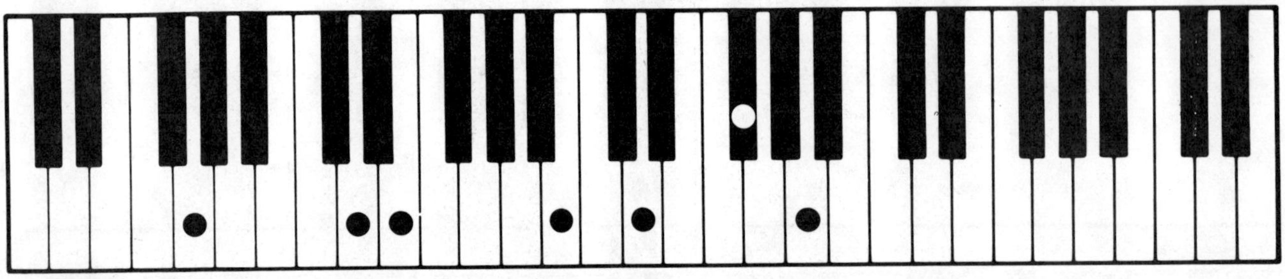

E11

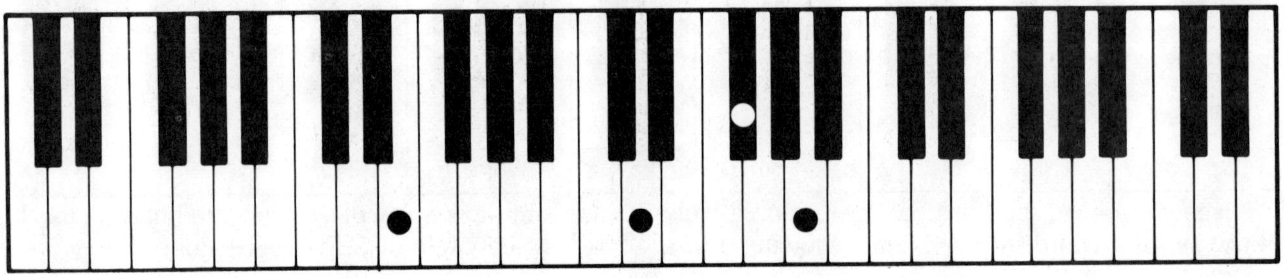

A+5+9

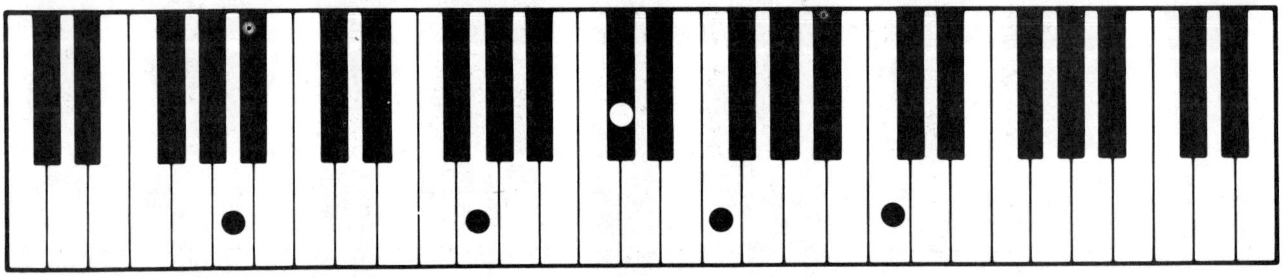

Dmaj79

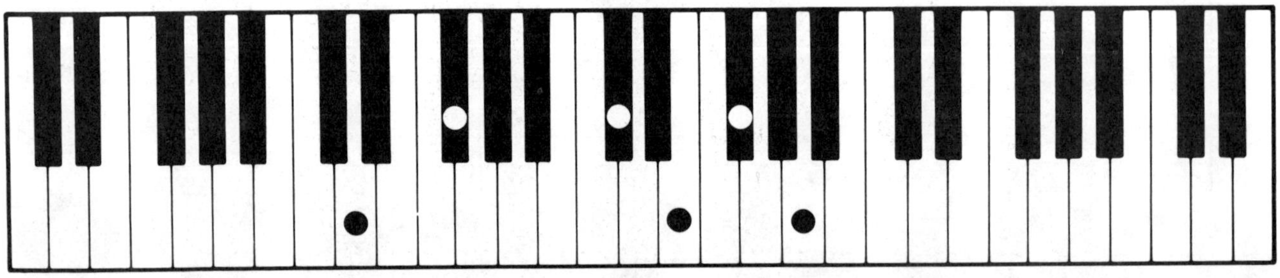

F+9

Bb13

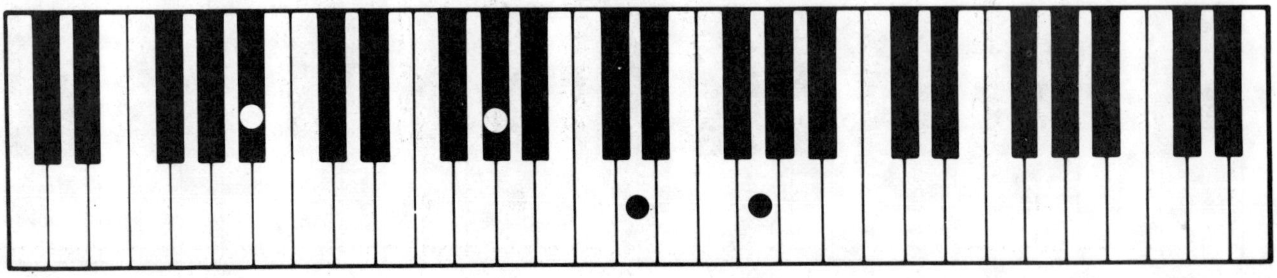

88

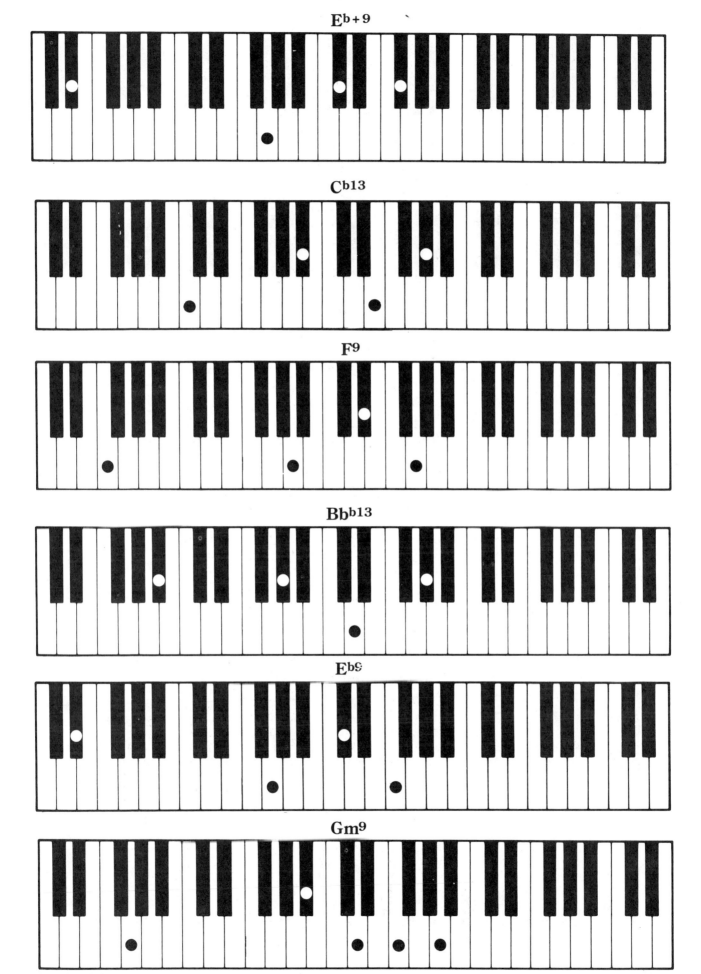

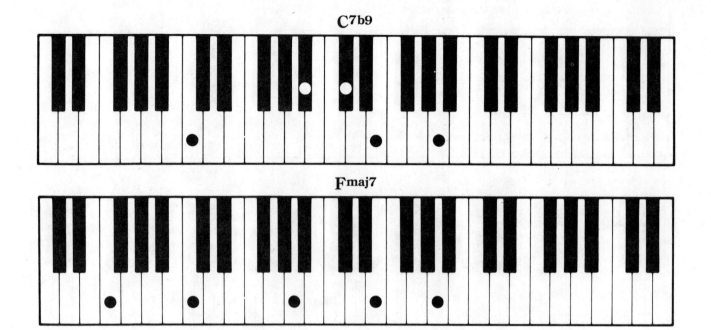

C7b9

Fmaj7

Often, these complex chords are voiced in a way that leaves out many of the chord tones. It takes a lot of experimentation and practice to achieve a complete command over these sounds, but in time they can become additional colors on your arranging palette. Use these examples as beginning guides to the world of chord voicing — the more you experiment, the better you'll sound!

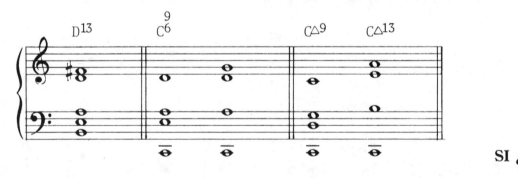

SI

# Striking A Common Chord

Many of who have studied the piano for years are now beginning to play organ, and vice versa. In fact, some people are choosing to become "multi-instrumentalists," which gives them the chance to experience the best of both worlds. As the saying goes, variety is the spice of life.

But keyboard instruments, though they may look alike, can sound very different. Playing full piano chords on a powerful, rich-toned console will reduce any piece of music to "Mud Gets in Your Eyes." After getting over the initial shock of that murky sound, a pianist would have to consider certain elements of chord voicing, especially the concept of "optimum range."

Take this piano voicing, for instance:

An organist would use much simpler voicings, which fall within the "optimum" register:

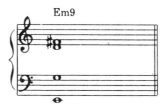

In fact, organists often play chords in inversion so that the notes of the harmony lie in a good-sounding place on the keyboard.

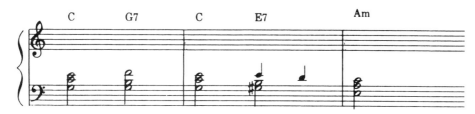

Some pop pianists do follow a similar routine; early swing players made sure that the chords they played fell so that middle C rested somewhere near the middle of the harmony. This helped to make the "swing piano" sound distinctive.

An organist, however, who plays his voicings on a piano will also run into a problem: some of the simple organ voicings will sound too bare. Pianists will tend to include half-steps and altered chord tones. It is possible, however, to develop a chord vocabulary that will fit either instrument. The following examples are useful in the song "I Love Paris"  **SI** ♩

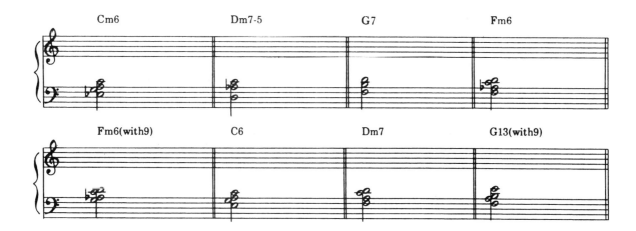

# POP CHORD PROGRESSIONS
## The Basics

Most pop tunes are based on a few simple chord progressions; even the most complex contemporary songs are variations, or sophisticated "twists" on basic harmonic relationships. We can begin examining some of the simple progressions used in songwriting with a review of the chords which occur naturally in any major key. These chords are built from the notes of the major scale.

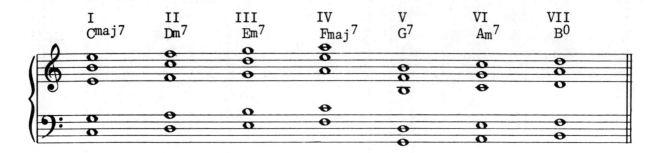

Sometimes a song is constructed by simply moving up and down the chord series I, II, III, etc.

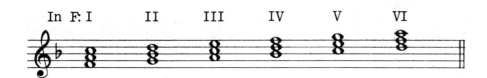

But most often the chords in a song will revolve around the use of a "cadence" — a formula for giving the impression of a momentary or permanent conclusion. The two types of cadence most encountered in pop music are IV to I (plagal or "gospel" cadence), and V to I (authentic cadence).

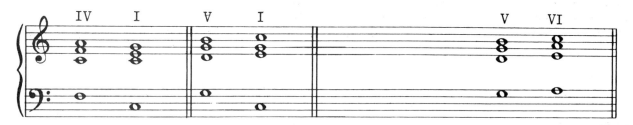

The sound of the IV-I cadence is illustrated nicely in the opening of "Swing Low."

Many well-known tunes make use of the V-I cadence; in "Skip To My Lou," the entire song is built on I going to V, returning to I.

"Hot Time In The Old Town Tonight" stays on the I chord (G) for most of the tune, then switches briefly to V in order to end with the V-I cadence.

Another example of a tune based solely on I-V-I is "La Bamba." Many Latin tunes follow this simple formula.

There are also songs, though, which use both types of cadence. Think of all the times you've played a tune (especially rock and folk songs) which uses only three chords. More than likely, those three chords are the I, IV, and V! "Morning Has Broken" is a good example.

# Longer Progressions

The V-I cadence is so strong that whole progressions can be formed by simply placing the V of any chord before that chord, wherever it appears in a sequence. If we stay within a key, C for example, the II chord (Dm) can act as the V of the V chord (G), since it is located a fifth above that G. The VI chord (Am) can act as the V of the II chord (Dm). So, the progression VI-II-V-I is really a series of V going to I over and over. When we string out all the chords in a key so that their roots keep descending a fifth, we have the "circle of fifths" in that key.

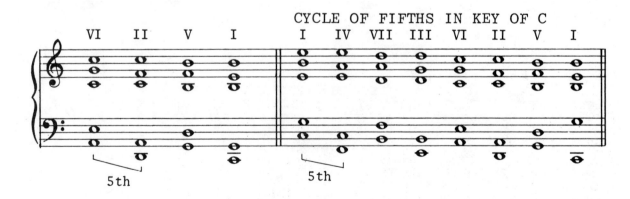

One piece of this circle, II-V-I, is so commonly used that you should be able to spot it in just about any popular song you play.

In C     In A
II    V    I (no 7th)    II    V    I (with a dominant 7th this time!)

In fact, you can create your own tunes easily just by writing down a series of II-V-I progressions, and finding a melody to fit the chords!

Dm7    G7    Cmaj7        Bbm7    Eb7    Abmaj7

2x                        2x

Gm7    C7    Fmaj7    Em7    A7    Dmaj7    Dm7    G7    C

2x                   1x                    1x

Occasionally you'll spot a song that uses just the II-V section of the progression; a number of rock tunes (such as George Harrison's "My Sweet Lord") make use of this "partial" progression.

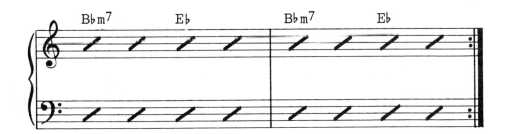

Bbm7    Eb        Bbm7    Eb

# Circles of Dominants

The strongest possible cadence is a V-I progression in which the V is a major chord with a dominant seventh added (in the key of C, for example, a $G^7$ leading to a C major chord). We can easily create a chain of V-I sequences, therefore, in which each chord is a dominant seventh chord. (We saw earlier how II-V-I in the key of C — Dm-G-C — works as a kind of V to I sequence. $D^7$-$G^7$-C is even stronger.)

*Continued*

The resulting sound should be very familiar, as the following example, using a "Charleston" rhythm, demonstrates.

The last two lines from the next example show a sequence of dominant seventh chords which form a chain of V-I patterns leading back to the original D chord.

# Variations

Looking back at the VI-II-V-I progression, let's add the I chord onto the beginning. The resulting I-VI-II-V-I was used for practically every song written in the 1950's! Note the movement from I to VI — it doesn't fit any of our previous categories of chord motion. We've now covered harmonic motion of IV-I, V-I, step-wise movement, and, in this last case, third relations.

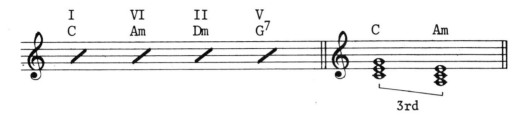

One variation on the I-VI-II-V-I progression is I-VI-IV-I (we've changed the cadence to our "plagal" alternate).

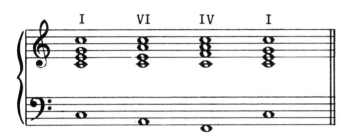

Here is a section of "Jeanie With The Light Brown Hair." Note the opening progression: I-VI-IV-I, followed by II (Major) -V-I.

Another type of variation can be formed by inserting the $V^7$ of any chord before that chord is played. One example of this would be to place an $E^7$ before the Am in the progression C-Am.

In "Wait Till The Sun Shines Nellie," this technique is used in several places.

*Continued*

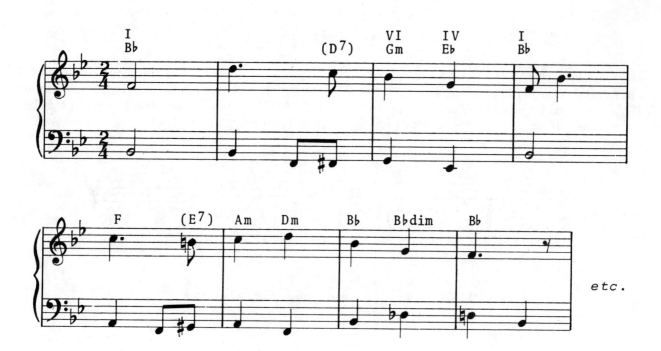

## Voice Leading

One other consideration in harmonizing pop melodies is the use of voice leading: the smooth transition from one note to another in changing harmonies. "We Wish You A Merry Christmas" utilizes a series of V-I patterns, but the harmonic movement is solidified through a bass line which moves smoothly through the chord changes through the use of inversion.

More extended variations on these basic pop progressions can be created through creative voice leading, and through chord substitution — a topic investigated on the following pages.

SI ♩

# Advanced Harmony

# CHORD SUBSTITUTION & HARMONY WITH THE CIRCLE OF FIFTHS

## PART I

An exercise to help familiarize you with the 'circle' is to play it on the keyboard as single notes, selecting any random location on the keyboard. For example: starting at the top of the circle you play a C, any C. Say Middle C. The next note in the circle is F. Play any F. It doesn't necessarily have to be the F below Middle C. Next play any B♭, to any E♭, etc. Memorize it as you play. Once you've done that you know the fifth below every note in the scale and you are on your way to changing your entire concept of pop harmony, which is really traditional harmony as epitomized by Bach.

*The following exercises will help familiarize you with the circle of fifths and perfect its use in your playing.*

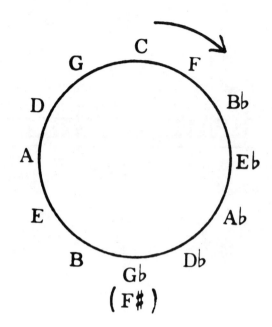

**A.** The circle of fifths starts with the top note of the keyboard and descends a fifth on each succeeding note, never repeating a note until it winds up on the lowest C of the keyboard. It progresses through all twelve tones of the scale before repeating a tone.

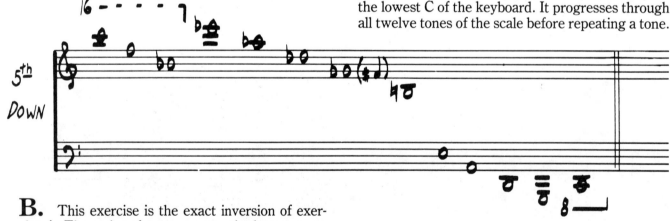

**B.** This exercise is the exact inversion of exercise A. The series of notes are exactly the same, except you are ascending. It is still called the circle of fifths because it is a fifth descending, but you are playing it upside down so it becomes a fourth ascending. Start memorizing the circle of fifths, beginning with the first four notes.

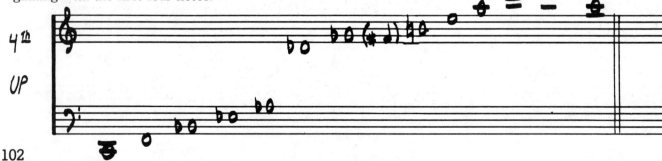

**C.** This exercise is a combination of descending and ascending fifths, alternating between the two. This is used in the base line of many pop songs and recordings.

**D.** This exercise is a mixed bag of descending and ascending fifths without any particular pattern. Memorize the first six notes of the circle and play them without looking.

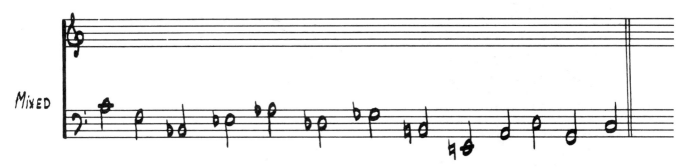

**E.** This exercise is a series of major chords built on a root which travels a fifth with each succeeding chord. Alternate ascending and descending fifths are found in many pop pieces.

**F.** This is an exercise to warm up your fingers and to develop your technique, as well as to help you memorize the circle of fifths. This exercise will also help you to use arpeggios in your playing. By now you should have memorized the first eight notes of the circle of fifths and can get this exercise up to speed.

**G.** This exercise shows the progression of dominant seventh chords structured on each root in the circle of fifths. It can also be called a series of secondary dominants. You should have memorized the entire circle of fifths by now.

**H.** This exercise is the same series of dominant chords as in exercise G, but it creates finger exercises to help you learn runs and put them into your playing. Play the exercise slowly with two hands. Only the first four chords have been written, the rest are left to you. If you have not yet memorized the rest of the chords in the progression, refer to exercise G for the next chords. Practice until you get it up to speed.

**I.** This combination of ascending and descending fifths loosens fingers and is good for practicing the circle of fifths. Again, only the first four chords are written. Repeat this exercise and progressively make it faster until it is up to speed.

**J.** This exercise is an important element for chords which travel through the circle of fifths. It is a combination of a minor seventh chord and a dominant seventh chord. It is sometimes called the II-V[7] progression in harmony. Repeat the progression until fully memorized.

**K.** This exercise is one of many ways to practice the circle of fifths. It uses thirteenth chords, but augmented ninth, or dominant ninth chords can also be used.

# PART II

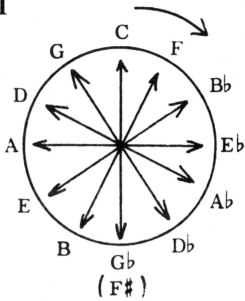

The illustration above is the one you will use to find chord substitutions and passing chords. Here are the three rules to remember:

Rule 1: You can often use the chord directly across the circle as a substitute for the chord you are playing.

(Example: If you are playing an F7 chord, follow the arrow across to find the likely substitute: B7.)

Rule 2: You can often use that same chord, the one directly across the circle, as a passing chord in addition to the original chord. (Example: If you are playing an F7 to a Bb progression, as written in a piece of sheet music, you can slip that same B7 in between as a passing chord.)

Rule 3: You can often precede the chord you are playing with the chord which precedes it in the circle. (Example: You are playing a G7 chord for two beats and would like to "fill" a chord before you hit the G7. Delay the G7 until the second beat and play the chord which precedes it in the circle on the first beat. The chord which precedes it in the circle is a D. In the example below we use a Dm7.)

105

Let us now apply these rules to a portion of Jerome Kern's "All The Things You Are."

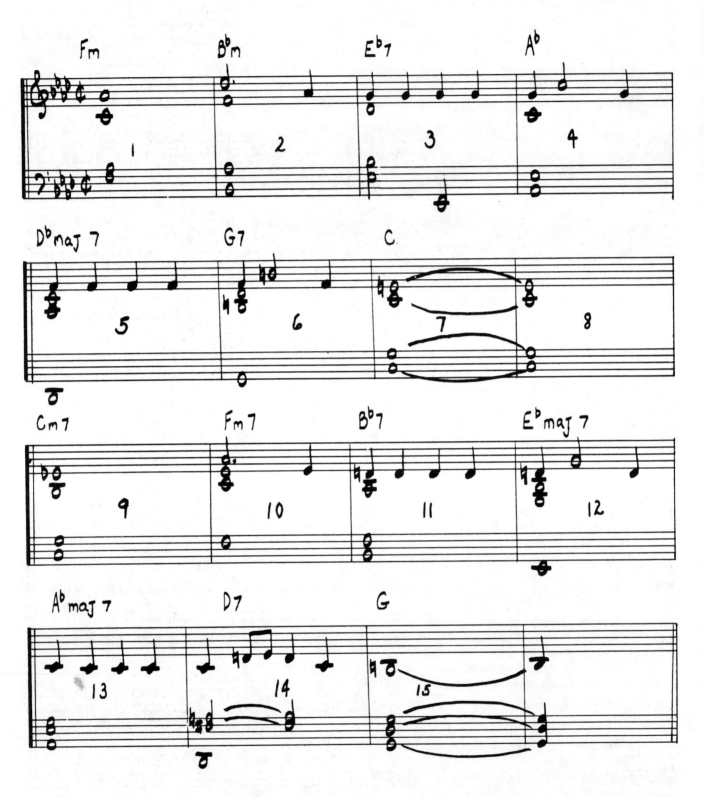

Before we substitute chords, take a quick look at how Kern composed this song around the circle of fifths, and also uses the 'jump-across-the-circle' technique we've discussed. His first chord is Fm. Next chord if Bᵇm (next in circle); his next chord Eᵇ7 (next chord in circle); next chord (can you guess?) is also the next chord in the circle, an Aᵇ: the next chord is (how can you miss?) a Dᵇ, the next chord in the circle. (You could practically play this song 'by ear' if you knew the circle of fifths.)

On the next chord, Kern throws a little curve. He gives us a G7. The G7 is not the next chord in the circle after D♭7 ... but it is the chord which is located directly across (follow the arrows) from the D♭7. He has used the 'jump-across' technique to continue his song. And now he starts using the circle all over again beginning on the G7. The next chord is C. It changes to Cm before going on to Fm,

the next circle chord. Analyze the rest of the example yourself to see Kern follow the circle and jump across.

Now let's put in some of our own chords using the rules we discussed here.

In the third measure we will use another chord instead of the E♭7. To find a possible substitute, look directly across the circle. An A7.

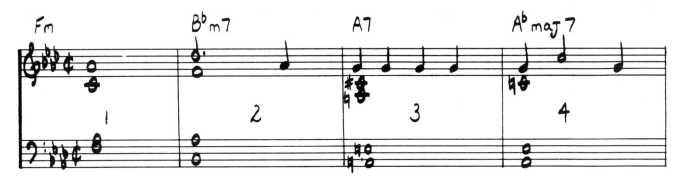

Now that we have that A7, let's apply Rule 3 to put a 'filler' or 'passing' chord in front of it. Find the

chord which precedes A7 in the circle, and use it just before you use the A7.

By using the circle, we have substituted two chords for the E♭7, and now you are leaving the sheet music arrangement for your own styled interpretation.

In measure 11, there is a B♭7 chord and we can apply the same technique. First find the substitute by looking across the circle. The substitute is E7.

Now use a filler chord by finding the chord which precedes the E7 in the circle. A B chord. Since

there's a D in the melody, Bm chord is the logical choice.

107

And finally, in the 14th measure, we can apply all three rules.

There is a D11 for four beats. An Am7 played before the D11 (Rule 3) and an AB7 played after the D7 (Rule 2):

Or you can simply ignore the original D7 altogether by substituting the A♭7 for it (Rule 1) but still keeping the Am7 as a filler chord.

This demonstrates how the filler chord (Am7) for the D7 can also become the filler chord for the D7's substitute. Another DISCOVERY! Ah, the circle is full of 'em!                                    **ES**

# Substitute Changes
## Helpful Hints

Many tunes share common progressions, and, depending on the particular melody being used, they can all be varied according to the principles outlined in the preceding articles.

Take the I-VI-II-V progression, for example. This chord sequence has been used in tunes such as "I Got Rhythm," "Cottontail," "Blue Moon," and "Tuxedo Junction." The original sequence,

$$\textbf{B}^\flat \text{ - } \textbf{Gm} \text{ - } \textbf{Cm}^7 \text{ - } \textbf{F}^7$$

can be varied in many ways. It sometimes appears as:

$$\textbf{B}^\flat \text{ - } \textbf{Gm} \text{ - } \textbf{Cm}^7 \text{ - } \textbf{F}^7 \text{ - } \textbf{Gm}^7 \text{ - } \textbf{E}^{dim} \text{ - } \textbf{Cm}^7 \text{ -} \textbf{F}^7.$$

The last four chords, however, can be substituted with the chords

$$\textbf{A}^{\flat 7} \text{ - } \textbf{G}^7 \text{ - } \textbf{B}^{\flat 7} \text{ - } \textbf{F}^7$$

as a circle of fifths progression leading to $\text{F}^7$ (with substitutions borrowed from across the "circle"):

Even the Blues progression can be spruced up through chord substitution. The typical Blues in F would look like this:

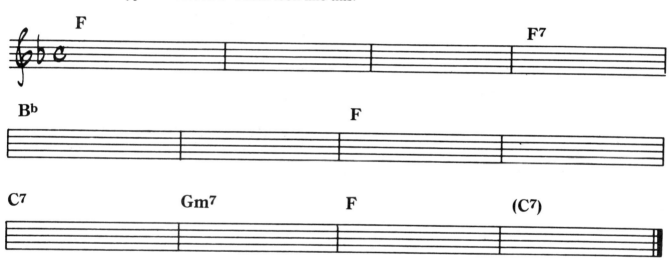

Here is a revised version using chord substitution:

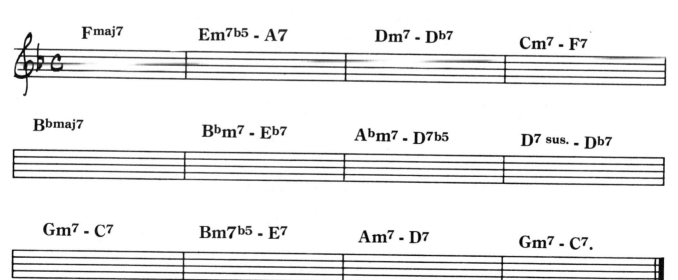

Try using substitutions on your favorite tunes. There is always a new way to play any song — the fun is in finding one you never thought of before!

# Keyboard Workshop

## Old Pants and New Suspenders

### —Suspensions add a different flavor to worn chord progressions

There was a time when pop music relied on very simple harmonies and straightforward rhythms; it's hard to imagine a George M. Cohan tune arranged with the kind of contemporary, sophisticated panache associated with Christopher Cross and Burt Bacharach. Today's music is something else entirely. But the new sounds we find in songs like "Best That You Can Do" (theme from the movie *Authur*) are not too difficult to understand. They just make use of a kind of harmonic tension that occurs when some of the well-worn simple progressions of Cohan's time are placed over unexpected additional tones.

Any tone can be a part of a countless range of harmonies. The note C, for example, can be part of a C chord, or of an F chord, or of a $D^7$, or a $G^{11}$, or a $Bb^9$. By the same token, a simple F chord takes on a new identity if you place a D below it: $Dm^7$. If you place a G below it, it will miraculously transform into a $G^{11}$.

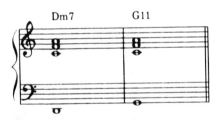

That sound of harmonies shifting over a steady bass is an important part of the contemporary sound; inevitably, the shifting treble harmonies create a "suspension"—a chord in search of resolution. There are plenty of examples of suspensions sprinkled throughout "Best That You Can Do."

In the above example, no sooner does the E chord resolve than we find a new suspension on the A chord. Still another suspension of sorts occurs when the common progression E–A (V–I) is placed over a held A in the bass. The dissonant sound produced when the E chord is struck resolves pleasantly into an A major sound; this is similar to a classical technique called *acciaccatura*. If the held A in the bass were absent, the harmonies would sound quite ordinary.

At other points in the song, typical step-wise progressions in the key of A, such as F#m–E–D–E (VI–V–IV–V) or F#m–E–D–C#m (VI–V–IV–III) take on new dimensions because of the bass tones below them.

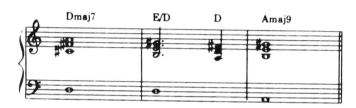

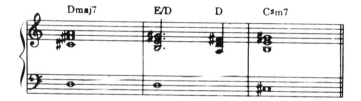

The technique of placing these simple harmonies over held bass tones results in chords with 9ths 11ths, 13ths, and so on. To continue this sound in sections where the held-bass approach is missing, simply add as many of these extra tones as possible to the chords indicated on the music.

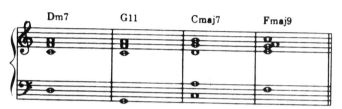

SI

# Harmony at the Keyboard

## *Transposing a Melody*

It is sometimes necessary to change the key of a song. You may be accompanying a singer who wants to take it higher or lower than written. Or you may want to add some variety to your rendition of a tune by playing the last chorus in a new tonal area. Moving a piece of music from one key to another is known as *transposition*. In this article we will explain how to transpose a melodic line.

Suppose you are dealing with a melody in the key of C major. The melody will make use, primarily, of the notes of the C major scale. Let us number the notes of that scale from one to seven. (The eighth note of the scale is, of course, the same as the first but an octave higher.)

Our next example shows the first four bars of the song *Careless Love* in the key of C major. We have given each note of the melody a number indicating its position in the scale. (The note below "one" is called "seven" since the scale is really continuous for the entire length of the keyboard.)

Now imagine that you want to transpose this melody to E flat major. Let us first write out the E flat major scale and, as before, number the scale degrees. The key signature has three flats: B flat, E flat, and A flat.

112

Look back at the original version of *Careless Love*. We saw that the notes of the tune could be represented by a series of numbers indicating scale degrees: 3, 1, 7, 5, 7, 2, 1. If we find these scale degrees in E flat major we will have the melody in the new key.

The process of transposition becomes slightly more complicated when accidentals are involved. Let us return to the C major version of *Careless Love*. A bit later in the tune we come across the note G sharp. We will label this note 5 +, since the fifth degree of the scale has been raised by a half step.

In the key of E flat major the fifth degree is B flat, so the raised fifth would be B *natural*. The principle here is that the actual accidental may be different when a melody is transposed, but the scale degree must be raised or lowered by exactly the same amount.

In summary: to transpose a melody you should first review the scale of the original key. Then label each note of the melody with a number indicating its position in the scale. Next review the scale of the new key. By finding the same degrees in this new scale you can reconstruct the melody in the new key. When accidentals are involved you should regard them as the raising or lowering of a particular scale degree.

If you want to acquire facility in this skill try writing out the transpositions of a few melodies, following the procedure we have outlined. Then work out some transpositions at the keyboard, without writing them down. If you practice doing this you will eventually be able to read off a melody in whatever key you wish; this is what is meant by "transposing at sight." In a later column we will deal with the transposition of chords.  SI ♩

# Harmony at the Keyboard

## Transposing A Chord Progression

In our previous column we discussed the transposition of a melodic line. As an illustration, we showed how the folksong *Careless Love* could be transposed from C major to E flat major. In this issue we will explain how the chord progression of the same tune can be similarly transposed.

In popular sheet music the chords are represented by symbols that appear over the vocal part. Our first example shows the opening bars of *Careless Love* in C major, together with the chord symbols. The letters C, G, and F refer to chord roots. The "7" after the "G" indicates a particular kind of chord—a dominant seventh.

To transpose the chords it is necessary to know their positions in the scale. Let us write out the C major scale and number each degree (it is customary to use the bass clef and Roman numerals when referring to chords).

Now we can return to *Careless Love* and give each chord a Roman numeral indicating its position in the scale.

Let us suppose that we want to transpose the song to E flat major. We must write out the E flat major scale and, once again, number the degrees.

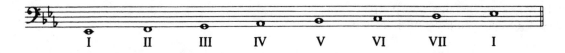

114

We have already—in the last issue—tranposed the melody to E flat. Now we can transpose the chords as well. "I" becomes an E flat chord, "V7" will be a B flat seventh, and "IV" will be A flat.

Notice that while the letter names change in transposition, the "7" remains the same because it specifies a *kind* of chord rather than a specific chord root.

Sometimes a chord appears that is not present in the scale. For example, later on in the C major version of *Careless Love* we encounter an A flat seventh chord. The note A flat does not appear in

the C major scale, but it can be considered the lowered sixth degree. So we have labelled that chord ♭VI7.

In E flat major the lowered sixth degree would be C flat (some players might prefer to consider

this a B natural). Here is the passage transposed to E flat:

As you can see, transposing a chord progression is very much like transposing a melody. Each chord is assigned a number corresponding to its position in the scale of the original key. By consulting the scale of the new key we can construct the transposed version of the chord progression. When a chord appears that is not present in the scale it should be considered a raised or lowered scale degree, such as the ♭VI7 in *Careless Love.*

In this article we have only dealt with chord *symbols.* Of course there are many possible ways to

play those chords at the keyboard, and some chords have rather complicated structures.

**RC** ♩

# Harmony at the Keyboard

## Introduction to Modulation

It is sometimes necessary to move from one key to another in the course of a piece. This kind of harmonic motion is known as "modulation." It should not be confused with transposition (which we discussed in the June/July '83 and Aug./Sept. '83 issues). While transposition involves taking a tune written in one key and playing it in another, modulation is the process by which you arrive at the new key.

Modulation is often useful when you are accompanying a singer or group of singers. Imagine you are accompanying the song "My Country 'Tis Of Thee" in the key of F major. Our first example shows the last four bars of the tune:

For the last verse, to provide some variety, you might want to move to a new key. Typically, the move is up a half step. This doesn't strain the singers' ranges much, but it provides a bright, new sound. Here are the first four bars of the tune in the key of F sharp major:

The problem is how to get from the end of the tune in F major, as shown in our first example, to the beginning of the tune in F sharp major, as shown in the second example. This is an harmonic problem, which calls for an harmonic solution. The strongest, most direct harmonic movement is from a "dominant" chord (the chord built on the fifth degree of the scale) to a "tonic" chord (built on the first degree). This is known as a V-I progression. A dominant seventh chord may also be used, and this is called a V7-I progression.

To move from F major to F sharp major, we can use the dominant chord of the new key to point the way. Our next example shows the last two bars of "My Country 'Tis Of Thee" in F major. After the final note, a C sharp chord has been inserted, which is the V chord of F sharp major. This establishes the new key, and the example concludes with the first two bars of the tune in F sharp major. The C sharp chord and the F sharp chord that begin the tune form a V-I progression. A little melodic phrase has also been added to guide the singers to the first note in the new key.

If, instead, we want to move up a whole step to the key of G major, we can use a D chord, which is the dominant in that key. Or, as in our next example, we can use a D7 chord so the progression is V7-I. Again a melodic phrase leads to the opening note. Notice that in both of our examples the modulation has been achieved without adding extra bars to the tune: This is the neatest way to do it.

We have been discussing the simplest form of modulation. In more complicated modulations a group of transitional chords may be involved, but almost always the dominant chord of the new key plays a major role.

If you would like to gain facility in modulation, you should become familiar with the V7-I progression in all keys. Our final example provides a pattern that can be extended up through all twelve tonalities. Practice it until it becomes automatic. When all of the dominants are (literally) at your fingertips, you will be ready to move the harmony in any direction.

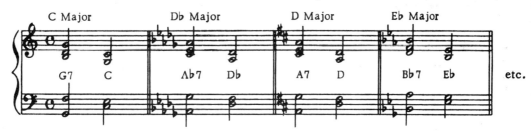

RC ♩

117

# pop piano

# Modulation
## Part 2: Voice Leading

Moving from one musical place to another involves much more than simply following a harmonic progression. A series of chords "works" only because there is an underlying melodic strain that "leads" from one voice to another. For example, let's take the common progression V - I. In the key of C, we will play $G^7$ to C:

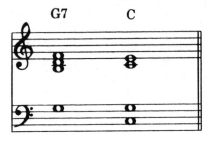

This movement sounds as solid as it does because the F in the G chord moves to the E in the C chord (a whole step); the note G acts as a "common tone" between the two harmonies (a common tone is the *strongest* possible connection between two musical moments); and the note B moves easily to the note C (a half step).

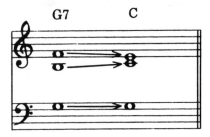

Such *voice leading* occurs often in popular music, and it can be spotted by looking for *stepwise* motion. The progression C to A to Dm, for instance, might appear this way:

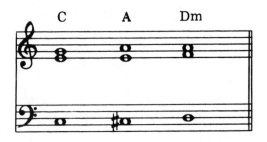

You'll notice that the bass line is moving chromatically stepwise, and that the right hand maintains a common tone: first the E, then the A.

This approach can be used in modulation, too. Last time we looked at certain chord progressions used to modulate from one key to another. This time, we'll explore the *voice-leading* approach.

Let's suppose we want to move from "Did You Ever See A Dream Walking?" (in G) to "Life Is Just A Bowl Of Cherries" (in B♭).

One way is to keep a common tone. The next example keeps the G in the bass, while the chords above move chromatically until reaching a B$^{b7}$ chord.

Here's another possibility, along the same lines: the common tone is in the uppermost voice, and the bottom voice descends. The last chord before the new E$^b$ harmony is a form of B$^{b7}$ — the V chord of E$^b$. The inner voices I chose just as a matter of personal taste. They could have appeared in endless combinations. Usually, however, *dominant* sounds are most successful.

The next examples omit the common tone altogether. Here, the method is to set up what is known as "contrary motion." The upper voice moves up toward the B$^b$ note of the new song,

while the bass voice moves downward towards the E$^b$.

Again, the inner harmonies are strictly a matter of choice. A B$^7$ harmony moves strongly to an E$^b$ harmony; like the V to I progression, the flat VI to I has both a common tone, and good voice leading.          SI ♩

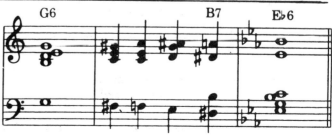

# *Style* at the Keyboard

## *Musical Form: The A-A-B-A Song*

A knowledge of musical form is very useful to the performer. Knowing the form of a tune can suggest ways of playing it, and it can also help you to remember the tune as you improvise upon it.

Many "standard" tunes fall into a particular form known as AABA. A good example of this in the present issue is *Darn That Dream*.

Let's analyze that tune. You should begin by numbering the bars of the sheet music, to refer to during the following discussion. Bars 1-4 constitute a short instrumental introduction. The "chorus," or tune proper, begins with bar 5. Bars 5-12 make up the first phrase of the tune, which we shall call "A":

Ex. 1

In bars 13-20 the "A" phrase is repeated, with a slight change in the ending. Then in bars 21-28 a new, contrasting phrase is introduced, which we shall call "B" (this is sometimes referred to as the "bridge" or "release" of the tune):

Ex. 2

Finally in bars 29-36 the "A" phrase returns. Bar 36 is provided with a "turnaround" chord progression to allow for a repetition of the tune, while bar 37 is an alternate, final, ending.

The overall form of the tune can be described as AABA. Each of the phrases is eight bars long, making a total of 32 bars. This is one of the fundamental forms of American popular music.

How can all of this help you to play *Darn That Dream?* You might decide to play the "A" phrases with a "stride piano" style accompaniment:

Ex. 3

The "B" phrase could be given a contrasting, broken-chord accompaniment. In this way the changes in keyboard arrangement will seem logical, and they will help to project the form of the song.

RC

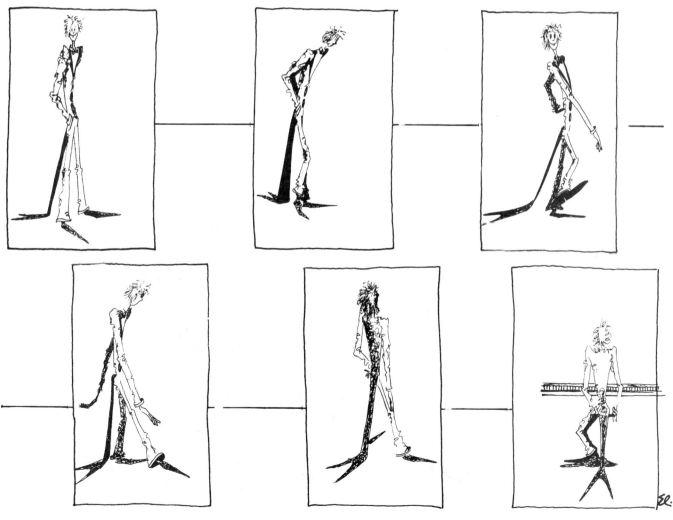

# Harmony at the Keyboard

## Minor Keys

Suppose you were to pick up the music for the old English folksong *Greensleeves.* Our first example shows the opening four bars. Looking at the key signature you would see one sharp, and you might assume that the key was G major. However, the opening bars seem to have very little to do with that key; there is not a single G major chord.

Then you might turn to the end of the song. As we pointed out in the previous issue, a tune almost always ends with a "I" chord, the chord that is built on the first note of the scale. In the key of G major that would be a G chord, but here the final chord is E minor.

Indeed the song is not in G major; it is in the key of E minor. We have come up against the fact that every key signature is shared by two keys: a major key, with which we are already familiar, and a minor key known as the "relative minor."

The relative minor is always a minor third lower than its associated major key. So a key signature of no sharps or flats can indicate either C major or, counting down a minor third, A minor. (You will recall that the interval of a minor third is made up of three half-steps.)

Our next example shows the signatures for the most commonly used sharp keys. In each case there are two possibilities: a major key and a relative minor that lies a minor third lower.

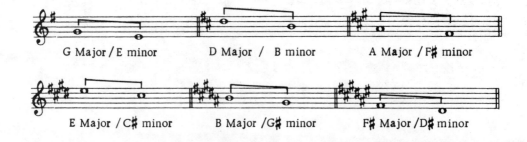

Now we can complete the harmonization of the second half of *Auld Lang Syne*, with a D-minor chord in the seventh bar. This chord is built on the sixth note of the scale. Because it is a minor chord it introduces a new, interesting sound. Another improvement would be to use an inversion of the F chord, with A in the bass, at the start of bar five.

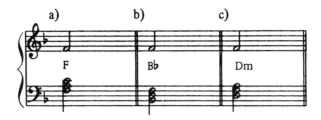

There is a system to be followed here. Begin the harmonization of a tune with the expectation that the three primary chords will play an important part. The tune often starts with the "I" chord, and almost always ends with it. When you come to a problem spot, try various chords that contain the main melody note. Once you hit on the best solution you will usually know immediately: your ear will tell you that it is right.

RC

# Harmony at the Keyboard

## The Three Minor Scales

We discussed the subject of minor keys. We saw that every key signature is shared by a major key and a minor key a third lower. Thus a signature of one sharp can indicate either G major or E minor.

Minor keys often include accidentals, so musicians have devised three different minor scales, to account for these. The basic minor scale is the "natural minor." It consists of the notes given in the signature, without accidentals.

E natural minor

A well-known tune that makes use of the natural minor throughout is "When Johnny comes Marching Home." Here are the first four bars:

It is common in minor keys for the seventh degree to be raised. This often happens for harmonic reasons, to create a V7 chord. So when we speak of an "harmonic minor" scale, that includes the raised seventh:

E harmonic minor

The following example shows the first four bars of the spiritual "Go Down Moses." Notice the D sharp in bar three: it is a raised seventh degree.

And, significantly, it is part of a B7 chord (which is V7 in E minor). Here, clearly, the raised seventh has an "harmonic" purpose.

Sometimes, in order to make for a smooth melodic line, the sixth as well as the seventh degree is raised. This usually happens when a melody is moving upward. On the way down it is more common for the seventh and sixth degrees to be lowered. This practice gave rise to a third scale, the "melodic minor." In its ascending form the sixth and seventh are raised, and in its descending form they are lowered:

E melodic minor

Our final example shows a phrase of John Philip Sousa's march, "The Picadore." In bar three, as the melody ascends, we find the notes C sharp and D sharp, the raised sixth and seventh degrees. This is an example of the melodic minor.

Bear in mind that a tune does not have to stick to only one form of the minor scale. It is just as common for the natural, harmonic, and melodic forms to be mixed together in one song. In a sense these scales are only theoretical: they are an attempt to codify the quirky behavior of melodies in minor keys. But they also serve a practical purpose: by practicing all three forms, the musician can prepare for many of the note-patterns that minor keys present.

RC ♪

# Keyboard Styles

# COUNTRY-STYLE AT THE KEYBOARD

The popularity of country music has grown so swiftly over the past few years that almost every musical style has been influenced by it in some way. Pop and rock artists often record in Nashville, and the little slides and fills which grew in the green hills of "Opry" country have now worked their way into urban music centers with pleasant insistence and rewarding results. While the elements of this style spring from the way certain instruments, notably the guitar, are played by country musicians, these techniques are easily transferred to the piano.

Let's look at some of the phrases and "frills" you can add to pieces to give them a country flavor, beginning with basic accompaniment patterns. Country back-up rhythms are usually very simple and straight-forward (like down-home country people!):

Ex. 1

Depending on the particular song, the accompaniment may have less movement in the left hand, and more in the right:

Ex. 2 & 3

Notice the bit of *walking bass* used in switching from the C chord to the F. Other forms of this movement occuring in country-style piano include the use of a *drone* note above:

Ex. 4

or parallel 3rds or 10ths:

Ex. 5

or triplets which arpeggiate or break up the individual harmonies:

Ex. 6

The walking line can move down, as well as up.

Ex. 7

Ornaments play a big role in this music and many of them duplicate sounds characteristic of the guitar. For example, guitarists sometimes "hammer on" notes, by striking a vibrating string down against the fingerboard; or they "pull off" notes by plucking a string with their fingering hand. The equivalent sounds on piano are these:

Ex.'s 8, 9, & 10

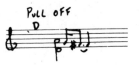

Floyd Cramer is famous for using these devices. The moving note always ends up on the third of the chord, starting from the second or the fourth.

Those *drone* notes can be used in many situations, and they often are:

Ex. 11

Other country sounds are the *tremelo* (used in slow songs very effectively):

Ex. 12

the quick chord *arpeggio* (like a guitar strum):

Ex. 13

and guitar-like "picking patterns":

Ex. 14

Applying these country "flavorings" to a song is simply a matter of looking for places to plug into the chord progression one or several of the "riffs" we've explored. It's important not to over-do it, but filling in with these sounds can be great fun:

Ex. 15

SI ♩

# Country Piano-Picking

A couple of years ago, we featured a column on country-style keyboard playing (October '80). As you'll recall, that introduction to country style contained several ornaments and guitarlike fills (made famous by Floyd Cramer and other Nashville artists).

Let's take another look at country playing, this time concentrating on "finger-picking" patterns. Standard country accompaniments to songs like *"Green, Green Grass of Home,"* may consist of just a simple chord arpeggiation like the one in example 1:

Note the bass line. It moves back and forth between the root and fifth of the chord; just before the chord changes from Bb to Eb, it moves up to the third of the chord, for smooth voice-leading to the Eb. This bass line can be made a little more animated through dotted rhythms and scale notes leading into the new chord:

Using these simple bass lines the right hand can be freed for even more energetic accompaniment patterns. Guitarists have a catalogue filled with different strum patterns, and keyboard players can easily adapt some of these. For instance, a favorite finger-picking routine of country guitarists is to play a chord arpeggio that is broken up into a series of 3 + 3 + 2:

It is easy to make up your own patterns, too. Take any chord and find a nice-sounding way to arpeggiate it; after a few repetitions, change the pattern, and you're all set:

It's not necessary to stick only to the notes of the chord, though. Remember this country ornament, similar to the "hammer on" technique of guitarists?

Strum patterns can make use of those notes which are extraneous to the chord, as long as they move into the chord tones, the way the "hammer on" pattern does:

By combining different patterns and breaking up the eighth notes into irregular groups of three and two, you'll produce "finger-pickin' " good sounds, perfect for backing up your favorite country tunes.

SI ♩

# *Style* at the Keyboard _____

## *Playing Country Music*

In the past decade country music has left its regional status behind to become the fastest-growing segment of American popular music, appealing to an international audience. At the same time the term *country music* has been extended to cover a wide range of styles. Still, there is a basic country music sound and feeling, as you can tell from the songs in this issue. Here are a few things to keep in mind as you play through these songs at the keyboard.

*Green, Green Grass Of Home* is an example of a traditional-sounding country song, with a straightforward four-beat rhythm. There are bass notes on the first and third beats of each bar, and you may want to add offbeat chords in the left hand on beats two and four. We have also moved the melody up an octave, for the sake of greater sonority.

In *The Gambler* the bass notes occur on every quarter note, so the chords should be added on the offbeat eighth notes. The rhythmic pattern here is not that different from our previous example; it is just notated in a different way.

In a mellow, country-pop ballad like *Snowbird* it is effective to add broken-chord figures in the right hand, suggesting the sound of a guitar. Notice that the rhythm of the melody is altered slightly to fit in with the figuration.

130

Another typical country device, also derived from guitar style, is the "slip note." This is an accented grace note, usually forming a second with the root of the chord and resolving to the third (i.e. in a C chord, a D resolving to an E). The "slip notes" give a country sound to the fills that we have added in bars two and four of *Rhinestone Cowboy*.

*Nine To Five* grows out of the "honkytonk" side of country music, and it calls for a more raucous and bluesy keyboard style. Dominant seventh chords, blue notes, tremolos, and a swinging stride-piano left hand are all appropriate here. Our example comes from the chorus of the song.

The harmony in country music should be kept simple. Notice that in all of our examples except for *Snowbird* (which is the most "pop" of the songs) the harmony is restricted to the three basic chords in each key. So, this is not the place for ninths, elevenths, thirteenths, substitute chords, etc. Instead, concentrate on the rhythmic vitality, the peppy fills and figures. Think of the sound of a guitar, banjo, and fiddle, and pay attention to the lyrics. The songs are sometimes happy, more often sad, but always expressive.

**RC** ♩

# pop piano

# The Sound of Soft Rock

Today's pop sounds are a hybrid of many musical styles. Music that once appealed to only limited numbers of people — such as rock and country — have taken their place alongside more traditional elements of the pop "melting pot." Now, more than ever, the pop musician must be familiar with the whole range of contemporary styles.

One modern style in common use is often labeled "soft rock." Contemporary ballads are almost always backed up with a strong, steady beat, and slightly syncopated rhythm—trademarks of the popular "soft" sound. Keyboard players who want to practice this style can do so with a tune like "We've Only Just Begun." (The complete music is in this issue.)

The bass is important in all pop music, and soft rock bass rhythms really help to set the right mood. Often, the rhythm is a simple repeating pattern based on a dotted quarter followed by an eighth:

Try this using the "We've Only Just Begun" chord progression:

This pattern can be spruced up at times by adding little connecting scales from one root to the next:

or by using "anticipation," the practice of hitting a main note earlier than expected:

The right hand can also play a basic pattern, which simply arpeggiates the notes of the chord being played:

To add more of a "kick" to the sound, this chord arpeggiation can be made more interesting through a bit of rhythmic "play." Practice this pattern for a while, and you'll have a basic "rock" approach that can be used over and over in countless songs:

132

Want to get even fancier? Try adding these sixteenth-note arpeggios every once in a while:

Now, let's put the whole package together, using the first few measures of our chord progression:

The only thing left to do is integrate these patterns with the melody of the song. Just keep in mind that you don't want to cover up the melody, so you'll want to save the fancy or busy background figures for times when the melody is static or silent:

# pop piano

## A Happy Marriage

It's no longer easy to classify a piece of music as simply "rock," or "pop," or "country," since in today's music world a whole rainbow of stylistic traits finds its way into almost every recording or performance. One very common mixture of musical influences can be found in songs like "Sweetheart" by the Brothers Gibb: a marriage of Nashville country-pop and urban soft-rock.

Here are some examples to help you with the "frills", and professional touches in this hybrid style. First, the country flavor: In previous articles, we've covered some of the elements of country playing. These include the "hammer-on" ornament (the second of the chord resolving to the root):

Chord arpeggio "fills" are also used. Most commonly, they will include the major chord tones, the sixth of the chord, and the second of the chord. In "Sweetheart," there are many possible places to insert arpeggios. Here are a couple of examples:

Our country-style embellishments can also be formed into short repeating patterns as an alternative to the arpeggio fills. In the example below we switch from a G chord to a D chord, then back to G (I-V-I) in order to produce the pattern on a G harmony:

There are a number of simple devices we can take from the sounds of soft rock to add yet another dimension to this song. One such device is the use of "pedal point." Find a section of the song which begins and ends on the same chord, and hold the root of that chord in the bass, even while other chords pass over it:

Try playing the song with this pedal point on D, and get that soft-rock flavor developed by artists such as Carole King.

One more rock element to keep in mind is the use of "anticipation." This means playing the downbeat of a measure (the strong, accented "1") slightly early:

Putting all of these devices together, we can come up with a rhythmic, country-swinging, down-home, rockabilly version of "Sweetheart" that will have everyone in the room jumping. Here's a sample starting at the fifth measure of the song:

SI

# RAGTIME RIFFS

In the introduction to his *Etudes,* Scott Joplin lashed out at those who threw bricks at "hateful ragtime," and announced with some pride that it is a music of often painful difficulty. He created his set of ragtime lessons, as he wrote, "to assist amateur players in giving the 'Joplin Rags' that weird and intoxicating effect intended by the composer."

Keyboardists who attempt ragtime rhythms are more likely to face confusion than intoxication, but with a little practice the weirdness of the music will seem no more jarring than falling down a flight of stairs. A good way to begin is to examine the music to see what the shortest note value is. If a sixteenth note is the shortest, count the entire measure in sixteenth notes.

### Ex. 1

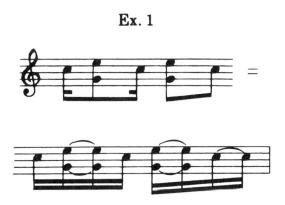

Using the sixteenth notes as a basis, the tricky rhythms that contradict the natural accents in each measure become less of a problem. Usually the left hand keeps up a steady, even pulse (although it will at times play a raggy counter-melody).

The right hand riffs of ragtime will most often fall into a few rhythmic combinations, all based on the syncopated feeling of example 1. These combinations place the "syncope" either before or after an even group of eighth or sixteenth notes; one of the key features of ragtime is the contrast set up between the syncopated figures and the "straight" figures surrounding them.

### Ex. 2a

### Ex. 2b

These combinations become a little more complicated through the use of ties.

### Ex. 3a

### Ex. 3b

### Ex. 3c

### Ex 3d

- or -

### Ex. 3e

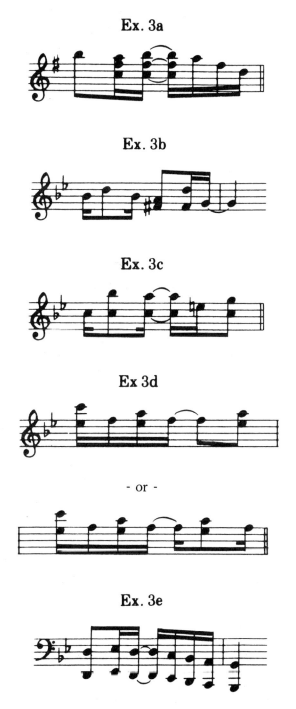

Again, the way to practice these is by counting them in sixteenth note divisions. Go through all the combinations above and then make up some additional ones yourself. After practicing each of the rhythmic possibilities, you'll be set to tackle any ragtime piece.

SI ♩

# Keyboard Workshop

## Playing Rock . . .
## What a Feeling!

Do you ever hear a great hit on the radio, go out to buy the sheet music for it, and wonder how the written version could possibly share the same title as the recording? This happens frequently in contemporary music because the "sound" produced in the recording studio is dependent on very stylized playing by some of today's top artists; the "bare bones" version of a song, as printed in the sheet music version, is always going to be a far cry from what you hear in the actual performance.

This is especially true in rock. For example, the standard sheet music version of "Flashdance . . . What A Feeling" doesn't convey the energy and excitement of the original soundtrack. One way to overcome this is to study some of the keyboard patterns studio musicians use to back up rock singers.

The basic approach used in playing this kind of contemporary song can be described in two steps: 1) keep a fast eighth-note feel going all the time; and 2) divide the rhythmic patterns between your right and left hands so that they take turns playing the accented notes. This leads to an occasional "surprise" in the sound, when the listener expects a strong bass note and hears a treble chord instead!

Here are four typical rhythm patterns for a funky rock keyboard sound. Try playing each one separately — slowly at first. You might want to tap your hands on a tabletop at the beginning, just to get the rhythms straight.

When you feel comfortable with all four of these examples, play them in order without stopping.

Then, try your hand at "Flashdance . . . What A Feeling," using similar patterns. You might try the next example to start:

Before long, you'll have friends asking, "Where can I get the music?" Imagine their disappointment when they find a copy!

SI

136

# Breaking Up Is Easy
# To Do

Tasteful arpeggios never seem out of place, and it is hard to imagine playing a contemporary pop ballad without them. Here are some ideas on approaching arpeggiation; the examples below use a chord progression similar to that of "What Are You Doing The Rest Of Your Life."

One simple way to decide on the pitches to use in your arpeggios is to pick out the harmony at any given point, and play it one note at a time. Keeping the arpeggio within a one-octave range is often a good idea; you may wish to establish a particular shape (up, down, up, down), and then add variations to it for increased excitement (up, up, up):

An arpeggio of sixteenth notes would also work well here. Notice that the points at which a "down" or "up" movement turns around occur at changes in the harmony. The transition is accomplished in a variety of ways: repetition of the same note; continuation of the chord arpeggio; or a smooth step-wise connection.

Placing the accents in an arpeggio on unexpected parts of the bar can make the accompaniment even more interesting. This technique brings to mind the guitar finger-picking patterns which add so much to the sound of country music.

Finally, arpeggio patterns can be pulled out of the nonstop motorific environment in which they are normally found, and placed here and there as melodic fragments. This will create a more sensitive, romantic effect.

SI

137

# $\mathcal{Style}$ at the Keyboard

## *Playing Contemporary Ballads*

Contemporary ballads have moderate to slow tempos, and often feature a bass line consisting of dotted quarters and eighth notes. This rhythmic pattern does not always appear in the sheet music, but you may want to add it, together with chords on the second and fourth beats. A good candidate for such treatment would be the song *Didn't We.* (The organist will play the bass line on the pedals, the chords with the left hand, and the melody with the right.)

When a more flowing accompaniment is called for, broken chords in eighth notes can be used in the left hand. (The organist can play the left hand figuration and also sustain the main bass notes with the pedals.) Here our example is from *The Way We Were.* Notice that the melody has been moved up an octave and thickened with chords.

Sometimes broken chord figures can be worked into the right hand and interwoven with the melody. Notice that here - in an example from the tune *If* - the rhythm of the melody has been slightly simplified, so that it combines more easily with the figuration.

138

In some contemporary ballads the rhythm of the melody looks very complicated, with many syncopations and sixteenth note patterns. This is due to the practice of basing the sheet music *exactly* on the popular record, preserving every nuance of the singer's style. It is often a good idea to simplify these rhythms for instrumental performance. Our next example shows the first phrase of *I'll Never Love This Way Again* as written (a), and in a simplified version (b).

*I'll Never Love This Way Again* is a ballad that can be given a stride piano accompaniment, with bass notes on the first and third beats, and middle register left-hand chords on the offbeats. This technique creates a soaring, expansive feeling for the chorus of the song:

RC

# Keyboard Workshop

## Stride and Rhythm Style
## At the Keyboard: Part I

Would you describe your playing as being "stuck in a rut?" Whether you are a pianist or organist, learning the stride or rhythm style can change your whole outlook on playing. Even if you never become a good stride player, working at it can add a lot of zip to your own style and get you out of that rut. The truth is that stride players seem to have more fun. So let's give it a whirl . . .

The best way to get started is to get the left hand going in some of the patterns that are found in stride. For organists, it is a combination pedal and left-hand drill. For pianists, it's all left hand . . . and it isn't as impossible as it first seems if you practice these drills very S-L-O-W-L-Y.

The left-hand rhythm is established by alternating bass notes, triads, and ascending and descending bass lines. See the 4th, 6th, and 9th measures of our drills for ascending and descending bass lines.

Learn these four drills in the "easy" keys as shown. Again, play them as S-L-O-W-L-Y as you can, gradually picking up speed when you have mastered the slow tempo. Your hands (and feet) are learning something new. Be patient with them. (You are free to move on to harder keys once you've mastered these.)

Note: Organists should play all the single notes on pedal. The ascending and descending lines may be doubled in the left hand if you wish.

Get these down pat before our next issue because we are going to add some right-hand licks . . . and you don't want to be thinking about the left hand. It should play almost automatically. Good luck. Remember to keep it S-L-O-W!

# Stride and Rhythm Style
# At the Keyboard
# (Part II)

Now that we have established a left-hand pattern via the four drills (January '84), it's time to superimpose some typical right hand patterns over them. The overall purpose of these exercises is to create the *feeling* of the stride style, not only in your head, but in your muscles. Keep it light. Try not to be tense and bangy. The music does not have to be played fast to be effective. And it should not be loud. Strive for the *light and easy* feeling as well as sound.

These drills constitute typical treatments of pop harmonies used in the stride style. Write out the right hand part for the other two keys practiced in the last article (G and Bb), and see if you can't create some simple variations or alterations on the original. This will be your first attempt at creating a stride arrangement.

**ES**

# Blues Sounds For Pianists

*"The Blues"* is a term which has been used to describe both a particular form in music, and a kind of sound which can color any piece, at the whim of a performer. Here is the form of a "12 bar blues."

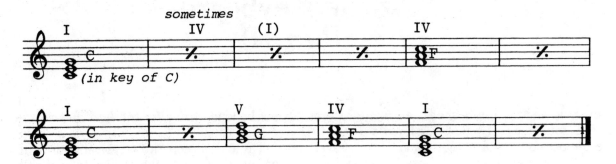

Most often, musicians use dominant seventh chords instead of the simple triads indicated above. The characteristic sound of the blues results from these dominant sevenths, and from so-called "blue notes." (We'll cover the blues scale shortly.) It is also closely tied to the "gospel" cadence (see below).

The best place to begin in describing the blues *flavor* is with the cadence IV-I. It is known by various names: the *plagal cadence* and the *gospel cadence* are both terms used to describe it.

It will certainly sound familiar as the basis of the "shuffle" pattern used in many blues and pop songs:

The IV-I cadence also serves as the foundation of many blues phrases and fills — those little professional "touches" added to an arrangement by blues musicians:

The switch from I to IV and back again will sometimes even occur over a steady harmony, as this shuffle study indicates:

There are other elements to the blues sound, however, and certain characteristic approaches for both the right hand and left hand in keyboard technique.

# Left Hand Patterns

Many of the left hand blues patterns were adopted by early rock and roll performers. Try each of the following, and then apply them to the 12 bar blues pattern you saw earlier.

# Right Hand Patterns

Over the rock-steady foundation of the left hand patterns above, blues players often insert little "fills" which are based on a few simple principles. Sometimes these fills are just arpeggiated chords or tremelos, played in repeating patterns.

These fills also make use of chromatic notes, especially the b3 and b5 of the chord being played.

These phrases can be practiced by going through the circle of fifths:

The b3 and b5 are prominent members of what is known as the "blues scale."

The blue notes found in this scale stand out because of the contrast between the notes of the normal major scale, and these alterations. Therefore, many blues phrases move back and forth between, for example, the major third of a chord and the minor third:

Right hand phrases will also employ the IV-I cadence, as well as chromatic movement (cited above):

# Advanced Harmonies

Contemporary, jazzy versions of the blues use advanced harmonies, such as the ones below:

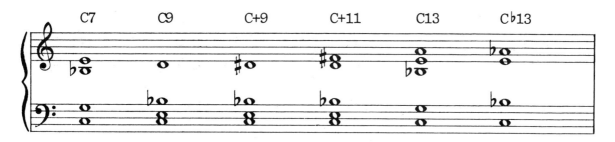

Note the left hand voicings in the following examples; modern pianists often omit the root of the chord. These sophisticated harmonies were unknown to the original blues players.

*Continued*

# Ornaments

One final technique is all you need to start playing blues sounds: grace notes. When a series of ornamental notes are played in blues style, a single finger is often used to slide across two or more. Try the following examples, and slide across the grace notes as smoothly as possible.

SI♩

# pop piano
## TIPS ON ACCOMPANYING A SINGER

Accompanying a singer is an aspect of musicianship that is often ignored or taken for granted. Yet if one simply reads the sheet music arrangement of a tune along with a singer, the results frequently tend to have an 'amateuriso' quality. If each of you is stating the tune without paying attention to what your partner is doing, you are, in effect, in musical competition, instead of working together to make a balanced musical statement. Let us look at some general guidelines for the accompanist.

First and foremost, we must realize that the accompanist's role is primarily supportive. If the singer wishes to have a rubato feel, don't try to impose a strict tempo. If the vocalist is building dynamically to a climax, support it in the accompaniment; conversely, if the singing drops down to a whisper, don't ruin this effect by overplaying. A sensitive accompanist often suggests directions in which to take the song (both verbally and in actual performance), but does so without trying to dominate.

What specifically does a good accompanist do to function as this sensitive musical support? One important principle is not to attempt to play the whole tune as if it were a solo piece. The accompanist generally avoids doubling the melody line that is being sung, except when it is specifically desired for emphasis. Chordal patterns, in block form, broken chords, or arpeggios, are common types of accompaniment. Using different inversions and voicings of the chords, and variety in the way the chord is broken up or arpeggiated is essential. It is helpful to change the rhythm of the accompaniment figure when there is a change of phrase or section. Also, don't restrict everything to a small section of the keyboard; a simple arpeggio figure can suddenly achieve a shimmering effect by moving it into a higher octave.

When the sung melody has a lot of movement, the accompanist might choose to play rather sparsely to emphasize this. When the tune comes to a rest or a long sustained note, the accompanist may then play a 'fill,' perhaps with an arpeggio, a scale line, or an answering melody derived from what just preceeded it.

While the supporting part will usually play on the strong beats, it is not necessary for it to be present on every beat, or on every note of the melody. Similarly, chords don't have to have all their notes played; the vocal part can fill out or suggest some of the harmony.

Let us look at how we can apply some of these ideas to "Always On My Mind."

In general, a pop-country ballad such as this should have a simple, straight-forward accompaniment. Notice the even bass figures and the simple chord figuration except when there is a fill figure. In the first measure of the first example (measure 3 of the sheet music) there is a right hand figure on the last two beats that echoes the three opening notes of the tune; echoing or answering the melody is often effective when there is a sustained note or rest. In the last two beats of the following measure there is scale-like line in sixteenth notes that fills while the vocal has a half note rest. Two measures later there is another half note rest in the melody; here the fill is a brokenchord pattern that has a pedal-steel guitar effect.

The second example (measure 10 in the sheet music) has a combined arpeggio and scale fill on the G# half-diminished chord which starts high and runs downward. When accompanying a simple tune such as this, a little of this kind of 'flashiness' goes a long way.

In the final example (measures 15-17 in the sheet music), the bass line moves in octaves, which adds drama and richness. Here the 'hook line' of the tune is harmonized in rhythmic synchronization by the piano part, adding emphasis. When the line is repeated two measures later, the rhythm of the accompaniment becomes sparse. This emphasizes the vocal line in a different way, by making it more soloistic. Note that the piano plays a plain A major triad while the vocalist sings a G note, completing the full A7 chord. This gives a more pleasing effect in this case than if the seventh of the chord appeared in both parts.

Take a song you are familiar with and play it in an accompaniment version. Have someone else sing the melody. **Listen to the total sound**. Good listening is the prerequisite to the development of the flexibility, sensitivity, and taste that is the hallmark of a skilled accompanist.

# *Style* at the Keyboard

## Accompanying Group Singing

'Tis the season for group singing, and keyboard players will be very much in demand on such occasions. Accompanying singers is a specialized skill, and we thought that some tips on the subject might be worthwhile.

If you can transpose, or are playing by ear, you will want to choose the best key for each song. A safe, average vocal range is the octave C to C, which can be exceeded by one or two notes in either direction when necessary. Suppose you are accompanying *Auld Lang Syne*. A good key would be F, which makes the lowest note C and the highest note D.

A short introduction will serve to announce the song, establish the key, and set the tempo. This last is especially important for keeping the group together. A typical introduction can be fashioned from the last four or two bars of the song. (Since *Auld Lang Syne* is relatively slow, two bars are sufficient.)

When accompanying a group it is often wise to pound out the melody, doubling it in octaves if possible.

Once you are sure that the group knows the tune you can stop playing melody and use a more rhythmic form of accompaniment. But notice that the right hand still touches on the *main* melody notes, to keep the singers on pitch.

When you come to the end of the tune you may want the singers to go on to another verse. You can signal them to do so by playing a "turnaround" emphasizing the dominant (i.e. the fifth note of the scale, which would be C in the key of F).

To create a final ending for the song, slow the tempo slightly, hold the last note (we have added a tremolo in the left hand), and then cut it off with a sharp "button" consisting of a tonic chord (i.e. a chord on the first note of the scale). Notice that as the tempo broadens we have provided an upper octave doubling, to give a fuller sound.

When you are invited to play at a party, it is a good idea to do some advance preparation. Make a list of the songs you expect to use (try to guess what tunes will be requested) and decide on the keys for all of them. Have your music easily accessible, to eliminate fumbling between songs. Then relax, sing along as you play, and enjoy the party. 'Tis the season. . . ♩ RC

# Secrets of a Musical
# "COLLABORATOR"

Dan Routh

*There's more to being an accompanist than meets the eye. Though pianist partners of leading soloists often remain far back from the gleam of stage lights, they exert a powerful influence on every musical performance; and they must call on special skills and talents to bring these collaborations off.*

---

*When music greats Itzhak Perlman, Pinchas Zukerman, Mstislav Rostropovich, or Beverly Sills perform at New York's Carnegie Hall or Washington's Kennedy Center, chances are they will ask pianist Samuel Sanders to join them. Sanders has been recognized for more than a decade as one of America's leading "collaborative" pianists. In addition to performing nearly one hundred concerts a year, he teaches accompanying at the Juilliard School, records extensively (two recent albums with Perlman and Zukerman have won Grammy awards), and acts as music director of both the Cape and Islands Chamber Music Festival, and the chamber ensemble Musica Camerit. Mr. Sanders has performed at the summer festivals of Marlboro, Ravinia, Wolf Trap, Saratoga, and at the Mostly Mozart Festival in New York, in addition to six performances at The White House.*

*Born with a serious heart defect, Samuel Sanders began piano lessons as a way to staying safely occupied through his childhood. He had several pioneering heart operations, and carried on a normal life until the spring of 1980, when he began having heart failure just before a concert. Since it was the inaugural season of the Cape and Island Chamber Music Festival, he continued on with the aid of drugs until twenty-four more concerts had passed! In the fall of that year he underwent open heart surgery twice, remaining in intensive care for a month and in the hospital for two*

*months more, during which time violinist Itzhak Perlman called him every day. One month after being out of bed, he made a recording with Perlman, and his career resumed at the same hectic pace.*

*Outwardly shy and modest, Sanders nevertheless takes musical command with ease. He likens his position to that of a catcher in baseball: "He's in on every single play," explains the pianist. "He has an overview and that's what you get at the piano because you are looking at all of the parts simultaneously, controlling many aspects, just as the catcher controls the flow of the game."*

*Keyboard Classics asked Samuel Sanders to write about the life and art of an accompanist, and he provided the following advice for our readers.*

I have been an accompanist for over twenty years, and during most of that time I have taught music courses on the art of accompanying. People often ask me just what that means, and how one gets involved in my field.

I've never been able to answer those questions to my own satisfaction. I do know one thing: the use of the term "accompany" is unfortunate, but I really can't think of a better word. For example, if I were to say that I was a collaborator, it could be taken that I sided with an enemy government. "Partner" is nice, but no soloist would ever put up with that. "Assistant" is possible, but one doesn't really "assist" in any significant Beethoven, Brahms, or Strauss work that I know of. So we're stuck with "accompanist."

The real problem is the public's misunderstanding of the word "accompany." The dictionary defines it in some of the following ways: to go with; to add to; to support. Yet, any musician who plays one of the great song cycles or instrumental works knows that the piano and the voice (or instrument) are coexisting in that work on an equal basis; the pianist is not simply "going with" or "adding to."

In fact, anyone who wants to make his livelihood as a concert accompanist should be aware that he or she will need a first-rate piano technique, as just one of a number of essential skills. The physical requirements of a song like Schubert's "Erlkönig" or a piece like the Rachmaninoff Sonata for cello and piano demand the same total command of the keyboard that one must possess to play a large portion of the solo piano repertoire.

Let me give you a few examples. This fragment from the first movement of the Rachmaninoff *Cello Sonata* shows the difficulty one may find in an "accompanying" part. Note the leaps in the left hand while the right hand negotiates an unwieldy stretching passage. Rachmaninoff had a large hand and huge span; others of us are not so fortunate.

Here's another difficult accompanying situation. In the extremely brief song "Ich hab in Penna einen Liebsten wohnen," by Hugo Wolf, the pianist's concluding passage is a sort of high-wire act. This passage must be executed brilliantly, with seeming total abandon: the slightest mishap can cause the pianist (*and* the song) to fall flat on his or her face.

Beethoven's *Sonata No.9* in A Major (Op.47) for violin — Beethoven actually labeled it "for piano and violin"—has a passage which is noteworthy in another respect. The technical difficulty of this piano part is compounded by the need to synchronize with the violinist. *Both* players must listen carefully and phrase as one—not an easy matter!

The most renowned accompanists in the field today are indeed people who have fluent command of the piano from the purely digital standpoint. They include, among others, John Wustman, Geoffrey Parsons, Martin Katz, Sandra Rivers, Graham Johnson, Brook Smith, and Margot Garrett.

Now that we have established that one must be a very fine pianist to play both the instrumental and vocal repertoire, we can tackle the question of what accompanying is, and how one becomes an accompanist.

---

## "Accompanists have to tackle problems that soloists never face. Here are some of them."

---

**A**ccompanying is a profession that can be an end in itself, or it can lead to other aspects of music-making. Accompanists who play in recital can expect to play up to twenty-five or thirty programs a year. In general, concert accompanists, in spite of a busy travel schedule, also do a certain amount of teaching and/or coaching. For the concert accompanist, there is yet further specialization. Some pianists prefer to work only with singers; others feel they make their best music with instrumentalists.

In either case, there will be requirements that a solo performer does not have to deal with. Very often, for example, an accompanying pianist must play in concert a section of an opera or oratorio, or the ensemble part of a concerto. This brings up the problem of substituting for an entire orchestra.

These works were not intended for the piano, and piano reductions are often written by editors who do not play the piano. Naturally, the reductions are unplayable. For example, take a look at the second movement of the Prokofieff *Violin Concerto No.2.* The passage printed here ideally requires three hands!

151

Faking is part of a musician's stock in trade; usually, pianists just go for the outer voices and fill in as much as possible. Certain notes must be left out to bring about maximum comfort, enabling the pianist to convey the *illusion* of an orchestra. My suggestion is to listen to the piece the way it was originally written so that you can extract an aural picture of the music. Once you know how it is supposed to sound, you can more convincingly create the right effect on the piano.

Pianists who specialize in accompanying singers will have more problems to contend with than one who just accompanies instrumentalists; for instance, he or she must have a command of French, German, and to some extent Italian. How can one expect to phrase and tonally inflect any song without understanding the text?

There is another difficulty in working with vocalists: one might master a tricky piece like Chausson's "Les Papillons" in the key of G Major (quite comfortable for that piece), and then have to perform it again in F Major (clumsy and awkward). Here it is in G:

Notice, in the new key, the discomfort in trying to fit your fingers between the black keys at a rapid pace!

In addition, many singers need a little more tender loving care—and justifiably; they are working with only their bodies and are more susceptible to the vagaries of weather,

*Samuel Sanders performing with violinist Itzhak Perlman.*

time, and place. An instrumentalist with a fever of 102 degrees might be able to gut his way through a recital, but a singer attempting such a feat risks an entire career.

Another skill that is helpful in accompanying situations is the ability to keep a straight face—or at least to maintain a sense of humor. Traveling with other artists can sometimes bring more than you bargained for.

I remember the time, for instance, when I was performing with cellist Mstislav Rostropovich in Cincinnati. He usually charges onto a stage and doesn't take time to tune; he just attacks the podium. At this performance, he was about to start when a very beautiful female latecomer sat down in the second row, center. Rostropovich turned to me, and in the most earnest but quiet manner said: "Not bad!" I was not able to recover in time for the opening of the piece.

That was mild, however, when compared to a concert we gave at the Kennedy Center in Washington, D.C. Backstage, Rostropovich cautioned me not to fumble around with the music; he wanted to rush out and begin immediately. When I arrived at the piano and opened the music, I discovered that he had pasted a centerfold from *Playboy* magazine across the first two pages. He sat on stage and pretended to be waiting impatiently for me to get ready. Frantically I tried to pry the centerfold loose without ripping the music, while the audience sat wondering what the trouble was.

On another occasion, I phoned violinist Itzhak Perlman on a beautiful Sunday afternoon in May to find out what time our concert was scheduled for. "We have to be there..." he began, then, with increasing panic, "We *had* to be there five minutes ago!" We arrived one and a half hours late, pulled the milling crowd back inside the theater, and apologized profusely.

Accompanists have to be prepared for *any* eventuality! Once I played for a soprano who started to go flat in the middle of a piece. She turned white as a sheet and asked me to help her offstage. I had to play a solo recital while a doctor attended her.

*Musica Camerit, the chamber group in residence at Merkin Concert Hall in New York. Samuel Sanders is the ensemble's music director.*

Some pianists who accompany do not enjoy that special feeling of panic that can greet one on the stage of Carnegie Hall. They prefer to do private coaching, playing for opera, choral, or dance rehearsals, and playing for students at their lessons. The vocal coach must know languages well enough to correct pronunciation and diction. A coach should guide a singer to repertoire which is particularly suitable to that individual's voice and help in program building—no small task. It is hard to differentiate between a coach and a rehearsal pianist, and often the two overlap. A coach must be a watchdog in matters of intonation. Ideally, a coach should work with singers on matters of interpretation. I remember with pain the earlier days of my career when I would often pound out notes of a song or an aria for a singer who had a fine voice and not much else.

> ## "When I arrived at the piano I discovered that Rostropovich had pasted a Playboy centerfold across the first two pages of the music!"

Accompanying is a field that can act as a springboard to other music-making activities. For example, a number of conductors such as Julius Rudel, Judith Somogi, and Richard Woitach labored as rehearsal pianists in opera companies before the baton replaced the piano as their means of musical expression. Charles Wadsworth has been for a number of years the artistic administrator of one of the most important chamber music societies in the world, The Chamber Society of Lincoln Center; at one time, he was one of the most active recital accompanists. My own teacher, Sergius Kagen, was renowned as a vocal coach, accompanist, and voice teacher, but he was becoming increasingly involved with composing at the time of his death.

If a person chooses accompanying as a livelihood, he should truly enjoy making music with others as a steady diet. The accompanist must be flexible in dealing with many schools of thought on how a piece should be interpreted. This flexibility will be strengthened by the accompanist's own knowledge and conviction of the music at hand. More and more, today's musician is one who not only can play his instrument or sing well, but is also stylistically and musicologically informed.

Fortunately, a great deal has happened in the accompanying field in the past twenty years, and the accompanist is no longer the black sheep in the musical community. A number of universities have degree programs, both graduate and undergraduate, in the field of accompanying and/or chamber music (in my own estimation, accompanying is chamber music). This trend seems to be growing. I always feel that the pianist who wishes to become a professional accompanist should understand certain basic facts: the repertoire is vast; certain skills such as transposition, ornamentation, and sight reading can be acquired (these are skills which improve simply by doing them frequently); and the love of music rather than the love of the limelight is needed to sustain an extremely difficult life with a financial reward that is hardly concomitant with the amount of labor and effort invested.

I would like to quote my dear English colleague Graham Johnson about our field. He says, "There is a double-edged sword between certain soloists and accompanists which requires total dedication, even intimacy in a musical context, which would seem to suggest equality and close friendship. But the confusing and saddening thing for many accompanists is that when the going is tough (over schedules, publicity credits, fees), the relationship evaporates to that of lordly employer and hired hand. The greatest pity is that trust and friendship are built into the character of chamber music, and it becomes increasingly difficult for an accompanist to function openheartedly when he or she has been too often disillusioned by disloyalty and lack of trust." When would-be accompanists understand these very real facts of life, they have already become professionals.

**SS**

# Harmony at the Keyboard

## An Introduction To Keyboard Arrangement

In the last issue we showed how to construct the chords for the first four bars of *The Twelve Days of Christmas*. We arrived at a very basic keyboard arrangement, with simple block chords in the left hand and the melody in the right. The chords were derived from chord symbols, which are shown here between the staves.

The same chords can be arranged in much more interesting ways. The notes making up the chords will stay the same, but they will be distributed around the keyboard in various configurations. To begin, we might use the left hand to play only the chord roots, and add chord tones in the right hand, underneath the melody. (Notice that on the second beat of the third bar the melody itself provides both the F and the D of the G7 chord.)

It is also possible to divide the chord tones more evenly so that there are two "voices" in the right hand and two in the left. This gives a fuller, more resonant sound, and exploits the various ranges of the keyboard.

A more rhythmic effect can be achieved by having the left hand play the chord roots in a low register on the strong beats, and then play chords in the middle register on the weak beats. This works out well for the first two bars, but in bars three and four the harmony changes too quickly to allow for up-beat chords, so it is necessary to put the chord tones into the right hand.

154

Another kind of arrangement makes use of what are called "broken chords." Here the notes of a chord are played in succession, rather than all at once. Usually the sustaining pedal is used to com- bine them. In our example the broken chords are played by the left hand, forming an accompani- ment that gives a lyrical, flowing quality to the music.

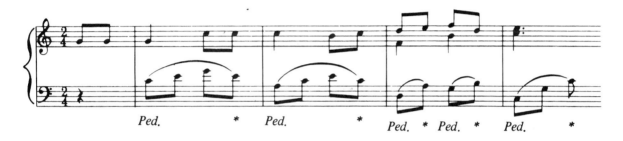

Of course there are many ways in which broken- chord figures can be arranged. The next ex- ample—utilizing exactly the same chords—shows a more widely spaced pattern. Now the effect is more sonorous, and in keeping with this the right- hand part has been thickened by the addition of chord tones.

In all our examples the harmonies have re- mained unchanged, but the notes of the chords have been arranged and rearranged to form a variety of musical textures. And we have only scratched the surface. The possibilities for key- board arrangements of a given tune are virtually endless. It is often amazing to see how many ways a resourceful musician can find to play the same melody and chords. In future issues we will discuss some more complicated, elaborate forms of ar- rangement.

**RC** ♩

# Style at the Keyboard

## Theme And Variations

Musicians have always enjoyed improvising variations on a leisurely tune with long note values, a tune that gives them a chance to "spread out." The practice is as old as the earliest Gregorian chants, and as current as tomorrow's rock or jazz album. A good example of such a tune in this issue is *The Rose,* and in this article we will suggest some of the many ways you can vary that song.

You might begin by adding a simple rocking figure in eighth notes as a lower voice in the right hand. Notice that we have slightly simplified the rhythm of the melody, and added a chromatic passing tone — the Db at the end of the second bar.

Somewhat more elaborate would be an accompaniment moving in triplets. Here the triplet rhythm is applied to broken chords in the left hand. It is worth pointing out that at the very bottom of the broken chords the thirds are omitted, because they sound muddy in the lower range.

Next we will fill in the long notes in the melody with sixteenth note broken chords in the right hand. Here the melody is present as an upper voice in the left hand, supported by a simple lower voice that supplies the bass notes.

Another approach to the tune would be to add a "counter-melody." Here the counter-melody appears in the lower middle register, as an upper voice in the left hand. It is the kind of line that, in an orchestral arrangement, might be assigned to the 'cellos. Notice that the counter-melody moves while the main melody is stationary; this provides continuous rhythmic activity.

In our next example the tune is in the lower voice in the right hand, while an upper voice harmonizes with the melody in sixths and thirds. This creates a texture something like a country music duet, where the tenor adds a "high harmony" part. We have added a few ornaments and blue notes to emphasize the country sound.

Finally we will make use of a device called a "pedal point." This is a single note which is held or repeated while many different harmonies pass over it. The best note for this purpose is usually the dominant, or fifth note of the scale (G in the key of C). In our example the dominant pedal gives the passage a suspended, hushed effect.

In all of our variations we have tried not to violate the spirit of the song — it remains a lyrical ballad with a country flavor. And we have not changed the basic tempo of the melody. The variations may introduce faster or slower note values, but the underlying quarter note pulse should remain constant. Keep this in mind as you invent your own variations on the tune.　　　RC ♩

# pop piano

# Christmas Carol Creations

There is a long history of pop performers using classical themes as jumping-off points for their own hit songs; old favorites such as *Strangers In Paradise* originated in the classical world, and even contemporary musicians like Barry Manilow have found the classical repertoire fertile ground for their creative endeavors.

In addition to culling the classical literature for tunes, it is also worthwhile to look at the way classical masters dealt with the "popular"

materials of their day. Often, we can find some fresh ideas that might lend themselves to contemporary arrangements. One musical source that never becomes dated is the Christmas Carol, and many of the masters offered their own versions of the carols which we still play and enjoy today.

A case in point is *In Dulci Jubilo* (*Good Christian Men Rejoice* in this issue). Here is the traditional four-part arrangement:

Franz Liszt produced this version, which makes use of a repeating figure in the bass:

Bach came up with a very different arrangement. The theme starts in the top voice, and then begins again a measure later in the bass, to pro-

duce a canon! Meanwhile, another countermelody plays along as an accompaniment, and it too is set up in canonic imitation:

158

We can learn from these composers, and go on to produce a new arrangement for ourselves. Let's look at Liszt's idea in the key of F:

We could create any number of similar patterns: the device is common enough. But we can also take Liszt's music as a starting point. One approach that springs to mind is to add harmony to the bass pattern—keeping the basic chords of the song intact, and adding a second line:

We can also add our own harmonies to the same pattern that Bach set up. First, let's create a canon with the melody, just as Bach did:

Now, let's play the countermelody in thirds.

When we place it all together, we will be left with something completely new — and perhaps not totally satisfying. Here is where we rely on our own ears and imagination; after all, we are using the older models only for inspiration.

When using harmony and counterpoint in this way, there will surely be times when we want to make changes or take certain liberties in order to produce a more satisfactory sound. That last E note in the second full measure, for example, will clash with the F in the melody; so, we can change it to an F. We may want to double some of the notes of the countermelody (in octaves). We might even add little bits of the countermelody in new places (see the top voice at the end of the second measure below):

In this way, we can take ideas from the masters and make them completely our own. Whenever you can, glance through the classical collections, and try to spot a phrase or technique that will come in handy. There is a treasure trove of material out there, and half the fun is in the finding! **SI**

# *Style* at the Keyboard

## *Playing Gershwin*

A bright, rhythmic song like *I Got Plenty O' Nuttin'* calls for a very clear and precise performance. You may want to "open up" the sheet music arrangement by moving the melody up an octave, and playing the off-beat chords with the left hand.

The long held note in the eighth bar of the tune (on the last syllable of "Got no mise*ry*") can be replaced by a "fill" using a typical Gershwin syncopation. Notice how the figure of three eighth notes is continuously repeated against a background of regular duple time, to produce a shifting pattern of accents.

Be on the lookout for possible inner parts, or "lines," to add interest to the keyboard texture. In *It Ain't Necessarily So* the harmony suggests a stepwise line which we have assigned to the thumb of the right hand.

160

Another way of handling such a line would be to give it to the thumb of the *left* hand. This is technically more difficult, but it has the advantage of creating some melodic activity in an often-neglected part of the keyboard: the lower middle range. (Sustain the left-hand line with the pedal, and roll the tenths if necessary.)

In a romantic ballad like *Bess You Is My Woman* you may want a more lush sound. But even here a rhythmically precise approach is rewarding. In the next example the sixteenth-note broken chords should be played in exact time, rather than as free arpeggios.

Gershwin wrote that American popular music "asks for *staccato* effects, for an almost stencilled style," and he warned against an overuse of the sustaining pedal. **RC**

# Style at the Keyboard

## Playing Jerome Kern

Jerome Kern, whose songs are featured in this issue, was the father of the American musical theater. His music also preserves much of the European operetta tradition, and it demands a sensitive keyboard style to bring out its special charm.

Many of his soaring melodies call for a full, lush treatment, with the right hand playing sonorous chords and octaves. Our first example is from *Can't Help Lovin' Dat Man.*

Long notes and rests in the melody can be filled in with broken-chord figuration. This technique works well for the middle section of *Can't Help Lovin' Dat Man.*

Sometimes the broken chords can flow from one hand to another, as in this passage from *Long Ago And Far Away* (our example begins with the fifth bar of the tune). In classical music this kind of keyboard texture is associated with the composer Schumann.

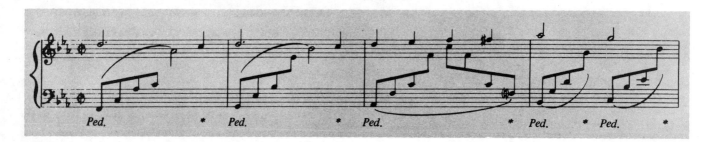

A typical accompaniment device in the Kern/ operetta style is the syncopated "push-beat," consisting of the pattern eighth note-quarter note-eighth note. That rhythm gives an urgent, passionate quality to the left hand of *The Song Is You.*

When a swing or blues feeling is implied, the sheet music arrangements of the Kern period sometimes seem awkward and old-fashioned today. In *The Folks Who Live On The Hill* you might want to replace the somewhat quirkly left hand pattern with a regular stride-piano accompaniment.

In a song like *Bill,* with its simple, unaffected, almost speechlike melody, the keyboard arrangement should be as straightforward and unadorned as possible. This is surely a case where "less is more."

RC ♩

# Intros And Endings
## Part I: Endings

While you can memorize set intros and endings, learning the musical theory and chord structures behind them will allow you to create your own, based on standard chord progressions and harmonic principles. Here are some ideas to help you along.

---

Example 1 is a deceptive cadence, or delayed ending—an ending where the tonic chord is momentarily avoided and substituted with other chords before returning to the tonic. The following series of progressions are for deceptive cadences.

In the key of F, a $G^9$ chord and a $C^9$ will bring the piece to the final F. If this were a typical ending, the $F^6$ would follow directly after the $C^9$ chord. However, you can delay the $F^6$ chord by first hitting the chord exactly one whole tone lower, an $E^{b6}$ chord, then going to the $F^6$ chord.

Try to transpose this to at least one other standard key, ie: C, $B^b$, G, $E^b$.

Not only can the $F^6$ chord be delayed by going to a tone a whole tone below, it is also possible to go a tone above the $F^6$. The $G^{b6}$ chord is exactly one half tone above the $F^6$ chord. This technique uses "neighboring tones" (tones which neighbor the tonic).

Transpose this exercise to the key of C, plus one other standard key.

This example takes both chords in the previous two examples (the $E^{b6}$ and the $G^{b6}$) and uses them in connection with each other, to create a deceptive cadence. Through these examples you are learning some standard simple endings, but you are also learning the thought processes behind them, such as how to use neighboring tones. In order to become thoroughly comfortable with these concepts, though, continue to practice transpositions of intros and endings. This will increase your ability to play them in other keys.

This is an example of another neighboring tone, the one exactly one half tone below the tonic. The last measure in example 4 shows an E⁶ chord going to an F⁶ chord. In example 1, the neighboring tone is a whole tone below the F⁶ chord for the deceptive cadence. This time it is only a half tone below the F⁶ chord. Play the entire progression and then transpose it to the key of B♭.

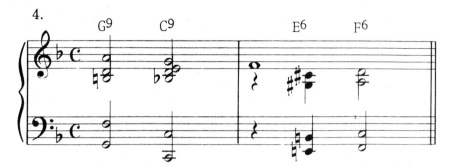

Example 5 uses all the neighboring tones previously discussed in this article (E♭⁶, G♭⁶, E⁶) and puts them together in one deceptive cadence. If you can play this ending in the standard keys of C, G, B♭ as well as F, and memorize it, you will be well on your way to being able to use it in your playing (in place of the uninspiring endings found in conventional sheet music).

Example 6 moves from the sixth chords we have been dealing with so far, to the major seventh chord. To create a major seventh chord, delete the sixth tone of the chord and put in the major seventh. For example, for an E♭ᵐᵃʲ⁷ chord, substitute a D for the C. In a G♭ᵐᵃʲ⁷ chord, substitute an F for the E. The major seventh chord is a jazzier, more modern sound. Transpose the major seventh chord progression to several familiar standard keys.

This example is also a deceptive ending, but instead of going to a neighboring tone on the last note, it goes to a tone a major third below the tonic chord. This ending could go directly from the D⁹ chord to the G⁹ chord to the C⁹ chord, but instead goes to the chord a major third lower — an A♭ chord — and from there to a D♭ᵐᵃʲ⁷ chord, before winding up at the Cᵐᵃʲ⁷ chord. This is the basic harmony of the deceptive cadence. Most pianists will arpeggiate or put runs in on the last three chords. Try playing this progression with some arpeggiated notes. It is a good ending to use when a singer is ending on the tonic note. In C, let the singer hit the C while you play the A♭. It is a dramatic effect.

*Continued*

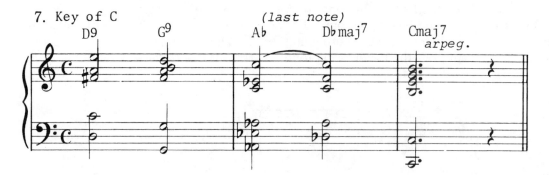

**7. Key of C**

The next to the last measure in this example is a neighboring tone chord, a half tone above the C: a Db maj7. This can be used in an up-tempo song such as "Lady Is A Tramp."

**8. Key of C**

In this example the second measure should have been an E♭ chord, going from Fm⁷ to E⁷ to E♭maj⁹ to the end of the song. Instead, a chord which is exactly an augmented fourth above has been inserted. This is an Am⁷ chord with an E♭ in it. This technique is used by pianists, arrangers and composers as an effective ending when the tonic note is the melody note—the E♭ in this case. All you need do from here is to take every tone in the Am⁷♭⁵ chord and lower it. If you analyze the seven chords from the Am⁷ to the E♭maj⁹, you will see they are basically a chromatic progression downward until the final chord is reached.

This progression is used often and you should learn it in as many keys as you can. Once you learn the progression well, you can improvise on it by simply rolling some of the chords, or by playing neighboring notes within the chord.

**9. Key of E♭**

# Part II: Introductions

This exercise uses the same chord progression as example 9. Once you have learned it, it can be effectively used as an introduction. You can write any melody over it while playing the progression with your left hand.

10. Key of E♭
Same progression as Intro:

Example 11 is an intro which uses the III chord (in the key of C, the III chord is an Em based chord with D as the seventh) and progresses chromatically downward until you reach the C chord. The first chord is a minor chord. The second chord, while it can be a minor chord, is usually a dominant seventh, i.e. an E♭7, B♭7, D♭7. Play this exercise with two hands and play the chords over and over until you are very familiar with them.

The right side is a variation on the basic chords. It is a good finger exercise and can be used as either an intro, an ending or a fill. Play the arpeggiated variation slowly with two hands to begin with and work up to speed. Move on to the keys of F, B♭, E♭, A♭ and G and play both the chords and the variation with both hands. Your left hand should not be neglected in any exercise. Remember that the first and third chords are minor sevenths and the second and fourth chords are dominant seventh chords.

11.
IIIm7 ♭III7 IIm7 ♭II7    VARIATION

*Continued*

The original sheet music ending in example 12 is dull. Substitute example 12a which uses the chord progression you have been practicing. Although it has a slightly different voicing than you have been practicing, it is essentially the same progression. 12b can be used as well, and is closer to what you have been practicing.

12. Original ending:

12a. Delayed ending:

12b. Or...

Example 13 is a II-V chord progression. In the key of C, a $Dm^7$ chord would move to a $G^7$ chord, which would normally progress to the I chord, C (not written in your example).

Variation I: this uses a $Dm^9$ chord (an E on top), instead of the $Dm^7$ chord, which lends a more modern sound to the II chord.

In the next example, which is in the key of F, the II chord is a $Gm^9$ (A on top).

Look at the first measure of each of these examples, and learn the II chord for a few different keys.

Go back to variation I. A $Dm^9$ progresses to a $G^{13}$. Learn this chord progression (the minor ninth chord to the thirteenth) and memorize it in each key. This is a good way of playing the II-V-I progression rather than in using the simple triad or the seventh chord. Now play this progression in the keys of $B^b$, $E^b$, $A^b$ and G. Write them out yourself in the space provided.

Variation II is a more modern sound than variation I, although the first chord is exactly the same. In the key of C, the B in the $G^{13}$ chord in variation I becomes a C in the G chord in variation II. It looks like an $F^{maj7}$ in the right hand over a G. This is often the way you will see the chord written in modern music. Learn variation II in every key and memorize it.

168

We are now getting into a very modern sound that will take your piano into another dimension of contemporary music. Try to play these variations in some kind of rhythm, not just half notes, or alternate between keys, perhaps from the key of B♭ to the key of E♭.

You can create many different kinds of intros with ninth and thirteenth chords. Another good way to use these chords is to skip around from one key to another and then return to the key that you are going to play your song in.

In the last example, the first two measures are in the key of C. This key is established with a II chord, going to the V chord. The second half of the second measure has a chromatic chord progression up to the key of E♭. In the third and fourth measures the II chord of E♭ (an Fm chord) going to the V chord (a B♭ chord) establishes the key of E♭ momentarily,

while the fifth and sixth measures reestablish the key of C with the II-V progression. The final two measures have the III chord descending to the flatted III, to the II, to the flatted II. These elements are what make up this intro.

Now that you understand the theory behind creating intros like this, you can do them in many keys for many songs, instead of imitating this one note for note. The key to success is to reread this article and redo the exercises until the theory and principles become a part of your playing.

13.

VARIATION I  VARIATION II

# pop piano

## Happy Endings—
### *Finish your songs with flair*

Let's continue our catalog of well-known "fills" with a look at some stock\endings. There you are, at the finish of a song. The last chord is coming up. You have a choice: play the final chord and move on to the next tune; or, add a little something extra to go out with a bang, or with a stylish flourish.

Many musicians use "tag" endings, in which they repeat the last musical phrase over three times before stopping. The following "cliché" endings work on a similar principle: they use a chord progression which begins and ends on the same chord, so they can be "tagged" on to the song you are playing.

Here is a familiar progression which can be used as an extra "tag" to finish off a fast, bouncy tune ending in B♭:

Here's a variation with a dixieland feel:

To spruce this up even more, try adding *another* little fill onto the ending of the last example:

170

Let's look at another chord progression used for
dixieland and swing endings:

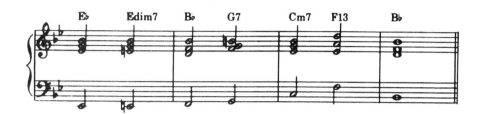

Adding rhythmic variety to this produces a fun
variant:

Here is a full-blown arrangement of this progression:

For more variety, try this substitute in the second measure:

or this in the last measure:

SI ♩

# pop piano

## Fill 'er Up!

### A catalog of musical "hooks"

One of the fun things about pop music is that there are little phrases — intros, endings, and fills — that can be used all the time, but which don't become boring. In fact, such pop "clichés" are expected — they're a regular part of the style — and never fail to bring a smile to those listeners within earshot of the piano or organ.

With this column, we're going to begin a catalog of great pop "one liners." Use them wherever, and as often, as you like.

There are hundreds. For example, think of those little figures played at ball games, or at the race track. Then there are silent movie themes, and Irish, Hawaiian, Jewish, bluesy, country, rock, and Oriental gimmicks, too.

Here's a typical honky-tonk introduction:

Ex. 1

You'll notice that it leads into a song beginning on a C chord. Suppose the song we're leading into is not quite so exuberant. Here's a variation of the last three measures:

Ex. 2

Part of the enjoyment of these little phrases is that there is always one to fit just the mood you are looking for. Here's an often-used ending on C:

Ex. 3

If Lawrence Welk were playing, the ending might come out more like this:

Ex. 4

If a blues player were performing, we might hear this ending to a tune:

Ex. 5

Or, perhaps we would hear this slightly more sophisticated approach:

Ex. 6

# RUNS AND FILLS FOR RIGHT HAND

Have you ever sat and listened to a professional pianist and said to yourself, "What was that wonderful run he just played? Wish I could do that?" If you ever got up the courage to ask, (and pianists *love* to be asked, by the way) you would probably discover that the fill or run was truly based on a very basic concept, such as an arpeggio, or a major scale. One of the tricks, however, is that the scale or

arpeggio he or she used is not exactly the most obvious. For example, the left hand might play a G7 chord, while the right hand plays a Db scale.

As our first example, we will play the very last chord of a song in the key of C with one final flourish: an arpeggio ascending. You have heard pianists use this, but may never have known exactly what it was.

The left hand changes the C Major sound to a C dominant 7th sound, but the right hand plays a D7 chord ascending. To transpose this run to other keys simply change the tonic chord, the final chord, to a dominant 7th (by lowering the 7th), play it with the left hand. And then arpeggiate with the right

hand a dominant 7th chord whose root is a whole tone higher than the left hand chord. In the key of F, for example, the left hand would play an F7, and the right hand would arpeggiate a G7. Learn this ending in several keys by transposing it yourself.

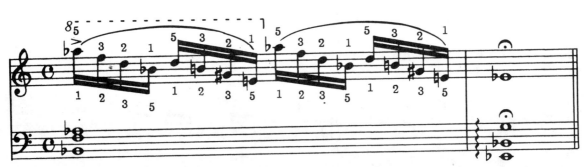

In this example two arpeggios are being used. The left hand chord is a Bb7, and the right hand alternates between a Bb7 arpeggio and an E7 arpeggio descending. Once you have mastered this run,

you can use it in connection with the first example to create a very fancy ending for a hundred songs. See example 3.

174

In order to transpose this run to other keys, let's analyze the method used: Example 2 uses a B♭7 in the left hand which is the V chord in the key of E♭. If we were to transpose this to the key of C, the left hand would play a V7 or G7 chord. The right hand starts on a B♭7 arpeggio, or a V7 arpeggio, and it begins the arpeggio on A♭ (the 7th of the chord). Therefore, in the new key of C we must also start on the V7 chord, the G7, and begin the descending arpeggio on the 7th of the chord, an F. The second arpeggio used by the right hand in Example 2 is an E7. This is one half-tone higher than the Tonic E♭.

(called a raised tonic or lowered 2nd). And it also begins on the 7th of the E7 chord. In the new key of C, the chord which is one half-tone higher than the Tonic (C) is D♭ (or C#). The second arpeggio, therefore, in the new key is a D♭7. And we start the new arpeggio on the 7th of the chord, a C♭, or B. You should continue to transpose these runs and fills by analyzing them in this manner, and playing them in those keys in which they feel comfortable. There are many keys where this and other runs do not fit the hand. Don't force the issue in these cases. Play the runs in those keys where they are comfortable.

(Key of C using both runs)

The example above can be used wherever you think it fits. Trial and error is the only way you can decide what is appropriate. Starting on a B♭ as it does, it can be played over a 1) D♭7 resolving to a C chord, 2) a G7 resolving to a C chord, 3) a G♭7 resolving to an F chord, 4) a C7 resolving to an F chord.

This is essentially the same run starting, however, on an E♭. It can be played over a 1) G♭7 resolving to an F chord, 2) a C7 resolving to an F chord, 3) a B7 or F7 resolving to a B♭ chord.

(Use Same Fingering)

The above starts on an A♭ and can be used over a B7 or F7 resolving to a B♭ chord, or over a B♭7 or E7 resolving to an E♭ chord.

175

Starting on a D♭ this can be played over a B♭7 or
E7 resolving to an E♭, or over an E♭7 or A7 resolving to A♭.

The above can be played over an E♭7 or A7 resolving to A♭, or over an A♭7 or D7 resolving to D♭.

You can make this run as long as you want simply by always going to the next black note with your second finger:

Now that you have learned and mastered this run, a good sounding variation is to go up a major third from each black note as follows:

Our next run is a scale variation and can be used as a fill with a C7 chord or a C7♭9. Be patient and practice these slowly. Once you master them, you will use them all the time.

This same run can be used with an A♭7 chord as follows:

Here is the same run transposed to an F7 chord, which can also be played over a Db7 chord:

Here is a great two-handed "white key" exercise which will do wonders for your finger technique and becomes a very impressive fill when you need it. It can be used as a one or two-handed run on any "white note" chord such as C, G7, Dm7, Am7, Em7, and sometimes an F or FMaj7.

If you wish to play this same run in the key of F, simply remember to flat all the B's:

etc.

177

The following example is once again a great finger exercise and a marvelous run that's been used by everyone from Frederic Chopin, to Art Tatum, to Errol Garner. It will take a great deal of slow practice for the right hand to be accurate with the thumb under when you wish to play it at a good speed. Play over a G Major chord, or G7.

Here is the same run over an F chord:

# USE THESE RUNS AS EXERCISES

Most people hate to practice finger exercises. Well here's a new method, and a new outlook: use these runs and fills as your exercises by playing them with two hands (to help keep the left hand active) and by practicing them very slowly to get evenness of tone and finger strength. The fun part of this kind of exercise is that you are mastering a stylized run or fill while improving your technique as well. Use the left hand fingering indicated below the notes, so that you may practice the right hand run with two hands.

Add these runs to your favorite arrangements, and before long someone will ask: "What was that fill you just played? Wish I could do that!"     **ES**

# Organ Technique
# & Styles

# organ studio

## Position Is Everything In Life (Especially If You Play The Organ)     Part I

There is one subject in my keyboard workshops that appeals to all mature organists . . . position at the console.

Some of the problems that can be cured by sitting correctly at the organ console are aches and pains occuring at the base of the neck, below the shoulder blades, small of the back and occasionally a "charley horse" (muscle contraction or spasm) in the left leg; inaccurate performance on the bass pedals; "riding" the Swell Pedal; inability to perform with both feet on the pedals; the inability to maintain a sustained melody note without jerking the Swell Pedal and hesitancy in making registration changes.

Most adult players are eager to "play now and learn later" and this impatience is quite often transmitted to the teacher who, in an effort to please the adult student-in-a-hurry, quite often overlooks the necessity to use some conventional building blocks in the areas of acquiring performing technique and learning theory and harmony.

In checking both private and class students, I find the tendency of the average player is to sit too far back from the console.

In the case of the former piano player turned organist, I can understand the casual approach to the lower keyboard/manual, assuming the same relationship as the piano keyboard, then simply reaching up to the upper keyboard without adjusting the original position. Longer legged players feel they have to be farther away from the manuals in order to fit their legs under the overhang of the console. (Sometimes it's true, but not all the time.) I certainly can't go along with the "teacher" who wrote, some years ago, "Pull back the bench so you can see the pedals easier."(!)

Let's go through the position routine I demonstrate at my workshops. First, examine the two drawings showing the "before and after" results of sitting too far back from the console and sitting close enough to allow proper balance, relieve muscle strain and encourage changing registrations.

**Sitting too far back**

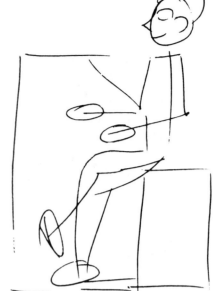

**Sitting Closer**

1. Place the bench (spinet or console) parallel to the keyboards and relatively close to the organ. Slide onto the bench, seating yourself about in the middle, and with your right arm reach for the upper keyboard/manual (the Swell Manual). Sit as close as necessary to maintain as large a break at the elbow as possible. Not ⌒⁄, or ₒ⁄ , but ₒ⌐ . Quite often, as the student adjusts the body closer to the organ to provide the bigger break at the elbow, it is necessary to pull the bench forward to provide support and avoid falling forward.

2. After moving close enough to reach out to the upper manual without leaning forward excessively, adjust the bench so that you have the majority of your thighs off the bench, but enough support under you to enable you to take the balance test.

3. The Balance Test is simple. Place both feet flat on the pedalboard. Without tucking the feet in under you, attempt to raise both feet/legs straight up into the air. If you have too little bench under you, you will have to lean back in order to counter-balance yourself. The more you lean back, the more you need additional support. Continue to pull the bench forward, in very small increments, until you have maximum freedom under your thighs with the ability to raise both your legs straight up without leaning backwards.

4. After the bench has been moved to accommodate both freedom of the thighs and support of the balanced body, take notice of where the bench is situated in relation to the organ. It can be marked on the pedals of the console organ. It is more difficult to remember with a spinet

organ. I advise relating the placement of the bench to a pattern on the carpet or hard tile, marking a blank floor or leaving the bench in place on a thick carpet until it makes its own mark on the surface. Be sure to place the bench in its proper position BEFORE sitting down at the organ.

**Not enough bench support**

**Adequate support with freedom**

BI

# organ studio

## Position Is Everything In Life (Especially If You Play The Organ)

## Part II

Alright, you've spent the time reading Part I in the April/May '83 issue, sat on the bench trying to follow the instructions to place yourself comfortably close to the keyboards, balanced on the bench so that you don't pump the Swell Pedal or fall on your face the first time you try to use both feet on the pedals.

Now you're ready to continue the position-at-the-console routine and locate the proper place for your body on the bench, moving from side to side instead of forward and backward.

Before we start to position your body, a few words about the bench.

Although we don't (for goodness sake!) wax the bench . . . we do want to be able to slide comfortably around on it. When the bench is new, it comes with either a slick wood surface or a smooth vinyl surface. The idea is to permit you to twist your body around easily while you are playing. If you do a lot of practicing you are bound to perspire onto the wood surface, which, in time, will destroy the slick finish. The result will not only be an eye-sore, but also you won't be able to slide around as easily as before. I suggest that if your bench didn't come with a vinyl plastic padded seat cover you get one and attach it firmly to the bench to prevent it slipping around underneath you. Avoid the fabric covers that tend to grab your clothes and not let go. If possible, try to find a tufted vinyl cover, as the air pockets created by the tufting will not only give you good support with less surface friction, but will also have additional pockets of air to keep you cooler while on the bench.

## Ready students?

Place the bench in position in front of the console and slide onto the seat to about the middle of the organ. I certainly don't recommend that you sit directly in front of middle C on the keyboards. That's a misconception, even if you happen to wind up in that position on your own instrument. The physical placement of the keyboards and the bass pedalboard varies from manufacturer to manufacturer and from model to model. It isn't possible to sit in the same relationship to the pedalboard each time by relating to a particular place on the keyboard.

After sitting in approximately the center of the instrument, don't look down at the bass pedals . . . just think of putting your foot on the pedal key "G" and with no effort at locating the G, simply lift your left foot and casually step down onto what you hope will be the bass pedal G. If your left hip is in line with the G on the pedalboard, your left foot will naturally fall on the G. After you touch the pedal (you should have registered the 16' and 8' bass pedals), keep your foot down on it and listen to the note you are producing. Then, without looking down to check your accuracy, use your left hand to sound the note G in the second octave below middle C on the lower manual . . . and listen to determine if the two notes sounding are the same. If they are, you know you have played the G in the bass correctly and are probably sitting where your playing of the pedals will be comfortable and fairly accurate. If the bass note clashes with the G on the manual, try to find the correct G in the bass . . *without looking down.*

If you find you've touched the F pedal, it will be necessary to move your body very slightly to the right, to bring your left foot comfortably over the G pedal. If, when you check the sound, you find that you had been touching the A pedal, then it will be necessary for you to move slightly to the left, in order for your foot to fall easily, without effort, onto the G pedal. When I say "move slightly", I mean just that. All movement on the bench, whether forward or backward, or side to side, should be made in very small increments, as the resulting change will be much greater than expected.

When you can easily lift your left leg off the bench foot rest, or lift it off the floor (if you're at a spinet organ) and step down directly onto the G

pedal, you've found a simple key position for your left foot—a place where you can return your left foot by simply stepping directly forward. Then, of course, the F pedal is slightly to the left and the A pedal is slightly to the right. In your initial rhythm pedaling, you will probably alternate between the low C and G pedals and once again, you'll find it easy and comfortable returning to G.

That's the easy, quick way to establish your position on the bench from side to side.

A slightly more complex approach is to use the area between the low Eb and F# black pedals and on a console, the space between the Bb and C# black pedals. These "key positions" give you an even more accurate check of your position on the bench.

## Try this routine...

Sit in approximately the middle of the bench with your right foot on the Swell Pedal, left foot resting on the foot rest of a console or on the floor with a spinet organ. With your left foot, reach down to the low C pedal and notice if there is any pulling or straining in your hip area. If you notice any discomfort, simply wiggle your hips slightly to ease any strain. *Don't move around on the bench any more than is absolutely necessary.* Next, move your left foot up to the C pedal an octave higher and again notice if you feel any strain or tension in your hip area. If you do, again wiggle your hips to relieve the strain but avoid moving unless you feel you have to do it.

When you feel that you can comfortably cover an octave of pedals with your left foot, place your left foot down on the pedals and slide it into the space between the lower Eb and F#.

It is not necessary to look down. It just isn't possible to slide your foot into any other place on the lower part of the pedalboard. At this point, stop and try to feel the relationship of your left foot to your body. In my studio, I take a pencil and run it from the student's foot all the way up the leg and thigh to the left hip, while asking the student to note the relationship of the left foot to the rest of the body. Truthfully, at this point, it doesn't make a great impression on the student, but it's a beginning. Here's how it becomes a real help in establishing position on the bench...

*Continued*

183

When you are pedaling, for example, C to G with your left foot and you notice that you are consistently pedaling the F instead of the G, or undershooting the mark, pause . . . wiggle very slightly to the right and then resume your pedaling without trying to change anything. You'll find that the movement on the bench has corrected the foot interval. Conversely, if you find you are consistently hitting the A instead of the G, or overshooting the pedal, pause . . . wiggle slightly to the left and then resume your pedaling without trying to make any changes with your foot. Once again, you'll find that you will be playing the correct pedals because of the slight change in your position on the bench.

IMPORTANT! Every time you make a change in your position on the bench and find that you are then playing the pedals more accurately, slide your left foot into the lower key position between Eb and F# and notice how the foot feels in relation to the rest of your body. After just a few weeks of this routine, you will notice a specific relationship to the key position.

Then we can summarize the position routine by
1.) placing the bench in position in front of the console where you have determined it is best for *your* body;
2.) slide onto the bench to approximately the middle and then;
3.) slide your left foot into the lower key position.

When you slide your left foot into the space between Eb and F#, if you touch the Eb, wiggle a bit to the right. If you touch the F#, wiggle a bit to the left. If your foot slides into the space without hitting either black pedal, you know you are sitting in exactly the right place on the bench for you.

The use of the upper key position between Bb and C# aids in helping both the left foot and the right foot become oriented in that area of the pedalboard. Then the key position between Eb and F# below the Swell Pedal is used to help the right foot move correctly when the student is just beginning to use both feet on the pedals.

If you've worked your way through Parts I and II of this position routine and applied yourself, you should, in a short time, notice an improvement in your bass pedal accuracy, easier registration changes, less fatigue (resulting in more time spent at the organ) and hopefully, less aches and pains from improper balance. Write and let me know if these suggestions have helped you or have me check your position at the console during one of my national workshops. 'Bye now. ♩ **BI**

# organ studio

## The "Joy" Of Performing

Anyone who plays a musical instrument is likely to be in a position of performing his or her art at some time or another. It can be a feeling of stark terror, terrible stomach pains, ice cube hands, nausea, and probably a feeling that you would rather be in a dentist's chair than in front of your listeners

Performing can also bring a great feeling of satisfaction. The arts are talents that should be shared if possible. That doesn't mean that you should go out and concertize for thousands of people. If you are comfortable playing the organ for your family and friends, you're on the right track. Many organ clubs ask their members to perform at meetings. This can be traumatic, but keep in mind that those you are playing for can sympathize with you, because they have been in the same boat.

In many cases the nervous mistakes you might make are minor, and possibly unnoticeable to your audience. If that first mistake happens, don't let it throw you. Take a deep breath, calm down and, above all else, KEEP GOING! Everyone makes mistakes. The true musician is the one who can cover that mistake smoothly.

Unfortunately, there is no magic cure for nerves. Some people feel that a few minutes of concentration prior to performing can help. Some people prefer a stiff drink. I feel the only answer to the problem is to take the bull by the horns, so to speak. Each time you play for someone, you gain a bit more confidence and experience. A bad experience can set you back. For instance, you play

*Tico-Tico* for a friend and really blow it. You'll probably be afraid to try that tune again. The best way to avoid these setbacks is to carefully select the tunes you want to perform. Try to pick numbers that are a bit under the ability level you have reached. Although you may be able to play a challenging piece perfectly at home, you'll probably have trouble under the pressure of performing.

---

*"The true musician is the one who can cover the mistake smoothly."*

---

The more experience you gain performing, the higher the ability level will be. The best way to gain that experience is to accept every challenge of performance. When friends ask you to play during the holiday season, don't make them beg you. Smile, grit your teeth and dive in. The first thing you play should be something you can almost play in your sleep. As the "encores" continue, gradually work up to something a little more challenging.

If you are comfortable in memorizing, I highly suggest playing from memory. Your argument might be: "What if my mind goes blank?" That usually only happens to those who dwell on that mental block, so don't even think about it. Playing with music can cause problems too. You might look down at your hands, or make a registration change and find yourself totally lost in the music. Or you might reach the end of the page and the extra adrenalin causes you to pull the music right off the stand.

The problems can seem monumental, but until you can comfortably share what you have to give musically, you're missing a really satisfying experience.

DC ♪

# Stop, Listen, and Learn!

*Take a private lesson from
your favorite organist*

When I was a high school student, I would make a special effort to attend concerts by those organists I considered to have really exceptional "styling" in their playing. I would sit through the performance listening, enjoying, envying, but never examining the music for the special features which made it musical and set it apart from the playing of other organists.

The very same thing was true when I listened to recordings. Again and again, I'd listen to my favorite organist making some really wonderful music. But all I did was listen, enjoy, and *envy*! Never did I examine the arrangements or actually try to duplicate the styling of the organist in my own playing.

Eventually, by way of some general music appreciation classes, I understood that the reason that I did not learn from the playing of these organists was because I did not know how to listen for specific musical elements. I was listening only to the musical whole and not to the individual parts that comprise a complete arrangement of a song. There is an endless number of excellent private organ lessons in every recording you own. The purpose of this workshop is to help you, the organist, learn everything you can from your organ recordings simply by helping you learn HOW TO LISTEN.

Let's start by breaking down our listening procedure into specific musical elements.

## I. LISTENING TO THE WHOLE SONG:

Even when you are planning to concentrate on specific elements in a recorded arrangement, it's a good idea to listen to the complete song at least two or three times. Get out your sheet music (you need to have the song in print even if you play strictly by ear) and listen to how many times the organist plays the verse and chorus. Listen, too, for any bridges which might be included.

## II. PLAYING THE SONG THROUGH:

Now go back to the organ and play the song yourself. Try to play the song at about the same tempo and with the same phrasing that you heard when you listened to the recording. In short, try to imitate the feeling which the recording artist gave the song on the record! At this point don't worry about introductions or endings—we'll get to those later.

## III. LISTENING FOR REGISTRATION:

All good organists are known for their use of registration. This includes initial registration and any changes which might be made at the beginning of the chorus or in the repeat of a verse, etc. Play the recording this time and try to analyze the registration being used. Is it a full organ sound including all pitches 16' - 1? Is it a solo stop: trumpet, clarinet, kinura, tibia, bells, xylophone, etc.? Are there percussion sounds being used: drums, cymbals, tamborines, sleigh bells, etc.? When, if at all, does the organist make registration changes? These are all aspects of the musical element of registration. Listen carefully and make some notations on your copy of the song so that you can try to imitate it when you play the song again yourself.

## IV. LISTENING FOR SINGLE NOTE AND HARMONIC TREATMENT OF THE MELODY:

Play the recording again. This time try to determine if the arrangement includes a single-note approach in the melody or a harmonic one. Does the artist play the song with one note in the right hand or more than one note?

## V. LISTENING FOR LEFT HAND AND PEDAL TREATMENT:

What does the organist do with the left hand and pedal? How does he or she "accompany" the melody? Is there a rhythmic accompaniment? If so, what kind of rhythm is it? Tango, Fox Trot, March, etc. Does it include a counter-melody? Before listening for anything else, try to duplicate the accompaniment you hear in your own playing of the song.

## VI. LISTENING FOR INTRODUCTIONS AND ENDINGS:

Introductions and endings are extremely important elements of an arrangement. Listen to see what the recording artist does with the introduction and ending. Is there some sort of melodic idea which the artist develops in the introduction that ties it in to the verse or chorus of the song? Is there some special registration that is employed to set the mood for what is to follow? How about the ending. Does the song end with a big full-sounding chord in the right hand? Maybe it ends with a soft restatement of the melody, or perhaps there is a "repeat and fade" ending.

Once again try to duplicate the introduction and ending in your own playing of the song. This may take some time, but be exacting! Try to imitate the introduction and ending exactly as you heard them in the recording.

## VII. LISTENING FOR KEY CHANGES:

This is probably the easiest of all elements to listen for in a recording. Unfortunately, it is probably the most difficult thing to do when playing the song yourself. Key changes add "new life" to a repeated bridge or chorus in an arrangement. If you feel sufficiently challenged by the recorded arrangement, maybe you will want to take the time to actually transpose the song so that you, too, can make a key change.

## VIII. FINAL NOTE:

Don't ever be afraid of "copying" another organist's arrangement ideas. So much can be learned from imitating. Every great musician will admit to having consciously imitated either a teacher or some other great musician. Nothing is ever truly original. All ideas, musical or otherwise, owe their inception to some previous idea. If you want to develop original stylings of your own learn to imitate others. Imitation really is the best teacher. But remember, in order to imitate successfully you must KNOW HOW TO LISTEN!

DK ♩

# organ studio

## Playing Like The "Real Thing"

### *Using solo stops more effectively*

Without exception, everyone who owns a home organ has at one time or another experienced what I like to call the "demonstration — WOW!" This usually occurs when one ventures into an organ showroom and hears a demonstrator put the latest electronic organ through its paces. The successful "demonstration WOW!" (which inevitably leads to a successful sale) is made largely by the art of using solo stops effectively. By "using" we don't simply mean turning the stop on or off but rather playing the keys in a manner which best imitates the sound characteristic of the musical instrument named by the stop. In this workshop we are going to examine this playing technique more carefully.

First, what is a solo stop? A solo stop is a stop on the organ which duplicates the sound of an orchestral instrument. These stops include: trumpet, clarinet, oboe, orchestra bells, xylophone, violin, piano, accordion, harp, and chimes, to name a few. Selecting any one of these stops is simple; the difficult part is knowing how to imitate the way the actual instrument is played. The way an orchestral or actual instrument sounds is governed first by its timbre or tone color, and second by the characteristic way the performer plays that instrument. On the organ, the timbre of the solo stop is predetermined by the organ you are playing. The characteristic way that instrument is played, however, is governed by the manner in which the organist interprets the melody of a given song on the keyboard.

As our first example let's say we've decided to use a bell stop to play the following song. To make the solo stand out more clearly use a soft accompaniment at 8' only, and a soft pedal stop at 8'. (I'm assuming your organ has some sort of bell effect; if not, register a flute at 8' and 1' with long sustain and no vibrato.)

(Original)

Upper: Bells (00 6000 006)

(Altered)

Notice how the rhythm of the melody was altered to make the organ's bell stop sound more like the real thing. This same rhythmic alteration would be made if we were using the chime or xylophone stop.

Now, here are some general rules for some of the other solo stops we mentioned:

**Piano:** Short, detached attack: alternate between single note and two note intervals in melody line (4ths, 5ths, and 6ths). Best effects obtained in octaves of middle C and treble C. No vibrato.

Upper: Piano 8'

**Trumpet:** Short, staccato attack; each note accentuated with slight volume pedal increase; usually single note solo, register with flute stop at octave pitch; give longer notes (whole, half, quarter) 1/2 their written rhythm value.

Upper: Trumpet 8' (00-8880-000)

**Clarinet** and **Saxophone:** Smooth, legato; usually single note solo, but can be effective in chords; register with flute stop at octave pitch, best single note effects obtained when played in octave of middle C; give notes their full written rhythm value. Full vibrato for saxophone, light vibrato for clarinet.

Upper: Clarinet 8' (00 8060 401) or Saxophone 8' (16 7662 310)

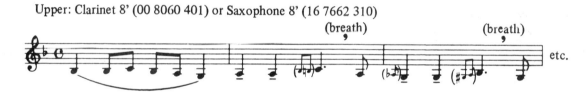

**Oboe:** same as clarinet except that the oboe, since it always plays alone in the orchestra, should never play more than one note. Oboes don't play melodies in chords! Once again, as with most reed stops, register the oboe along with a flute at octave pitch. Little or no vibrato.

**Violin:** Smooth, legato: single note solo; for more body try registering with a flute stop at sub-octave pitch (ex. 8' violin with 16' flute, or 4' violin with 8' flute); best effects obtained when played in upper three octaves on manual. Give notes full rhythm value or double value. Alternate between heavy and light vibrato.

Upper: Violin 8' (08 4663 000)

*freely*

These examples should give you a good idea of what is meant by imitating the "way an instrument sounds" by playing the melody of a song in a special way for each solo stop. Remember, the designers of electronic organs have done their best to duplicate the timbre of orchestral instruments, but timbre is only half of the overall effect. To make the organ sound like that instrument you have to do your best as a keyboardist to play like the instrument you are imitating. This applies to all keyboard instruments which attempt to duplicate other instruments: drawbar organs, standard organs, electronic pianos, and synthesizers!

DK ♩

# LEFT HAND AND PEDAL RHYTHMS FOR ORGAN

One of the essential ingredients of music is rhythm. We will discuss ways to create rhythm by using the left hand, the pedals, or both together.

The rhythms written out on the following pages start from the very simplest accompaniment and gradually become more difficult. No matter what level you are on, there are rhythms given here that you can incorporate into your music.

Several measures of each rhythm are written using chord progressions made up of these chords: C, Am, Dm7, G7 and back to C. Hopefully, this will help you to become comfortable with the rhythms using several different chords. The chord inversion used in strictly a matter of personal taste, although it is best to keep the chords somewhere between the E below middle C and F above middle C. The pedals are identified by scale degrees of the chord (used to make it easier to play these patterns with other chords). For instance, when the C chord is played, he pedals used are C(R), E(3), and G(). R stands for root, E is the *third* note of the C scale and G is the *fifth* note of the C scale.

The rhythms are divided into four sectons. Part 1 contains sustained left hand chords, with movement in the pedal. Part 2 contains the easier combination left hand and pedal rhythms. Part 3 consists of the more syncopated rhythms, mostly the latin rhyms. Part 4 is the most advanced.

The pedal notes in parentheses are for spinet organs only. Those of you who have consoles should use the higher notes.

These are by no means all the possibilities for left hand and pedal rhythms, but it should give you some ideas to dress up some of those old, boring arrangements that you're tired of playing—D.C.

191

*One half-step below the root of the next chord.

192

PART 2

193

PART 3

196

PART 4

198

199

200

DC

# organ studio _____

## Let's Do Something About Those Ho-Hum, Hum-Drum Pedals—Part 1

Do you remember when you finally got the right and left hand and pedals together? My gosh, wasn't that great? Such co-ordination! A "C" pedal with a "C" chord, a "G" pedal with a "G" chord, etc. That was some accomplishment, wasn't it?

Next was learning rhythm or pedal-chord, pedal-chord; that is, a pedal on the 1st count, a chord on the 2nd count, a pedal on the third count, and a chord on the 4th count (see example). For those who have never seen what this rhythm looks like in notation, here it is:

This is an example of what a person who has been taught correctly would be reading. However, many *so-called* qualified teachers do this pedal pattern by showing PCPC (pedal, chord, pedal, chord) for 4/4 rhythm or PCC (pedal, chord, chord) for 3/4 rhythm. It is usually taught as a verbal lesson, as opposed to a well-laid-out and prepared lesson so that you can visually see and hear what the rhythm is supposed to be.

Well, I hope you have progressed at least to that stage. Next is pedal, chord, pedal, chord, with alternating pedal. What? Alternating pedals? Are you crazy? I can just about get PCPC together. Say that out loud. Sounds weird, doesn't it? PCPC! PCPC! Or for those who want to be really different, how about PIC-PIC, PIC-PIC?

Enough jest! Alternating pedals is when you use the root of the chord on the first count on the pedal; the shown chord on the second count in the left hand or accompaniment manual as it is properly termed; the third count is what we call the alternating pedal; and then the shown chord on the fourth count on the accompaniment manual. (The alternating pedal for any given chord in the music is based on the 5th tone of the given chord's scales.)

For example, the fifth tone in the "C" scale is "G". So when you play in 4/4 rhythm, the pedal, chord, pedal, chord rhythm, the two pedals in the measure are going to be C and G on the first and third count respectively (see example).

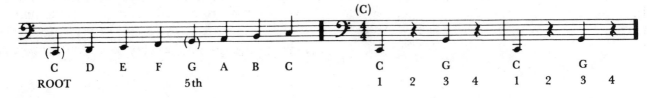

If you move to a "G" chord, and want to play alternating pedals on the first and third counts, you must use the "G" scale as your guide and find out what the fifth tone of the "G" is. If you know your scales, you will have already picked out the tone "D" as the alternating pedal for a "G" chord (see example).

(G) A B C (D) E F♯ G    G D G D
ROOT        5th

When this is shown in music as a complete pattern, pedal, chord, pedal, chord, with alternating pedals, it will look like this in 4/4 rhythm:

Key of "C"

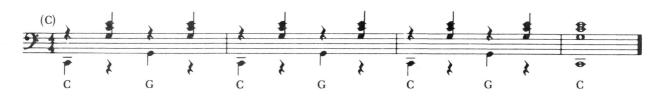

C G C G C G C

Key of "G"

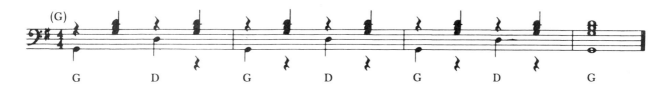

G D G D G D G

If you have been struggling with the pedals, be not dismayed! In the next few articles, I will try to clear up some misconceptions about pedal playing and will try to help you realize what your mistakes have been and show you how to correct those mistakes. Just remember that if you want to play alternating pedals and have not done so before you can find the alternating pedal by finding the fifth tone in the scale of the given chord. If you have not been taught good scale training, get yourself a scale book of which there are many on the market. In your major scales, find the fifth tone and you should begin to help your pedal playing sound better!

Here are two suggestions for pedal technique books that you might find helpful. I use them in my teaching program, and even though they are classically oriented, the material presented in them is invaluable.

1. *Joyce Jones (Pedal Mastery) for the Organ.* There are two editions: one for Spinet and one for full pedalboard. This is a Richard Bradley publications book.

2. *An Organ Instruction Book for the Organ and the Hammond Organ,* by J. F. Alderfer and Charles R. Cronham. This is a J. Fischer and Bros. publication.

BH

# organ studio

## Let's Do Something About Those Pedals — Part 2

If you still find that playing the right hand, left hand and pedals is a problem, explore with me some other possibilities that should help.

1. BENCH POSITION — This aspect of organ (and all keyboard) playing is often overlooked both by teachers and students. Although there are some texts that suggest that the left foot should be suspended over the low G pedal, I do not recommend this position, nor do most qualified teachers. Such a position prevents you from sitting in the middle of the bench, equidistant from each end of the console. Instead, sit so that the left foot is (approximately) over the high B and C pedals (for spinets), or the B and C pedals in the middle of the full pedalboard.

Sitting in this position, your body and arms are in the middle of the console — your hands and feet are positioned comfortably, and you won't have to contort the left hand to play chords.

Now, how far forward or back on the bench should you sit? As a general rule, remember that your hands should be in a comfortable position when playing. Keeping that in mind, you should be able to sit at the console with your feet on the pedals without making them sound. Playing the pedals is the result of *ankle* movement, not the leg. Position yourself so that you don't feel as if you will fall forward or backward. Relax.

2. ALTERNATING PEDALS IN 3/4 TIME — In 4/4 we played the root pedal on the first count, the chord on the second count, the alternate pedal on the third count, and the chord again on the fourth count. What about 3/4 time?

First, see if the music specifies playing one chord for more than a single measure, as in this example:

Ex. 1

Normally, you would play this accompaniment for that example.

Ex. 2

To alternate the pedals in 3/4 time you would do this: play the root pedal on the first count and the chord on the second and third counts — for the first measure. For the second measure, play the alternating pedal (the note a fifth above the root) on the first count and the chord on the second and third counts, as shown in this example:

Ex. 3

Here are all four measures as you would play them:

Ex. 4

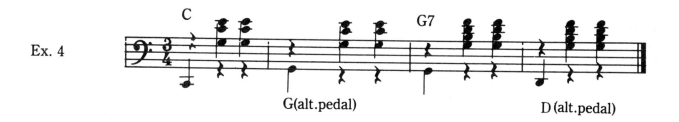

G(alt.pedal)                    D(alt.pedal)

There are other ways of playing alternating pedals in 3/4 time, which we will explore in future workshops. These are, of course, the basic patterns. Practice them slowly at first, building up speed little by little, until you can move smoothly and quickly from one chord to the next. Then, add the melody in example 1. More rhythms to come.

BH ♩

# organ studio

## *Instrumental Sounds at the Organ*

One of the wonderful aspects of today's electronic organs and synthesizers is the ability to produce authentic-sounding instrumental sounds. However, many players often overlook the limitations of range of the instruments they are registering, with the result that they sound anything but authentic!

So, here are some charts designed for quick and easy reference, to use when you are looking for the true sounds of the orchestral instruments at your command. If you play within the ranges shown, the tones of the violin, clarinet, trumpet - any or-chestral instrument - will fall within the tonal range in which the actual instrument would be played.

(If you have a spinet, do the best you can. This is one of those times when a full console is a desirable asset).

I hope you find this helpful in creating as many authentic sounds as possible on your instrument. Be sure to experiment with each individual instrument, and learn the full capability of the registrations on your particular keyboard.

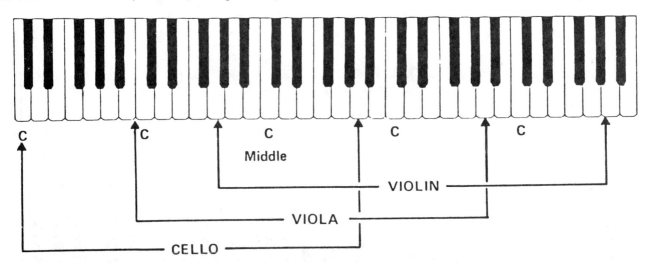

**String Instrument Ranges**

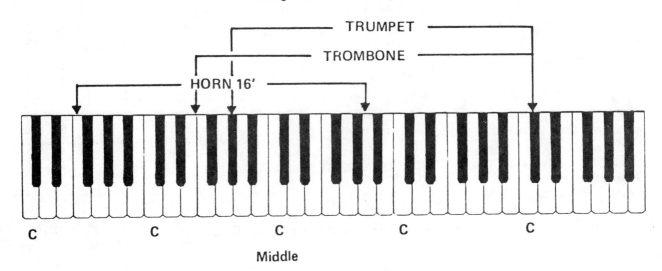

**Brass Instrument Ranges**

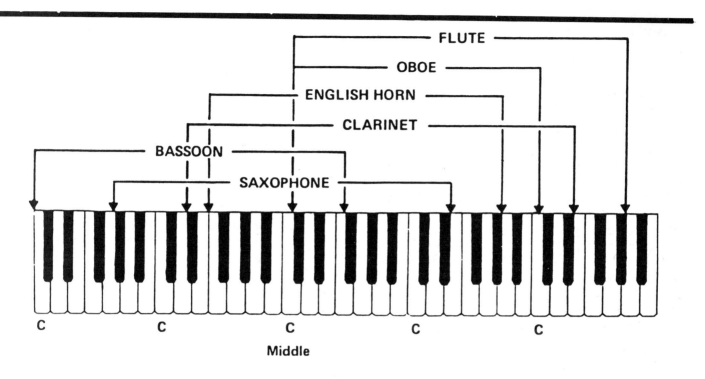

Woodwind Instrument Ranges

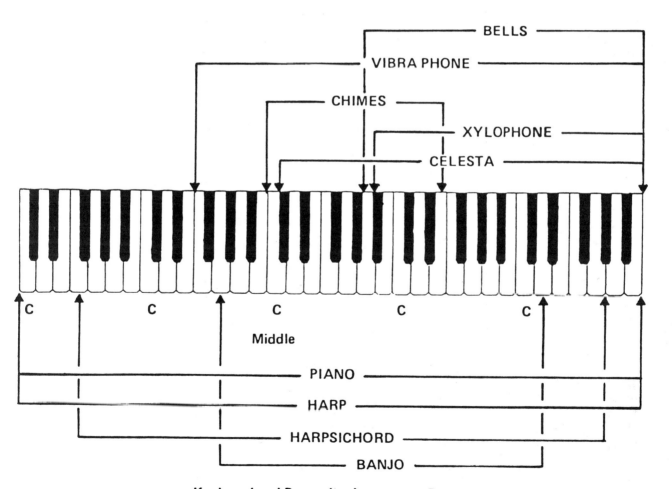

Keyboard and Percussion Instrument Ranges

# MAKING YOUR ORGAN AN ORCHESTRA

The sound of the organ has changed drastically over the years. Although we can still sound "like an organ" we can also authentically recreate almost every orchestral voice.

Many of us have listened to a salesman demonstrate "that beautiful violin," buy the instrument, and never find "that beautiful violin" again. That's because the salesman knew the tricks of not only pushing the correct button, but treating that voice as if it were a real violin.

We have to consider each instrument individually. It helps to know how the sound is produced, the instrument's range, type of vibrato used (if any) and any other special treatment necessary to make each voice sound as authentic as possible.

With the wide variety of organs on the market, it is impossible to be extremely specific in some cases. We will try to use general terms that will clue you as to the feature name on your instrument.

Keep in mind the idea of phrasing. Many instruments we will discuss are wind instruments—meaning that air produces the sound we hear. A trombone player who is not allowed to take a break every few measures will probably pass out!

The goal of this lesson is to help you to understand the instruments better, and, ultimately, to make the time you spend on the bench even more enjoyable.

VIOLIN

Range:

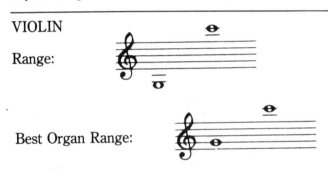

Best Organ Range:

The violin dates back to the early 16th century and can be used for a broad variety of musical styles. It can be played either legato or staccato, and you can play single notes or two, three, or more notes to create an entire string section. The vibrato is created when the player moves his hand against the strings.

If you listen to a violinist, notice that the sound intensifies as he draws the bow. On the organ, this effect can be imitated by backing off of the volume pedal and gradually adding volume as the note is played. (This only works for notes held for several beats.)

The vibrato is delayed—it comes in a short time after the note has been introduced. If your instrument has a "delay vibrato" feature, use it. On some organs, the vibrato's depth and speed can also be controlled. I would suggest a medium setting for both. The most realistic vibrato comes from the "touch vibrato" feature, where the vibrato is produced by physically moving the key.

Whichever vibrato you use, it will give the violin a much warmer tone and make it useful for many types of music.

The accompaniment should provide a contrast (unless you are duplicating a string ensemble), so use a flute 8' by itself or add a horn 8' to the flute.

SUGGESTED TUNES:

Fiddler On The Roof
The Godfather (Theme from)
Lara's Theme (Somewhere My Love)

These are by no means the only tunes to use with the violin. The sky's the limit!

CLARINET

Range:

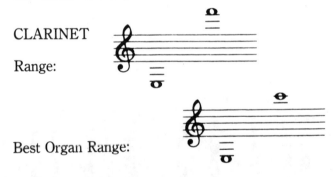

Best Organ Range:

The clarinet is a cylindrical tube with a single vibrating reed. It dates back to the very end of the 17th century. It can play only one note at a time and can be played either legato or staccato. The clarinet can jump easily from high to low notes and smooth runs are no problem for the experienced player.

The clarinet can be played with or without vibrato. If vibrato is used, use the delay vibrato if possible. If you have control of the depth and speed, they should be at a minimum setting.

A bass clarinet is created by using the clarinet voice in the lowest range of the organ keyboard. It can be effective, so experiment with it.

The clarinet player can "glide" from one note to another. Most organs have a glide feature, usually located on the expression pedal. Be sure to activate the glide first, then hit the note and finally release the glide when appropriate.

The accompaniment will vary depending on the kind of music you are playing. For the faster tempos, use a flute 8' so that the clarinet is emphasized. A flute 8' with the addition of a cello 8' would be effective for a ballad, where the accompaniment might include some nice harmony or moving lines.

SUGGESTED TUNES:

Begin The Beguine
Clarinet Polka

TROMBONE

Range:

Best Organ Range:

The trombone is one of the larger brass instruments, using a slide with seven positions to create the different pitches. It is not always capable of playing very legato, since the slide might be moved quite a distance at times, from the closest position to the farthest.

The vibrato is created when the player moves the slide slightly, and it is noticeably delayed. Use the delay vibrato if possible, with a medium to full depth and a medium speed. The amount of delay used will depend on the melody played. The longer delay should be used for melodies with many notes held for several beats. A short delay is best for those melodies with few or no sustained notes.

The trombone is known for the "glide" effect. As with the clarinet, be sure to engage the glide first, strike the note, and then allow the pitch to rise. Don't overuse the glide. Two or three times per chorus is usually enough. If the melody includes half steps upward, the glide can be incorporated into the melody, as demonstrated on the tape. When you reach the point in the melody with the two effected half steps, first engage the glide and play the *higher* note (it will sound like the half step below). When the melody's rhythm calls for the higher note to be played, simply release the glide control. This effect can be a challenging one to coordinate, but it is very useful in creating an authentic trombone.

Grace notes and fast runs are difficult for the trombone, again due to the seven position slide.

The accompaniment will vary depending on where you want the emphasis. A flute 8' by itself would be best if all the emphasis is to be on the trombone. If the accompaniment includes counter-melodies or interesting harmonies, try adding a cello 8' or string to the flute 8'.

SUGGESTED TUNES:

I'm Getting Sentimental Over You
Moonglow
Seventy-Six Trombones (no vibrato)

PIANO

Range: Entire Organ Keyboard

Best Organ Range: Avoid Highest Octave

The piano has been enjoyed by both players and listeners since the 18th century. The sound is created when the pushed key activates a hammer which strikes strings that vibrate.

No vibrato is used and any type of turning speaker should be avoided if possible. All of the orchestra voices will sound most realistic through a stationary speaker.

Since the piano tone dies away, don't attempt to play notes with long time values. Sustain can be used to add length to the tone. Strike the note and quickly let go, allowing the note to "ring." Use a medium amount of sustain for slow ballads and less for faster tempos or songs with a good deal of movement. Some instruments provide a damper feature, so that sustain can be added at any point and taken away when necessary. This feature allows the organist to play a very authentic piano, especially if he is also a pianist.

If you have no piano experience, begin by using the piano only for the melody, with your accompaniment sounding like a "normal" organ. The melody will be accented very nicely if you are able to play octaves (add the note one octave above the melody note).

The piano can also be used for the accompaniment registration. It can be played simply with a pedal-chord rhythm, or used with arpeggios. The accompaniment could be a variety of things; since the flute 8' is very similar to the piano tone, it might be best to accent it with a contrasting voice, such as a horn or string.

## SUGGESTED TUNES:

The Entertainer
Send In The Clowns (Use piano for arpeggio accompaniment)
Maple Leaf Rag

## TRUMPET

Range:

Best Organ Range:

An early version of the trumpet was used in the 17th century, and today's most popular version has three valves used alone or in combination to create the well known sound.

The trumpet player creates vibrato by moving his fingers on the valves. His lips also have a great deal to do with the tone he produces. Again, the vibrato is delayed. For those of you with a delay vibrato feature, a medium delay is best. The depth of the vibrato is medium and the speed slow to medium.

You can use the trumpet for both legato and staccato passages, as well as long jumps and runs. It is a very flexible instrument and is used for all types of music. Ballads, marches, country, big band and classics all sound authentic when played on the trumpet.

Although the trumpet plays only one note at a time, you can duplicate the entire trumpet section by playing full chords in the right hand.

A simple musical accompaniment should have a simple registration—possibly a flute 8' with a touch of flute 4'. An interesting musical accompaniment calls for the addition of an 8' string or cello.

## SUGGESTED TUNES:

Bugler's Holiday
Tenderly
Theme From "Ice Castles"

## OBOE

Range:

Best Organ Range:

The oboe dates back to the beginning of the Christian era and is a conical tube with a double reed. These reeds are positioned back to back and the player must "pinch" the reeds between his lips.

As the player blows into the oboe, the reeds vibrate and create the haunting, easily recognizable sound.

The oboe player uses a subtle, delayed vibrato. If your instrument has delay vibrato, use it. The depth and speed of the vibrato is usually at a minimum.

The best use for the oboe is as a single note melody, since only one note can be produced at a time. An "oboe choir" is extremely rare, so it is best to stay away from full chords with the oboe.

The accompaniment must be fairly soft, as the oboe is a soft instrument. I would suggest using a flute 8' by itself, or a flute 8' and horn 8'. The accompaniment should provide a rich background but be careful not to overpower it.

## SUGGESTED TUNES:

Stranger On The Shore
The Way We Were
Caravan

## FLUTE

Range:

Best Organ Range:

The flute is a cylindrical tube that is stopped at one end and has been a part of the orchestra family since the mid 18th century. It is not a particularly loud instrument, but it has a very pleasing tone.

The flute voice is probably the most used voice on any organ, since most organs include several flute pitch levels and some organs base all of their sounds on a flute foundation. The 8' flute is the pitch that should be used for the solo flute.

The vibrato is actually more of a tremolo or "wah" (a change in volume or tone, rather than the change in pitch that is vibrato). Vibrato (delayed if possible) will work just fine if your instrument does not include a "wah" control. The type of tremolo used for any turning speaker, such as Leslie, is not the tremolo necessary for an authentic flute.

The flute 4', used with a slight vibrato and played in the upper range of the keyboard will sound like a whistle. The flute 4' can also be used to create a piccolo (it plays one octave higher than the flute).

The accompaniment should provide a contrast, so try using a horn 8' or string 8' with the flute 8'.

## SUGGESTED TUNES:

Girl From Ipanema
Meditation
(Any Bossa Nova)
Sweet Georgia Brown (Use the flute 4' as a whistle)

DC

# organ studio

## Organ Registration — The Importance of Reverberation

What is reverberation? What purpose does it serve? We might define *reverberation* as that part of a sound that reaches the ear after being reflected from the floor, ceiling, or walls, as distinguished from the sound that reaches the ear by a direct path through the air. Think of a Swiss yodeler whose voice bounces off the mountain walls and rolls around in the valley below: now *that* is reverberation! In music, particularly organ music, reverberation can play a great role in creating a musical atmosphere, or ambience, that makes the music come alive. We organists are fortunate that we can create and control the extent of reverberation that we apply to our music — we can simulate, in the home, the acoustical effect of playing in a large concert hall.

In order to provide some insight into how we can use reverberation, I posed a few questions to a sound engineer at a major recording studio. I was told that the individual artists and instrumentalists are highly aware of the effect of reverberation, and in most cases indicate to what degree they wish it applied to their performance. In recording, reverberation is generally applied *after* the actual recording, using a variety of mechanical processes. One such mechanical device is the "plate reverb," which is actually a steel sheet 1/4 inch thick, measuring four feet by eight. The plate is suspended in a sealed box with a microphone at one end and a speaker at the other. The sound from the speaker travels through the plate, losing intensity as it goes, and the "delayed" signal is picked up by the microphone. Another device is the "spring reverb," which uses a long spring instead of a plate. The sound is transmitted through the spring, producing an artifical reverberation effect. Then there are electrical systems, such as "digital delay," in which a sound is stored momentarily by an electrical circuit, then released, producing an echo effect. In most of these systems, the decay time can be altered, producing a wide variety of effects.

So much for how reverberation is produced. Let us come now to its effect and purpose, as it applies to the organist. We can use reverberation to 1) RETARD the build-up of a tone (or soften the "attack"), or 2) to PROLONG the tone after the key is

released (increase the "sustain"). For instance, short detached chord structures do not have a chance of becoming excessively loud because the keys are released before the tones can accumulate or intensify. However, the experienced player can give life to such chords with a judicious use of reverberation — the rise and fall of the reverberant "echoes" of short chords create dynamic interest that may be lacking in the music itself.

As an example, try this on the organ you play. Set the reverb control on *maximum*. Using both manuals and both hands, strike a series of chords sharply, with the expression pedal well depressed. Release the keys prematurely as you go from chord to chord. Listen to how the reverberation picks up the sound, sustaining it well after the keys have been released. There is a sensation of spaciousness, perhaps even "hollowness." How can you use this effect to enhance your playing? Experiment with it. Don't use it all the time, and don't use it at maximum when you do use it, but think of it as a function of *registration,* not just as an effect. Even the slightest touch of reverberation can bring any music to life. ♩

**ML**

# organ studio

## How To Make — Registration Changes

Are you one of those conservative organists who luckily found·a nice-sounding registration on the instrument a few years ago and has been using it, and only it, for a long time?

Do you yell at your spouse not to go near the organ because it is set up just right and any touching will destory the nice sound?

When you are playing a piece, are you like the politician who promises a lot of changes but never makes any?

Do you take the equivalent of a television commercial break when you daringly reach for some tab, lever, drawbar, pressure-sensitive switch, knob, et cetera, to make a registration change during a performance?

Have you noticed how unrelated your playing is to the automatic rhythm unit after you pause to make a registration change?

If you are one of those poor unfortunate organ hobbyists who suffers from that dread disease "neverchangingregistrationitis," don't just start to cry and leave the room keep on reading. There is still hope for you, and we are going to discuss that

aspect of registration right now.

To begin, registration is an inherent part of playing the organ. It should be—it MUST be — studied and the knowledge applied if you are to have pleasure at the organ. It is a basic part of organ study. In fact, the only thing more basic, and certainly much less complicated, is knowing what switch turns on the organ. Sometimes, even that on/off switch is hard to find.

When the organ is first turned on, it is necessary to set up the registration for the manuals (keyboards) and the pedalboard. This is not a study of registration, so I will not go into the complexities of all the components of registration—families of tones, foot lengths, animations, contrast, balance, et cetera.

Instead, I'm going to concentrate on the various techniques I use and teach my students to enable them, and you, to make quick, accurate, smooth, acceptable and *noticeable* registration changes.

Why did I emphasize "noticeable"? Because registration changes that are too subtle are a waste of the organist's time and effort. Of course, I will not dictate or even suggest "taste" in the quality of your registrations. If you are reading traditional organ arrangements (I hope some of them are mine, published by Hal Leonard Publishing Corp.), then the registration is suggested. While it is, of necessity, a general suggestion (not all registration timbres [tone qualities] can be found on the various brands of organs), it is quite important that you make the effort to set up the organ as close to the suggestions as possible. Watch out particularly for the footages given for the different stops or settings. These are most important in relationship to the area of the keyboard where you will be playing. Then, if you are choosing your own registrations for chord work, where YOU are the arranger, your choices will depend on your knowledge of the various components of registration, your ability to hear the wide range of tones (known as your "ear"), and your "taste."

Now that you have set up the organ for whatever you're going to play, your first thought should be: Am I going to play the piece rhythmically or in a sustained (rubato, freely, ad-lib) manner?

If you are going to play without a steady beat, then registration changes are easy to make. They can almost be done leisurely. In nonrhythmic playing, pauses are acceptable and during them, either hand can usually be used to make the registration change. Prior to an actual pause, try ritarding the "tempo" (simply start to play even slower than you have been playing) so that the pause used to change the registration will seem natural, like a normal part of the performance. Even then, I would suggest that you practice making the planned change so that it can be made to look and feel as if it were done effortlessly. People do seem to enjoy performers "working" during a performance; that is, the more the performer perspires and appears to be working hard (not struggling) to please the audience, the more the audience responds to the show. However, there is always the audience who appreciates the music the artist is producing with no apparent effort. The words "You make it look so easy" are often heard at a concert, and the performer can take pride in knowing that all the effort put into the performance was concealed in the polished presentation witnessed by the audience.

The techniques used in making registration changes in the middle of a rhythmic performance run the gamut from simple to complicated and will depend quite often on your instrument.

First, there are some basic rules for changing registration while playing rhythmically.

If the tempo (speed) of the piece is slow, use your right hand to make registration changes. Generally, the accompaniment for slow ballads will have the left hand holding sustained chords while the pedals are played on all four beats of the measure. When the right hand is removed from the manual, the full background produced by the sustained chords in the left hand, plus the activity in the bass with the four pedal beats, will effectively maintain interest and continuity for the listener. However, when the left hand is used at a slow tempo, the bottom seems to fall out of the arrangement.

Conversely, if the tempo is moderate to fast, I suggest using the left hand to make the registration changes since the movement in the right hand will keep the listener's interest while the left hand is doing the work.

At all times, look for the opportunity to make a registration change during a pick-up, that is, melody notes in an incomplete measure. It is always effective in arranging to have pick-up notes played without accompaniment (N.C., Tacet, Soli). Of course, that is the ideal situation for the left hand to make the change while the right hand is busy.

When there is apparently no opportunity to try the above suggestions, moving the right hand down to the lower manual, usually playing the melody 8va (one octave higher than written to avoid running into the left hand) is a simple, quick, and generally satisfying way to make a registration change when there is no time to make mechanical changes.

It is also possible to move the left hand up to the upper manual to play the tune with both hands on the Swell manual. However, you must remain aware of the footages in the settings. With an 8' setting, you can use both hands in the middle register, but if there is a 16' setting, you will have to move both right- and left-hand parts one or two octaves higher to avoid a muddy sound in the left-hand accompaniment.

In my registration workshop, I show how several registration changes can be made without a lot of mechanical changes. For example: Always check to see what, if any, preset registrations are available, especially on the various brands you have not played before. Try them and notice what sound each preset produces. Quite often, the manufacturer sets up the presets so that the settings become bigger and fuller as you move from left to right. On several makes of organs, the manufacturer gives you the opportunity to set up your own special preset sounds. I suggest you follow the same order and have your adjustable presets expand from simple 8' settings to more complex 16' settings as you move from left to right.

BI

213

# organ studio

## How To Make — Registration Changes
### Part II

**1.** Look for solo pre-sets that can be set up with a single movement, such as a tablet/lever/switch for Piano, Vibraphone, Chime and any of the solo orchestral instruments. When more than one movement is necessary in order to set up a particular setting, it will take more time and greater dexterity of movement to accomplish the registration change. A case in point would be having first to cancel the present setting before the new setting can be used, or having to change the animation (tremulant or vibrato) to match the new setting. If you are having any difficulty in making changes, learn to handle the simplest changes quickly, cleanly, and in rhythm before attempting the more intricate changes.

**2.** Some instruments have knee levers that can be activated without removing your hands from the manuals. They are excellent for quick changes (they give you the equivalent of a third manual when they change the entire sound), but it takes a little practice to become accustomed to the coordination required. If you are playing another brand of organ that uses a knee lever, make sure that the movement to the right produces the same mechanical result with which you are familiar. Generally, the knee levers can be adjusted to the

most comfortable position for you. There are several effects for which a knee lever is used including changing the present registration back to an original setting, creating a glide, turning the animation off and on, etc.

**3.** On larger electronic and pipe organs, foot pistons are used to enable the player to make rapid changes with either foot.

**4.** There is generally only one switch to turn the tremulant or vibrato on and off. This can be a very valuable aid in helping you to change sounds. For example, if you are playing a melody in chords with the right hand, using full tremulant, try changing to a single-note melody with the trem turned off. The left hand can make the cancellation easily at most any time, particularly during a tacet (N.C.) pickup. When playing pop music with no trem on, use a light, disconnected touch to avoid sounding liturgical. You'll find that the orchestral instruments used in jazz numbers sound authentic when played without trem or vibrato. If you do use the vibrato for the orchestral instruments, then be sure to use the vibrato *delay*, and if it's adjustable, don't have it come on too soon.

214

**5.** Swell pedal switches are very valuable in making changes. When there is just one switch (it may be placed on either the right or left side of the pedal), it is generally used to turn the automatic rhythm unit on and off. However, there are organs on the market that have two switches in the form of short metal posts standing up on both sides of the swell pedal in the general area of the toes. One switch will control the starting and stopping of the automatic rhythm unit and the other will control a number of changes that are pre-set on a control panel. Remember that even the act of turning an automatic rhythm on and off constitutes a change and will enhance your presentation.

All right, let's get to the pièce de résistance that I offer in my workshops. How to make several changes during a piece without touching—or hardly touching—any mechanical switches, tabs, drawbars, or levers.

In speaking of different areas of the keyboard, we use the term "register". The area around middle C would be considered the middle register. Then the octaves above would be the higher register and the octaves below referred to as the lower register.

Playing single notes and chords in the different registers doesn't actually change the sound, but with the change of octaves, the sound seems to have a different quality. Let's explore that thought.

On the upper manual, set up a rather full 16′ setting, using 16′, 8′, 4′, 2′ flutes/tibias, with 8′ and 4′ strings and either an 8′ or 4′ reed. This will provide a variety of tonal textures that will enhance the effect of changing as we move the melody up and down the manual. Set up 8′ and 4′ flutes and strings on the lower manual with diapason 8′ added for "body," if available. Use 16′ and 8′ in the bass pedals with sustain. Tremulant or vibrato on, full.

Remember that with a 16′ setting, you must be very careful when playing even single-note melodies in the middle register, to avoid sounding muddy. With a 16′ setting, you must never play melodies in chords in the middle register. Even when you use single-note melodies, you must be careful unless you are performing heavy classical or dramatic pieces that call for that kind of sound.

Choose any simple piece for the following experiment.

Use your right hand to play a few single melody notes on the upper manual in the middle register and listen to the sound. Then move your hand to the highest octave on the upper manual and play the same single-note melody. It *does* sound different.

Then have your right hand repeat the single-note melodies in the same registers on the lower manual. If you have a spinet, your upper register will not extend as high, but there will still be a slight difference in sound between the melody played in the middle and upper registers.

Next, return to the upper manual and have the right hand play the melody in chords, legato, in the area around C an octave above middle C—between the middle and upper registers. Then repeat in the same area on the lower manual.

Return to the upper manual and this time, play the melody in chords in the same place, but play the chords *staccato,* in a crisp manner. (Note: In the accompaniment for this melody style, I suggest using a sustained countermelody with after-beats.) Again, repeat the melody in staccato chords in the same area on the lower manual.

With the right hand on the upper manual, play a single-note melody with the animation turned off, cancel the trem and/or the vibrato, and use a disconnected touch. Try playing the staccato melody in chords with the trem/vibrato off.

If you have a solo pre-set that can be turned on with a single movement (piano, virbraphone, chime, etc.), use it for the melody.

Try playing the melody in various styles, such as three-part open harmony, block chords, pyramid chords, etc., on either the upper or lower manuals, between the middle and upper registers.

For a big-theater effect, easily and quickly available to you with this type of approach, use the block harmony style of playing both hands close together on the upper manual, with the left hand holding the chord conventionally and the right hand playing a single-note melody.

Instead of the left hand holding the accompanying chord on the lower manual with the right playing the single-note melody on the upper manual, move the left-hand chord to the upper manual and play it an octave higher. Add the right-hand single-melody notes immediately above the left-hand chords and *voila!* . . .the sound of Radio City Music Hall! (I relate to that, having grown up in New York City listening to the pipe organ in that magnificent hall.)

Now that you have a variety of sounds at your command with very few physical movements or mechanical adjustments, choose a tune and at least every eight measures, make some sort of "registration change." For example, start with a single melody note in the middle register on the upper manual, next play the melody in chords or the single-note melody high on the lower manual. Follow with staccato chords on upper, followed by single-note melody in the middle register of the lower manual. You can certainly figure out several ways to utilize the changes.

For a big sound, I end the demonstration in my workshops with the full theater sound (Radio City). It's usually well received.

There's always more to say on a subject, but that's all on making registration changes for this time.

If you have a particular playing problem, write to me in care of *Sheet Music* and perhaps I can provide some instruction through these pages.

'Bye now. **BI**

# organ studio
## Gimme A Little Gliss!

The modern organ keyboard/manual with its gently rounded keys is a natural for performing the various glissandos used in pop music.

As with any embellishment technique, it's easy to overdo adding glissandos to your playing, so be sure to remain conservative when you use the basic three organ glissandos.

THE THUMB GLISSANDO is used when a single note or chord moves *up* the keyboard to the right. It is indicated with one wavy line like this:

With just enough pressure to make each white key sound, drag your right thumb from left to right over the white keys, keeping the angle at 45 degrees or less which will tend to push down the keys to the right. Too upright an angle will not allow movement. See illus.

R.H. THUMB  GOOD  BAD

Use the area between the center of the pad and the fingernail. When preparing to thumb gliss, practice moving from chord to chord without the gliss to be sure you know where you're going, then add the gliss. In general, avoid using the thumb gliss when the bottom note of the top chord has a black key at the bottom. Use the Palm Gliss instead.

THE LITTLE FINGER GLISSANDO is used when a single note or chord moves *down* the keyboard to the left. Use the fleshy part of the 5th finger and keep the angle low. Use enough strength to make the keys sound but not too much or the finger will stick to the keys. Once again, when the top note of the bottom chord is a black key, I suggest you use the Palm Gliss instead.

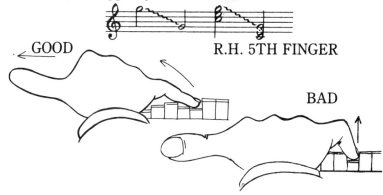

GOOD  R.H. 5TH FINGER  BAD

THE PALM GLISSANDO is the most versatile of the organ glisses as it is used both up and down the keyboard for glissing between chords. It isn't practical for a single note gliss. Use the base of the palm, I call it the "roller coaster". Depress the chord, hold the keys down while you move the hand forward to the back of the keys, continue to hold the chord down as the palm is placed just inside the edge of the keys. Place the palm in the center of the chord and when the keys have been depressed by the palm, keep the palm down and lift the fingers. The movement should be so smooth and the sound so sustained that it sounds as though the chord melted into the keys. Holding down the palm, raise the fingers and point them away from the direction of the gliss. Use just enough pressure to make the keys sound (too much and you won't be able to move your hand), and gliss up or down to the next chord.

When you arrive at the chord, the palm should have gotten there before your fingers. Hold the palm down in the middle of the chord while you swing your fingers around to depress the actual keys. After the keys of the chord have been depressed, hold the chord and slide your hand back towards you, raising the palm. Performed correctly, it should sound as though the first chord melted into the keyboard, traveled through the keys and smoothly emerged when the hand reached its destination.

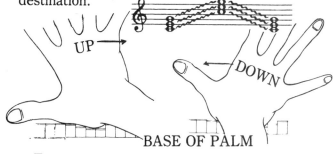

UP  DOWN  BASE OF PALM

Try to limit your use of glissandos to actually connecting two notes or chords. The three general exceptions are: 1. a splashy gliss up to an opening chord, such as the opening of *Jealousie*, 2. a splashy gliss down to a root note for an ending, 3. a gliss used after a note or chord as a "strain" (a dropping away of the pitch).

Wish I was there to demonstrate the techniques as they are both visual and audio techniques. However, any time you attend one of my pop concerts or keyboard workshops, I'll be happy to show you how they are done.

By the way, fingernails are generally used to gliss on the piano, not the organ, but you can gliss in third or sixth intervals by using 1st and 3rd or 1st and 5th fingers, using, from left to right, flesh and nail glissing up and the reverse, nail and flesh glissing down.

Are you ready to "gimmie a little gliss"? **BI**

# The Jesse Crawford Style

On a recent concert tour of New Zealand and Australia, I included on my program a theatre style interpretation of an old tune and was very pleased when the audiences reacted favorably to my mention of the man who was responsible for this style, and who became famous for his technique in performing three part open harmony with finger or chromatic glissandos. Of course, I'm referring to Jesse Crawford, who is often referred to as the "Dean of Theatre Organists." The technique became known as the "Jesse Crawford style." Traditional theatre organists usually included this style somewhere in their programs and I thought you'd enjoy trying your hand at this old-fashioned technique that still remains a favorite with modern exponents of the theatre organ style. (By the way, I didn't say it was easy to perform. It does require some skill, but I think it's a challenge that is well worth the effort. Besides, aren't you getting a bit tired of being told how easy everything is?)

Let's start with the simple idea of three part, open harmony. The simple melody line is:

Play the melody in three part harmony, adding the balance of the chord under the melody note. When using a four note chord, such as the G7th, in order to reduce the four parts to three parts, a simple rule is to omit the root when the melody is not on the root. The same rule applies to the fifth step. Play the melody in three parts. . . . .

Next, keeping both hands on the same manual . . . . usually the upper . . . physically remove the middle note of the chord and use your left hand to play it an octave lower. The reason for both hands on the same manual, is to maintain the balance of the notes in the chord. You can get some interesting effects with the middle note played on the other manual, but you have to make sure that the volume on each manual balances unless you are striving for some unusual sounds. Play the example.

You can approximate the sound of the J.C. style by using slides between the left hand notes. Use them when moving up to the right. You can keep it very simple by using the two half tones below the following note, like this. . .

Now that we've gotten this far, it's just a wee bit more involved to produce this style authentically.

Basically, the bottom two notes of the three part open chord move up (and sometimes down) chromatically, arriving at the following chord at the same time. Study the following example and then I'll discuss an approach to performing this technique. . .

Rarely do both hands have an even number of notes to be played in the chromatic movement. You are supposed to start together and then have the hand with the extra note(s) play slightly faster so that both hands arrive at the new chord at the same time.

When there is just one extra note in one hand (in the chromatic movement), try playing the extra note before starting the movement with the other hand, then play the remaining notes in both hands together. For example, you might start your practice in the first measure in this manner. . .

After a little practice, start the chromatics in both hands at the same time, but rush the hand with the extra note or notes so that both hands arrive at the next chord together.

Does that seem clear?

Obviously, you're going to want to try this technique with very slow tunes that have a lot of whole and half notes in the melody.

The next time I'm performing a pop concert in your area, come on up to the organ and I'll perform the chromatic glissandos for you. . . or I'll be happy to go over the whole approach for you during one of my workshops. Bye now. **BI**.

# An Organist's Guide To Latin Rhythms

# LATIN RHYTHM GUIDE
## (Tango)

To fully understand the unique quality of Latin Rhythms, we would do well to start at the origin of all rhythms.

The BEAT itself!

Students sometimes disregard the fact that the beat must conclude a full cycle, much like a bouncing ball. We will work with the quarter note as representing 1 beat, although other note values are used for this purpose. Thus, the quarter note would be counted ONE-AND, TWO-AND; "one" representing the DOWNBEAT, and "two," the UP, or AFTERBEAT.

Like this:

1 and 2 and, etc.

As you see, the elements that establish rhythm are missing.

The ACCENTED note (or beat) can provide to some degree, one of the important elements.

Like this:

A BAR line before each accented note establishes the time signature 3/4. The rhythm: WALTZ.
Accents can be applied at greater intervals, depending upon the "pulse," or rhythm desired.
As in our first rhythm - TANGO:

In the tango rhythm, the first and **fourth** beats are heavily accented, unlike the usual 4/4 pattern, in which the first and third beats are accented.

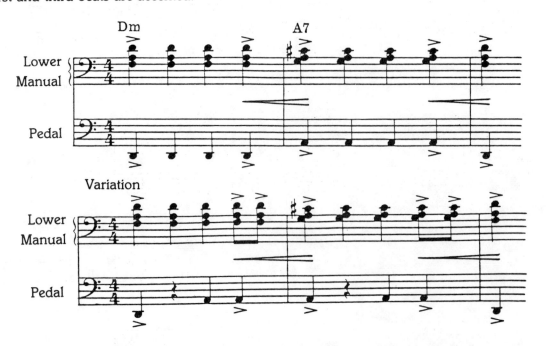

220

# LATIN RHYTHM GUIDE
## (Cha Cha)

The Cha, Cha, like the Tango, deals with ACCENTED DOWNBEATS.

Please refer to the illustration extracted from the arrangement of "Sweet And Gentle."
The Pedal/Bass pattern consists of 4 equal beats. The 2nd beat, denoted by a quarter rest, is silent, or "empty".
The resulting effect of this pattern is the basis for many Latin rhythms.
The Left Hand must perform figurations more complex.
The left "side," meaning the Pedals and Left Hand, should be practiced together as a team; since here lies the rhythmic support for the Right Hand. It is after this aspect has been mastered accurately, in tempo, that automated rhythm (if desired) may be applied with some assurance it will coordinate with the activities of the Pedal and Left Hand.

# LATIN RHYTHM GUIDE
## (Bossa Nova)

This extremely popular Latin rhythm is very "versatile" and lends itself to many forms of music in the popular and Jazz idiom. The bass (or pedal) line is most important. See Below:

VARIATION*    *This rhythm produced by automated unit.

# LATIN RHYTHM GUIDE
## (Rhumba - Beguine)

RHUMBA: The rhumba is another example of how we can produce a completely different rhythmic effect by altering the accent pattern of the four beats. In this rhythm, beat 1 is emphasized slightly, there is a rest for beat 2, and 3rd and 4th beats are accented more heavily than the first.

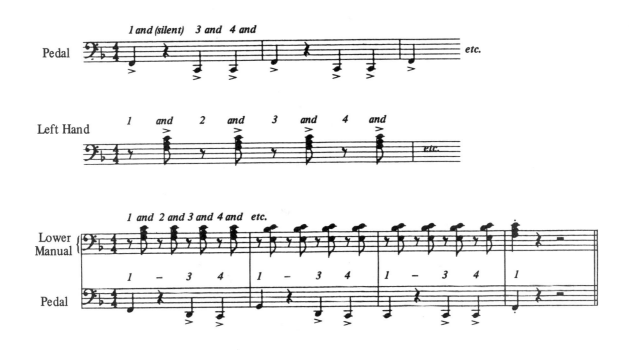

BEGUINE: The beguine is not unlike the rhumba in accent pattern. However, please note the "AND 2" in each bar. It is a quarter note and frequently can be of slightly longer duration. Also, the second beat is **not** silent in the pedal, but is consolidated with the first beat.

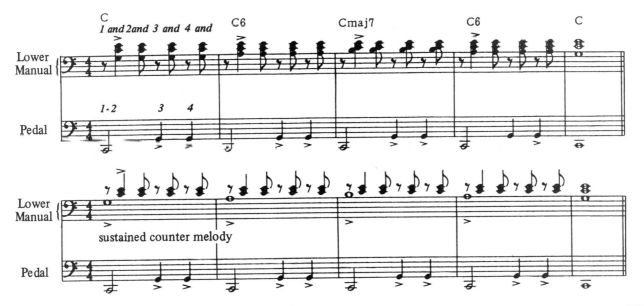

223

# LATIN RHYTHM GUIDE
## (Mambo)

The Mambo is played at a very bright and lively tempo. Below are some of the various Pedal patterns.

Accents on beats 1 and 3.

Accents on beats 1 - 3 and 4

Stationary

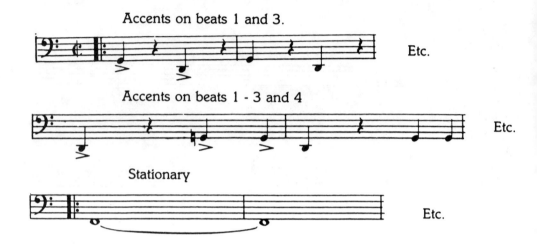

**RHYTHM ACCOMPANIMENTS:**

Melody and Accompaniment - I

Both Hands
Upper

Melody and Accompaniment.

**CHORD RHYTHM:**

# LATIN RHYTHM GUIDE
## (Samba)

1. PEDAL or BASS pattern: The heavily accented 2nd beat.
2. LEFT HAND: The "anticipated" beat preceding the 1st beat of each bar.

INTRO:

*Observe accent on 2nd beat throughout.

The anticipated beat is accomplished by placing the accent on the weak or second ("and") half of the beat cycle. This often involves the "borrowing" of time value from one beat and giving it to another.

1 & 2 & 3 & 4 &

1 & 2 & 3 & 4 & 1 & 2 & 3 & 4 &

ML

# organ studio

## *Chord Curiosity*

In my teaching experience, the organ student's fascination with any and all kinds of chord "tricks" never ceases to interest me. What surprises many students is that the Lower Manual was not constructed solely for the purpose of providing a place to play chords. In fact, chord accompaniments may be played on the Upper Manual with the right hand for a melody played on the Lower Manual with the left hand!

Be that as it may, let's get to the crux of "Chord Curiosity." It doesn't take very long for the old C-F-G chord approach to wear thin, especially when used in hundreds of song adaptations. It's true, everything does begin to sound the same.

When browsing around sheet music stores, inevitably the *Fake Book*, or some similar publication finds its way into the hand of the student organist. In an attempt to provide relief from the C-F-G approach, the publishers of these books often include the original unedited chords. Organists who say at first glance, "Ah, this is for me!" are soon faced with the task of finding someone, or some "thing" to interpret these unedited chords.

In an attempt to relieve some "chord curiosities" of both teachers and students, I'd like to offer some information concerning 9th chords and 9th chord alterations.

The playing diagrams outline 9th chord constructions in the key of C. The numbers to the right of the notes indicate Root, 3rd, 5th, etc. In each diagram the Pedal is assigned the Root of each chord. Fingering has not been suggested due to varying hand sizes. If the 5 Part 9th chords are too difficult, try the 4 Part diagrams instead.

### 5 Part 9th Chords

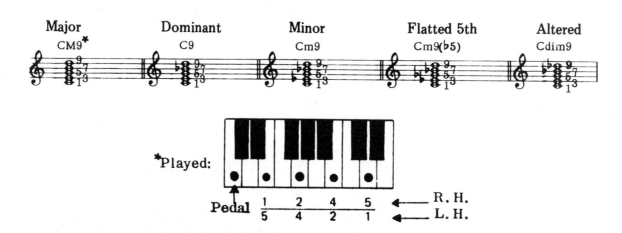

Professional, or unedited organ arrangements often indicate chord combinations such as these:

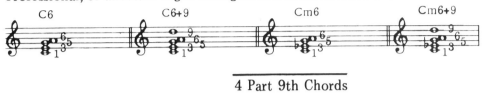

## 4 Part 9th Chords

As with 7th chords or other complex chord structures, the 5th is omitted permitting the important tones to prevail and be more easily managed.

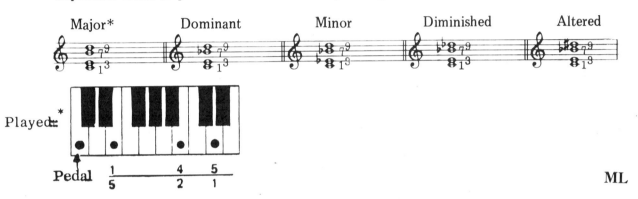

ML

# Keyboard Workshop

# THE ECHO TECHNIQUE IN EAR TRAINING

## Part I

One of the greatest statements I've heard about musicians was made by Champ Champagne, supertalented and very knowledgeable keyboardist, bassist and arranger, whose home is Hull, Quebec, Canada. The statement? "Musicians *see* with their *ears* and *hear* with their *eyes*."

In this article I'm going to discuss "seeing" with your ears; that is, *ear training*—the development of our ability to recognize pitch (the high or low sound of a note), rhythm (the time values of notes), and harmony (the types of chords used to accompany the melody).

When I refer to "seeing" with your ears, it's just another way of saying that you can develop the ability to hear a melody, analyze what you hear almost automatically, and relate it to the keys on the keyboard, almost as if you are looking at, or "seeing," the music. Actually, more than the idea of "seeing" the music, we're talking about "looking" at the keys on the keyboard and seeing what keys will make the sounds you hear. For example,

if you are very familiar with the simple tune "Mary Had a Little Lamb," you ought to be able to look at the keyboard and as your eyes move down from the physical keys of E, D, C, and up through the keys of D, E, E, E..., you ought to almost hear the melody in your head.

Have you noticed how many jazz and popular keyboardists hum or actually sing along with their playing? They're not frustrated vocalists. Rather, they are verbalizing what they hear in their head while re-creating those sounds on the keyboard with their fingers. Great examples of this technique are in the recordings made by the late Errol Garner, a jazz pianist who made jazz history. The verbal noises he made while performing have become part of his legend.

Ear training can't promise you greater musical creativity, but it can help you to listen to, assimilate, and re-create musical ideas expressed by more knowledgeable performers. As a result, you continually add more information to your musical computer, which, in turn, increases your ability to perform your present material better and leads you in new directions.

Let's get started.

The echo technique of ear training, which I am about to discuss, can be used easily with teacher and student working together in a studio. Even two students can help each other to practice this technique. However, I prefer the use of a tape recorder for the student. The aural dictation can be done by a teacher, another student, or by the student himself (or herself).

228

To maintain a steady tempo, use either a metronome or a very simple rhythm on the automatic rhythm unit. Quite often, unless the auto rhythm unit has a metronome setting, it is difficult to find a rhythm setting that will just sound four steady beats in a measure. Experience has shown that many students find it difficult to hear or feel the basic four beats in a measure when an automatic rhythm setting adds extra percussive effects to the basic beat. Hand clapping to the beat, under supervision, can help a student hear and feel the basic beats in any automatic rhythm.

Set the tempo (speed) of the metronome or auto rhythm so that it is slow enough for you to maintain the exercise from measure to measure. We'll start with 4/4 time, common time. Of course, the same exercises can be performed in 3/4 and 6/8 time later on.

Set up the organ registration with flutes or tibias, 16', 8', 4', 2', 1', if available, on the upper manual (keyboard). The use of animation, that is, tremulant or vibrato, is optional. Some traditionalists believe that the pitch of the notes can be heard more easily when there is no animation used (one of the reasons that animation is reduced, or not used at all in accompanying congregational singing). We'll start with the C major triad (three-note chord).

Knowing that you are going to be using those three specific pitches of C, E, and G will make it easier for you to concentrate on the time value given each note in the performance.

**Important.** If you are a beginner and have not had the experience of performing and listening to steps of the various major scales, which automatically increases your ability to recognize melodic movement up or down, and gives some background for the more complicated movement in intervals (the distances between notes), you may wish to have someone help you with this initial step. Simply have someone play the C major scale and verbally identify the names of the steps: then, while not looking at the keyboard, you name the notes the pianist plays at random. That should help. Now, back to the ear exercises.

Whoever is going to do the playing examples—your teacher, friend or you—will play one measure, using the three notes of the C major chord, in any order and with any time values. This is done while the metronome is sounding the beats of the measure.

At the end of the measure, the player rests for the following measure, four beats, and resumes the playing in the following measure. This technique of performing a measure followed by a blank measure allows the student to try to imitate the preceding measure WHILE MAINTAINING A STEADY BEAT. That's the important part. There is no time to try all the notes, hunting for the right ones and then trying to play them with the correct values. The constant beating of the metronome or rhythm unit forces the student to pay attention and replay immediately the example heard. The initial performing measures might be played as follows:

The initial level, using the three notes of the C major chord, is determined by the playing ability of the student and how rapidly the student can imitate the examples. I have numbered the illustrations from 1 to 5 to indicate the growing level of difficulty in the performed measures. A teacher should not have the student working at a level beyond the ability to hear and perform the examples. (That's where the expertise of the teacher is of value to the student.)

For example, if you have trouble imitating the quarter note examples (1), then, of course, you should not be attempting to imitate the even eighths, dotted eighths, triplets, etc. (I haven't shown any examples of sixteenth notes.)

All right, let's get set up for the actual performance of the exercise at this level.

Whoever is going to do the recording of the musical examples should set the speed of the rhythm device, turn on the tape recorder (having the microphone, which is built in to most of the modern portable cassette tape recorders, close to the organ, usually on the bench), and prepare the listener by counting off four beats before performing the first example. The statement may be "Are you ready? Here we go. One, Two, Three, Four" and start the first measure. I tend to say, "One, Two, Three, Listen," and then start to play.

While the metronome/auto rhythm unit is beating, play the measure and sit quietly through the following measure, recording only the beating of the rhythm device. Record as many measures as desired, using the three notes in any order and slowly increasing the rapidity of the movement by using notes of less value.

This level can be maintained for weeks or months, depending on the ability of the student to perform the examples correctly at speeds from slow to moderately fast.

When the student cannot imitate the measure, do not stop the tape to review. Continue on, concentrating on the following measure.

There is no age limit to this ear training technique. Youngsters to senior citizens find it entertaining, a challenge and fun!

I'll show you how to continue this exercise to higher levels in Part II in the next issue. Did you *hear* that?

**BI**  ♩

# organ studio

## THE ECHO TECHNIQUE IN EAR TRAINING

### Part II

If you've been working on the beginning level of the echo technique in ear training, as explained in Part I in the Aug./Sept. '83 issue, you should be ready to continue with a slightly higher level of the ear-training routine.

We can take a short side trip and advise that if you have some difficulty in recognizing time values — the length of time the melody notes are held — you might turn to the tried and proved method of imitating hand clapping. When you try

to imitate hand-clapping patterns in rhythm, you are not concerned with relating aural pitch to specific keys on the keyboard. This allows you to pay closer attention to the rhythms being clapped. Of course, using the hand-clapping technique, you would either need to have someone in the room with you — a teacher or an advanced player — or have someone use hand clapping on the tape for you to imitate at home. It is necessary for you to be monitored at some point in order to be sure you are imitating correctly the original hand-clapping patterns.

Let's get back to the second level of difficulty with the echo technique.

This time, we'll use the five notes/keys from middle C through G on the staff. The routine is the same. Start the beat (metronome or rhythm unit), count off the four beats ("One, two, three, four"), and begin the alternate measures of the performed example followed by the measure of rest for the imitation.

Here are some examples of the possibilities in pitch and rhythm when you are using five notes instead of the original three.

You'll find that moving in odd intervals, even with easy note values, is more difficult than moving straight up or down the five notes.

At this level, we're talking about weeks and months of work on the various examples.

Don't rush the different levels: take plenty of time. If this material is incorporated into your regular lessons, it will just take a few minutes to sharpen your ears in preparation for the rest of the lesson. In my private lessons, I usually start with finger and foot exercises, followed by ear training, before getting to the traditional reading and key-board harmony work.

Ready for the next level? Here we go.

We'll add to the five notes/keys we've been using from C through G, by including all the half steps, the black keys of C#/Db, D#/Eb, and F#/Gb in our examples. This is the first level that is fairly difficult with even the easiest of time values. When we play straight up or down all the white and black keys—moving in half tones/steps—it is called chromatic movement.

Here are some playing suggestions for the third level.

How are you doing? I hope you're not going to try to do this level of work at this time just because it's all shown in this little amount of space. It's just the outline of months of work at each level and should be taken in small degrees.

Don't be impatient. Learn to imitate successfully the various musical phrases at each level before proceeding to the next level.

Okay, just two more levels to go.

The fourth level encompasses one entire octave of notes using the C-major scale, from middle C to C on the staff. This level will include a greater number of pitches and bigger intervals. Remember, when we are doing the full octave at this level, it is using the white keys only. Ready? Let's try some.

If you have taken your time and spent many hours listening to the musical examples and then repeating them in the blank measures, you're ready for the top level in this group of ear-training exercises.

We're going to take the same full octave we used in the preceding level, and for the fifth and final level, we're going to add all the half tones/steps in between. In other words, you're going to attempt to imitate the musical phrases created by the use of the chromatic scale in a complete octave.

For the fifth level, try recording the following measures and then have whoever makes the recording create many additional measures of phrases to really challenge you. When you are working at this level, you are at the point where instead of saying, "I wish I knew what the organist/- pianist was playing with the right hand," you should be following the melody along, or imagining what notes/ keys are being used to produce a certain phrase.

Have fun(?) with these suggestions.

Another reward for developing your ear is finding that you are beginning to hear original melodies. You'll be tempted to compose your own tunes as well as pick out the tunes you hear played.

I hope you've enjoyed (enjoyed) this echo (echo) approach to ear training (ear training) . . . hmmmmmm . . . must be the acoustics.

Anyway, perhaps you now have a greater understanding of the phrase "seeing with your ears."

As for "hearing with your eyes" . . . we'll discuss that subject soon.

'Bye now.

BI

# organ studio

# IT'S ALL IN THE GAME

## crowd-clapping foot-stamping inspiration!

Spring is not long in coming and soon the lure of the baseball park will again attract the fans and aficianados of America's biggest professional sport. Soon, too, the keydesks of countless numbers of organs will be dusted off and again the familiar sounds and strains of the stadium organist will be heard over the cheers and crys of the home-team crowd.

Actually music and professional sports go back a long way. The Greeks used music extensively at the Olympic games and the Romans were probably the first to use a type of organ at events in the Colosseum. The hydraulus, originally an Egyptian invention, was a water-powered pipe organ that was used to inspire competitors and spectators alike at the Colosseum. Never let it be said that stadium organists have no place in the history of music!

But, let's get back to baseball. What about the music itself? On what sources do these musicians draw for all those quick little musical quips and crowd rousers.

This workshop will outline and notate some of the most popular musical devices in a stadium organist's repertoire.

## LET'S GO _____:

This works well with teams whose name contains only one syllable, like Cubs, Sox, Mets, etc.

## CHARGE:

Probably the most popular and often used. Never to be played when the opposing team is at bat!

## REVELRY:

Another "bugle call" which is often substituted for CHARGE.

## THE OLD ONE-TWO-THREE-FOUR:

First credited to New York Yankee's Eddie Layton, this one is a particular success when the score is close and the home team needs some real crowd-clapping/foot-stamping inspiration!

## MEXICAN HAT DANCE:

A great break or fill during a lull in the action. The younger spectators really go for the hand-clapping inserts.

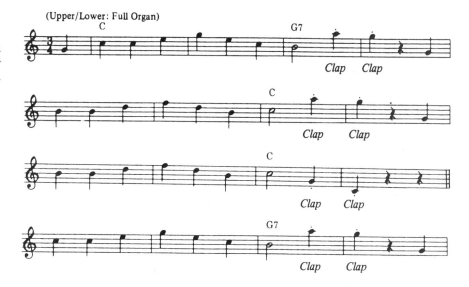

## SPANISH DANCE:

One of the "Hall of Fame." A real crowd rouser, especially when the pressure is on for a run!

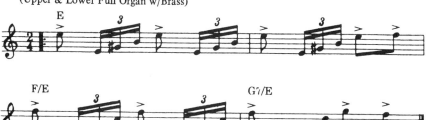

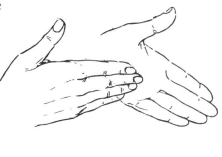

## ENTERTAINING:

Apart from these little devices—and there are hundreds of others—stadium organists must have a wide and varied repertoire of pop standards, well-known classics, and Top 40 tunes. Even the hydraulus player at the Colosseum back in the good old days had to be an entertainer at half-time! The popular requests of the day are all part of the job. "You Light Up Meus Lifus" and "I Don't Want to Set the Sphinx on Firus" were known to be particular favorites of the Colosseum crowds at the time of the Emperor Nero.

Seriously, though, to know when to use a musical interlude is just as important as to know how to play it. A good stadium organist has to have a keen and detailed understanding of the game itself. He has to know the players and the crowd he's working with. What works well with one team in one city may fail completely in another!

Use this workshop for your fun and enjoyment. Try envisioning your own game situations, or better yet, watch a game on TV and try playing for it as you might if you were "On the Bench." Until next time, see you at the game! **DK**

# organ studio

## The "Soapy" Side of Life, Playing For Daytime Drama

### An Interview With Eddie Layton

*For many dozens of years the organ has been closely associated with dramatic serials or "soap operas" on both radio and television.* Sheet Music Magazine *thought it would be fun and informative to visit with Eddie Layton, well-known New York organist of soap and stadium fame.*

**SMM:** When did you start playing for radio?

**EL:** I began my radio career playing the piano for the "Horn and Hardart Hour" and the "Uncle WIP Show" both broadcast from Philadelphia. Later, my trio was featured on CBS in coast-to-coast broadcasts from the Mermaid Room and the Ritz Hotel, in New York City.

**SMM:** What about TV?

**EL:** My first "soap" began in 1966 when I played for the brand-new "Love Is a Many Splendored Thing". That was followed by "The Secret Storm", "Where the Heart Is", and "Love of Life."

**SMM:** When was the organ first used in TV soaps?

**EL:** From the very beginning. The organ was used to accompany soaps on radio. It was easily and successfully transferred from radio to TV.

**SMM:** Was the organ music live or prerecorded?

**EL:** The music was live or miked to a tape. I played as the camera saw the action.

**SMM:** How did you view your job in relation to the show?

**EL:** The organ was an important part of the soap opera, accenting the dramatic action with "stings," themes, and musical bridges. It provided complete background and fill music.

**SMM:** How did the schedule work for TV soaps?

**EL:** After the actors finished their preliminary rehearsals, I would play along with the dress rehearsal and then we would do the live broadcast or tape the show. I would play for three or four complete shows everyday.

**SMM:** Did you consult with the director about the music?

**EL:** Yes, we exchanged ideas. The director might suggest that the music be more dramatic or I might suggest that there be little or no music at all. I believe the music should be just like an actor. That does not mean there must always be music. Silence or playing just one low note can be very dramatic.

**SMM:** Did you plan the music for each episode or was it spontaneous?

**EL:** All my music was spontaneous. I did not consult the script in advance. I responded to the action as I saw and felt it, as though I were in the audience. I wrote themes for some characters such as the hero, vamp, or heroine and then varied those themes by playing them in different keys, etc. I always tried to isolate each show using different organ sounds and themes for each one.

**SMM:** Would you illustrate a few examples of stings or interludes so that our readers could "hear" them?

**EL:** Sure. I'll show them several typical musical settings.

"Serious" - Change to a different scene (Upper/Lower 8' Flute)

"Tragedy" - Curtain (Upper: Strings & Flutes 16', 8', 4', 2', Pedal 16' & 8')

"Finale" - Curtain (Upper/Lower: Full Pedal 16', 8')

Game Show Playoff (Full Organ with 8' Brass)

**SMM:** Why were these dramas called "soap" operas?

**EL:** That's easy! "Ninety-nine and forty-four one-hundreths percent" of all soaps were originally sponsored by soap companies.

**SMM:** How is the music done today on soaps? Do you think live music will return to daytime drama?

**EL:** In order to meet the budget and to sound contemporary, a musical supervisor chooses orchestral tapes which are cued by a technician. When timing is the most important element, this method offers little coordination of timing or feeling to the action. Live music is better. It will return in an evolved state performed on a synthesizer, by an orchestra, or on an advanced technology organ.

**SMM:** As organist for the New York Yankees and Madison Square Garden, do you see anything in common between playing for sports events and soaps?

**EL:** They have much in common. When there is a man on third base, it's the bottom of the ninth, the Yankees are losing by one run, and a Yankee comes up to bat, the music has to be dramatic. The same thing is necessary when the evil vamp is plotting something against the hero.

**SMM:** Was there any evolution in the organ techniques or music used for playing soaps?

**EL:** Yes. Originally, the organists would use only major and minor chords depending upon the action or character. Later, they began using sixth and flatted-fifth chords. Finally, we used complicated harmonies. Diminished chords were always reserved for mystery, evil, and foreboding.

**SMM:** Were you the only soap organist?

**EL:** No. Rosa Rio played for seven soaps per day. They would hold the elevator for her at NBC so she could run from one studio to another.

**SMM:** Did you have any musical tricks or secrets that made you a successful soap organist?

**EL:** I gave only clues. I never gave away the scene musically. When the evil vamp was ensnaring the hero, I did not play dark, mysterious music. I played light, happy music with only an eventual touch or hint of evil or foreboding.

**SMM:** Tell us about some of your funny or unusual behind-the-scenes experiences.

**EL:** During one live broadcast, the female lead made her entrance and tripped. I instinctively struck a dramatic chord. She finished the scene with a broken ankle and no one guessed what had happened.

We had lots of fun in the studio. The technicians would try to make me laugh while I was playing for a very sad and serious scene.

The most tense moment was when the organ began smoking just before the first broadcast of "Love Is a Many Splendored Thing." The technician replaced the offending part with ten seconds until air time. There could have been some dramatic music written to accompany that scene!

# organ studio

## Swing Low Sweet Chariot

### Playing Tips and Educational Notes.

It's a pleasure to talk to you through the pages of *Sheet Music Magazine* and I'm proud that our first discussion is about the harmonically rich arrangement created by my student and associate teacher, Phyllis Bradshaw of San Pedro, CA.

When you set up the registration, I suggest you try the following: *Upper:* Full Organ 16',8',4',2'/ 60 8868 666. *Lower:* Diapason 8', Flutes 8',4', String 4'/ (00) 8764 432. *Pedal:* 16',8'/ 6-5. *Trem:* Full.

To accentuate the harmonic accompaniment, emphasize the 16' in the bass for the first theme and hold notes for full value. For the second theme, use a strong 8' bass. You can leave the bass sustain on for both themes. Use a crisp, light touch on the bass pedals when playing rhythmically. Return to the original bass setting for the final theme, both hands on the lower manual.

There's a variety of tonal "textures" in the arrangement as the harmonies are performed in both close and open structures.

I suggest that you number all the measures in the arrangement from 1 through 21, starting with the first complete measure. This will make it easier to follow the commentary.

As in most advanced arrangements, fingering has not been shown. However, if you are not working with a teacher (I never recommend the "do it yourself" approach), take the time to go through each measure, hands separately, and experiment to see which fingering would best suit your hand and then write it in, so that you're not casually using different fingers each time you play the same passages.

For example, in measure 1, if you simply leave the 3rd finger of the R.H. on the sustained melody note F, the moving notes underneath will be played detached. If you play the F with the 3rd finger and substitute the 5th finger, you will be able to perform the moving notes in a legato/connected manner, but before playing the R.H. chord on the 4th beat, you'll have to substitute the 3rd finger on the F to move smoothly and honor the tie.

Advanced players may wish to use heel and toe technique for the bass notes, moving from black to white/white to black, and sliding from black to black. The right foot can be used to play the interval jumps smoothly.

Take plenty of time performing the ad-lib (without a steady beat) sections. Don't rush all the harmonic changes. It may be too confusing for the average listener.

Prepare the auto rhythm unit by setting up the Swing or any "long-short" pattern that will complement the shuffle rhythm in the accompaniment in measures 9 through 16. Not too fast. If you have a rhythm switch on the Swell Pedal, turn on the rhythm unit on the 1st beat of measure 9 and kick it off on the first half of the 3rd beat in measure 16. If you don't have a switch on the Pedal, use your L.H. to turn on the rhythm on the 1st beat of measure 9 and try to get back to the lower manual in time to play the first sixteenth note chord. If you can't, simply wait to start playing with the next chord in the 2nd beat. Then reach over and turn the unit off immediately after the staccato chords on the 3rd beat in measure 16. Practice the handling of all the mechanical devices on the organ just as much as you would the performance of the music. Performance: Concentrate on a legato touch throughout, except for measures 9-11. However, strive for full value even when you have to lift the full chords. Meas. 2, the sign || is a lift or "breath." It is meant to disconnect the musical thoughts. To perform the Thumb Gliss. in meas. 3-4, concentrate on the movement to the correct chord with the hand and simply drag the thumb along with just enough pressure to make the white keys sound. Meas. 8, ritard broadly and accent the syncopated pick-up chord by pushing the Swell Pedal forward immediately before striking the keys and then pulling it back immediately *after* hearing the notes. The Thumb Gliss up from a black key will take a bit more pressure at the start. Meas. 12-13, the quarter note triplets are to be played perfectly evenly against the bass notes (three against two is generally quite difficult). If an auto rhythm unit is producing a "long-short" rhythm, you will have to ignore the distraction and concentrate on the even quarter notes in the bass. Meas. 17, return to the original ad-lib tempo used at the beginning of the arrangement. Meas.19-20, continue to slow down the tempo through the syncopation in meas. 20. Meas. 21, the Fermata ⌒ is an indefinite hold. Hold the note for at least twice its indicated value following the ritard.

Harmonic Notes: There isn't space for a detailed analysis of the harmonic structures and progressions used throughout the arr. For advanced students of harmony, I'll call your attention to general progressions. Meas. 1, the single melody note is harmonized by 9th chords moving down in whole tones, resolving to the root major chord on the 3rd beat. The Eb9 on the 4th beat was suggested by the bass pedal movement on the way to meas. 2 for the Db9 which progressed diatonically (around the Circle) to Gb9, which was again resolved by a chromatic movement to the root major, Fmaj9. Basic chord progressions include diatonic (around the Circle), chromatic (movement in half tones), movement in whole tones, substituted chords based on roots played in the bass (using the preceding three progressions to choose the bass pedal notes). Meas. 4, the simple C7 chord is made more interesting with the movement of the bV,V,VI and #V. Meas. 8, the technical name for the Gb chord is the Neapolitan 6th (major chord built on the bII of the scale). Notice when the melody is played rhythmically in meas. 9-11, the harmonies are kept simple. Meas. 12-16 uses melodic embellishment to lift the melody out of the ordinary. Meas. 15, the use of the Db9 before the C9 is a common substitution (using the 9th chord a half tone above the original) when the melody is on the 5th step of the original chord.

## SWING LOW SWEET CHARIOT

TRADITIONAL

ARR. BY PHYLLIS BRADSHAW
EDITED BY BILL IRWIN

**BI**

**RPF**

# Improvisation

# Keyboard Workshop

## PLAYING JAZZ—
### More tricks of the trade

Improvisation is like composing, except that it is done spontaneously. So, improvisors have to contend with the same musical problems that face composers. There must be enough variety in what is produced to keep things interesting; at the same time, there has to be a unified feeling, so that the music holds together. Then, there are different structural layers that should be kept in mind:

small-scale issues involve what notes to choose or what rhythm to play in any particular moment; but there are also large-scale aspects to consider, like how one phrase relates to another.

In this column, we'll look at one way to create order and balance in an improvised solo: it's called *sequence*.

Suppose we were improvising a solo using the song *Mona Lisa* . The opening chord is E♭. Here are the notes in that chord:

If we take those notes as our "melody" or basic material to embellish, we might add notes between the chord tones, or above them, or below them:

But we want some kind of form to emerge — a musical gesture that makes sense, that gives direction, and that satisfies. One such gesture can be constructed by repeating an idea:

If we take this idea and repeat it starting on different *pitches*, the result is called "sequence:"

Sequences can be extended over changing harmonies:

The improvisor who comes up with a spontaneous melodic idea can use the technique of sequence to extend that idea, and create a cohesive form within the solo.

SI

# Keyboard Workshop

## *Improvising with Jazz Rhythms*

Applying "jazzy" rhythms to standard melodies is not only a good way to pep up your old arrangements, it's actually the first step in building the ability to create jazz solos. "It don't mean a thing if it ain't got that swing," said Duke Ellington. Jazz rhythms give whatever you're playing that essential ingredient of "swing."

Let's look at some typical rhythms. One of the most common is the "charleston" effect, created by a dotted quarter note followed by an eighth note which is *accented*. Accenting a note which is normally unaccented is the secret behind all jazz rhythms. Example 1 starts with the "charleston" rhythm, and continues with a few more "off beat" phrases.

Ex 1

We can take a simple melody and *jazz* it up by applying these rhythms to it. Here is a melody, followed by a version that "anticipates" one of the notes; that is, it accents a note earlier than expected.

Ex. 2

Another way to jazz up that melody would be to delay the arrival of some of the notes, instead of playing them early. In each of these cases, we are sort of dancing around the normal pulse.

Ex 3

We can take the same approach with any tune we wish. Here is an example to try on a well-known melody. You can extend these ideas by toying with the rest of the song on your own. Next time, we'll apply these rhythms to improvised melodies based on the chords of common pop songs.

# Keyboard Workshop

## Jazz Improvisation: Melody and Rhythm

Last time we looked at how jazz rhythms can be used to add "swing" to standard melodies. Before that we created improvised melodies by adding notes to chord intervals. This month, let's combine our jazzy rhythms with those improvised lines.

Here are some of the rhythms. Notice that they make use of *syncopation;* that is, they place accents in unexpected places.

Ex. 1

Any series of notes can be made more interesting by keeping these peppy rhythms in mind. Suppose you want to play a *bluesy* scale:

Ex. 2

Used as a fill, this line is pleasant enough. But, it really comes to life when we add the "feel" of those syncopated figures:

Ex. 3

Earlier, we explored the idea of using *sequence* — repeating a musical idea on different pitches — to give direction to an improvisation.

Ex. 4

Idea      Sequence      Sequence

Watch what happens when we add rhythmic flair to those sequences. The change in accents balances out the sameness of the idea. The result is musically more exciting!

Ex. 5

Practice tapping or singing these rhythms, and they will naturally become a part of your playing. Once they are familiar enough, you'll be able to use just snatches here and there, so that even your improvised melodies will gain a flexibility and freedom that always sounds fresh. Look at the difference between the first sequence example above, and this possible end result:

Ex. 6

SI

# An Outline of Jazz Techniques

Jazz grew out of the cotton fields of Mississippi and the pleasure houses of St. Louis, through piano rolls and wandering brass bands, to smoky Harlem night clubs where player challenged player into the early hours of the morning. It is a music filled with tradition and bursting with excitement.

There are many different styles of playing jazz that have developed over its long history. Jazz masters play a very complex and difficult type of music. This article is going to outline very basic approaches to beginning jazz improvisation, in order to give you the tools and background to move ahead on your own.

## Rhythm

The best place to start in developing a feeling for jazz is to study jazz rhythm. Early jazz rhythm used an element called the Hornpipe. This consists of a dotted eighth note followed by a sixteenth note, as in example 1, using the C Scale.

You may be familiar with a sound called the "shuffle rhythm," a favorite among blues players. This uses the dotted rhythm as well. Blues musicians use it in a chordal pattern as shown in example 2.

Ex. 2

An early jazz style piece that uses this dotted rhythm is shown in example 3.

Ex. 3

The modern jazz feel, however, does *not* use the dotted rhythm; instead it uses more of a triplet feeling. Often though, as in the eighth note passage in example 4, the triplet feeling, which is very exaggerated, is replaced by the use of stress put on certain notes. In any group of two notes, the stress usually goes on the first.

Ex. 4

Sometimes the stress is reversed, as in example 5. When this happens, we have a feeling that something is not quite balanced. The result is called syncopation — stress on a normally weak note. Often, that stress will be turned back around to fall on the normally strong note. This happens in the second measure of example 5.

Ex. 5

The feeling of syncopation often occurs in jazz in a form of "anticipation." Example 6 has anticipation at the very end. The final E gets an accent that it ordinarily would not have.

Ex. 6

Exercise 7 shows other forms of anticipation. Some of these anticipatory or syncopated rhythms make up what is known as the "swing style." The following examples cover swing, or the big band era phrases.

Ex. 7

Example 8 uses syncopation quite a bit. Use a metronome to keep count as you try to play these complicated rhythms. Play this exercise several times until you are very familiar with these rhythms. If you are having trouble, eliminate the tie and try to play them as a series of eighth notes. When you are comfortable enough, put the ties back in.

*Continued*

Play example 9 with a metronome several times.

Ex. 9

Example 10 is a typical jazz run. Place the accents on the first note of every group of two, and note the anticipation on the very final note of the phrase.

Ex. 10

Example 11 is another typical jazz phrase which uses stress accents, but without any anticipation. Notice how important the use of stress is to bring out the flavor of the phrase.

Ex. 11

Example 12 is a simple tunc. Play it straight the first time, then use anticipation (12b). 12c shows the same tune, but this time, instead of anticipation, it features a slight delay.

Each of these approaches is just a way of loosening up the rhythm so that it does not sound stiff. The result is known as "swing."

Ex. 12

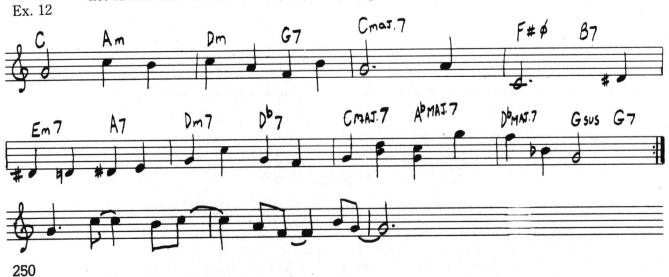

# Swing Rhythms

Turn your attention once again to a rhythm that places an accent on the weak beat in a very deliberate manner. One common rhythm that does this is shown in example 13, the "Charleston" rhythm. The Charleston rhythm is played in the right hand against a steady quarter note rhythm in the left. This rhythm is typical of the kind of figures that the brass played in the big bands of the swing era.

Example 13, the "Charleston" sounding rhythm, is a variation on the Hornpipe. Our original Hornpipe consisted of a dotted eighth note followed by a sixteenth note. Here, we have stretched out the rhythm so that it takes twice as much time: a dotted quarter is followed by an eighth. To complicate things a little more, the dotted quarter is silent in this example. But the syncopated feel is still very much present.

Ex. 13

Now look at some other rhythms that were typical of those brass sections. Example 14 shows a number of these rhythms. Look at each measure separately. In the first measure there are notes on one and four. The second measure is in a syncopated rhythm. The third measure is again on one and four. The Charleston rhythm follows. Now put the first four measures together.

These rhythms are difficult to read and play if they are unfamiliar. Use your metronome and play the rhythms on a single note. If you are having trouble playing these rhythms, try clapping them along with the metronome.

Move on to the next line. This line begins with the Charleston rhythm but it is tied over onto the next eighth note so it becomes even more complicated. Try the first two measures with the metronome. Then the next two measures, and repeat.

Play the last measure several times with the metronome to get a steady Charleston rhythm. Now play the entire phrase, both lines, with the metronome.

Ex. 14

Next is a series of patterns from the swing era. Look at the entire line and use the metronome while playing it. Repeat it over and over until you get the

right feeling. Remember, rhythm is the key to good-sounding improvised lines.

Ex. 15

# Selecting The Right Notes

We can now move on to selecting the notes in making up a jazz improvisation. Let's use a well-known tune as our basis. Example 16 is a well known song called "Worried Man's Blues."

Ex. 16

First we'll use variation in the rhythms of the original. Example 17 is a rhythmic alteration of the opening line using anticipation.

Ex. 17

Here are some of the swing rhythms you've practiced, applied to the melody. We are now beginning to form an improvisation, although the same notes are maintained. In the second measure of example 18, some notes are repeated in order to accommodate the rhythm. Try this with the metronome.

Ex. 18

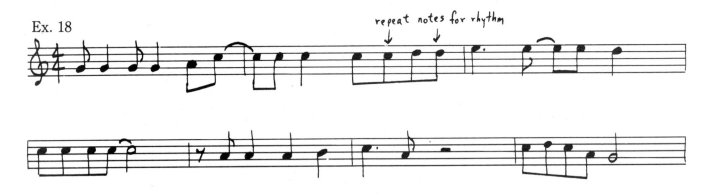

Look at the next phrase. If you clap these rhythms you will recognize them from the earlier swing exercises, numbers 14 and 15. Now play the third phrase. Put them all together, keeping the notes of the tune, yet altering the rhythm.

Sometimes, taking things out can be as important as putting them in. You might decide to leave most of the third measure out, for example, in order to bring in more of a resting balance with the activity of the eighth notes. Play example 18b.

Ex. 18b

Until now we have just been altering the rhythms. It's time to look at how to add notes of your own. Jazz improvisation is just a form of spontaneous composition, and as jazz musicians we should start composing while playing at the keyboard.

In order to find a way to embellish what's already on the page, it is possible to go as far back as the sixteenth century in Italian music when embellishment was very commonplace. At that time musicians were expected to add notes to what was on the written page.

Example 19 shows an interval, the note G and the note A, and three ways of embellishing that interval. Play each one. The three different kinds of embellishments that can be added to any interval are: adding notes which lie above the interval, in this case any note above the A; adding notes that lie below the interval, in this case any note below G; and adding notes that lie in between the two original notes, in this case, a G# or an Ab.

Ex. 19

Example 20 retains the original tune, yet notes have been added both above and below the intervals that occur within the tune. The passage begins with a G note and the next note of the tune is another G. A note above or below that G can be added. In this case, a note above has been added. Once you add a note higher than the interval, you might consider

adding a note lower than the next interval in order to create a weaving motion. This alternation between higher and lower notes (and those in between) will create an interesting melodic effect. In the following examples the H indicates a note higher than the interval, the L indicates a note lower, and the B indicates a note in between.

Ex. 20

Some of the notes of the melody have not been retained in example 21. Often jazz musicians will ignore the original melody all together when they are taking a solo and base an improvisation on the chords which underlie the melody. Notes from the original melody are circled.

Now we're going to use a similar approach to improvise on the chord structure of the tune. Take a $C^6$ chord and arpeggiate it. You can look at it as if it were the original melody. If you just add the swing rhythm without changing any of the notes in the $C^6$ harmony, you could end up with the phrase in example 22.

Example 23 shows the introduction of a C scale which adds more notes to choose from.

Example 24 shows what happens if notes lower than the intervals and higher than the intervals in the $C^6$ chord are used. The circled notes, the C, E, G and A are all part of the $C^6$ chord.

Choosing non-chord notes is really a matter of developing a personal style. It's important to use your ear to listen for the sounds you like. For example, rather than choosing the $D^\#$ at the beginning of example 24, a $C^\#$ could have been inserted. The key is to experiment as much as possible. See what happens if you add notes very close to the melody notes. Then try wide skips. Try several notes in a row that are higher than the melody notes, or several that are below them. Ideally, of course, you want to create melodic interest.

One way to organize your melodic improvisations so that you don't become repetitive is to think in terms of form. For example, your phrases can be shaped as questions and answers.

Example 25 shows this question and answer technique.

Ex. 25

Example 26 uses the original melody at times, and switches off to lines built from the harmonies.

Ex. 26

Example 27 shows an eighth note pattern used by Charlie Parker, who was one of the founders of the modern school of jazz. It shows a Gm$^7$ chord going to a C$^7$ chord. The notes that belong to the chords have been circled. Analyze which notes inserted in addition to the chord harmonies lie above the intervals and which notes lie below.

Ex. 27

# Patterns

Example 28 shows a pattern that takes you through the cycle of fifths. It is in the form of a *sequence*, a melodic idea that repeats over and over, beginning on a new pitch each time. Continue the sequence through the cycle of fifths.

Ex. 28

A rhythmic sequence can also be used, as is shown in example 29. Here, the rhythmic idea repeats.

Ex. 29

Once you know how to create sequences and are familiar with all the chord harmonies, you have a large palette of colors and shapes to choose from in your solos.

# More Jazz
# Pattern Examples

Example 30 uses some swing rhythms described earlier in combination with eighth note patterns which revolve around the chord tones.

Ex. 30

Example 31 uses scaler passages and then creates a weaving effect.

Ex. 31

Examine both examples 32 and 33 very carefully; circle the chord harmonies and analyze the other notes in relation to those chord harmonies.

Exs. 32 and 33

256

Example 34 returns to the tune "Worried Man's Blues," but now utilizes all of the concepts covered in this article. The harmony tones have been circled for the first several measures. Go through the rest of the song and circle the other harmony tones. You will be able to see where the non-harmonic tones come into play.

Ex. 34

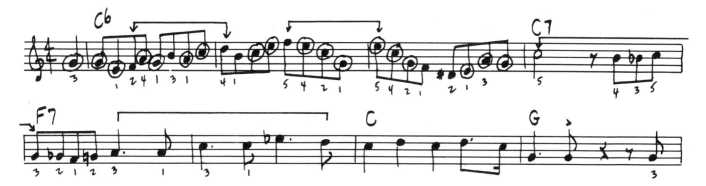

Here are some of the features of this improvisation: the phrase which begins the opening measure is repeated at the beginning of the second measure, starting on a different pitch. At the end of the second measure there is a phrase which finds a near relative at the beginning of the third measure. The pattern in the fourth measure with the $C^7$ chord is repeated at the beginning of the next measure, although the rhythm is different.

The ninth measure also contains a rhythmic pattern repeated in the eleventh measure. There are many other relationships in this improvisation like the ones just mentioned.

This is only one possibility, of course. From the standpoint of musicality, I would consider example 35 to be much too busy, although it does help to illustrate the principles involved in improvisation. As you practice the art of improvisation, you will tend to move further away from the strictness and rigidity of these examples, both in the notes chosen, and in the increasing flexibility of rhythm. We could vastly improve example 35 simply by editing out some of the notes, as in following example 36. Try this editing-out technique often, after you feel comfortable enough with the chord progression you are playing on.

Ex. 35

In order to find your own jazz style listen as much as possible to artists you like and appreciate, and continue to refer to this article on the basics of jazz improvisation.

# JAZZ RUNS FOR THE RIGHT HAND

Jazz runs are used in a variety of ways. They can form a catalog of sounds for a jazz or pop musician improvising on a song, and can be used as endings, intros or fillers. They can also help in modulating from one key to another.

Runs come in a wide variety of forms based on scales, arpeggiated chords, sequences (patterns which repeat on different notes), weaving lines and harmonic progressions. This article will examine all of these varieties and how they are used over single chords or with chord progressions. Once you have learned the entire range of runs, as well as the

theory behind creating them, you will be able to apply this to any music you play.

We will begin with scales. There are many different types of scales, the most common of which is the major scale. This can be used simply by inserting it as a run or fill over a simple major chord.

The scale can be varied in a number of ways. It can be broken into patterns of three notes at a time to create a simple sequence, as in example 1. Play the run in example 1 descending. Be sure to watch your fingering very carefully. Try playing this example in a few different keys.

## Ex. 1

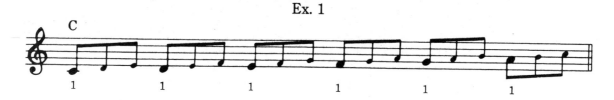

Example 2 is a sequence pattern which ascends first, then descends. The fingering is similar to the

fingering of the simple major scale. To play this, keep a relaxed hand and begin by playing it very slowly.

## Ex. 2

Example 3 is a slightly more sophisticated sequence.

## Ex. 3

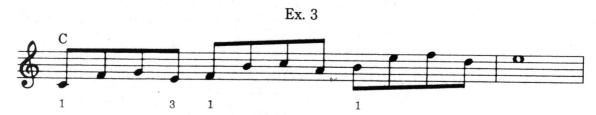

Example 4 is another scale passage which goes over a C major chord. The only member of this scale foreign to the C major scale is the D# which

acts as a leading tone into the E note. Begin by playing this slowly and practice the fingering very carefully.

## Ex. 4

Example 5 is another simple scale passage. It is written over a C chord.

258

Ex. 5

Simple sequences in scale passages can be made into weaving lines, as in example 6. This run is based on the E♭ major scale, used with a B♭7 chord. This is a simple arpeggiated pattern. Note that if this pattern were broken up it would be the weaving line shown in example 6a.

If this pattern is divided into groups of four, in the beginning of the pattern, the rise to the next member of the scale occurs on the first note of each group of four. By the end of the passage, the rise is on the second note in each group of four. This shift in accent keeps the pattern interesting.

Ex. 6

6a

Example 7 uses a weaving effect. Practice this exercise with the fingering indicated until you are comfortable with it.

Ex. 7

Example 8 is another example using the notes derived from a scale in order to create a weaving pattern.

Ex. 8

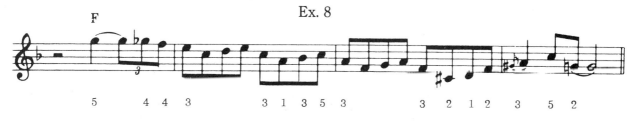

Example 9 makes use of the C major scale to create a weaving motion. Example 9a is another run based on the concept of using a scale to create a run or a sequence. Try creating your own pattern based on this idea.

*Continued*

259

9a

While the patterns previously mentioned in this article can be played over one chord, the pattern in example 10 can be played over a II-V-I progression. (In the key of C this would be over $Dm^7$ to a $G^7$ to a C.)

Ex. 10

Another scale that can be used is the blues scale shown in example 11. Blues notes often contrast with the notes normally found in a major scale. Patterns can be built using the blues scale in the same way that they were built using the major scale.

Ex. 11

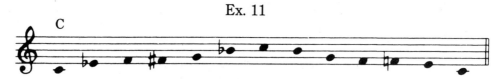

Play example 12 until you are familiar with it.

Ex. 12

Example 13 is a "whole tone" scale, so called because there is a whole tone between each of its members.

260

Ex. 13

Example 14 is a typical pattern built on a whole tone scale.

Ex. 14

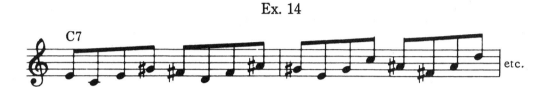

Example 15 features the half tone/whole tone scale, alternating from a half step between notes to a whole step. The scale in this example can be played over a B$^{b7}$ chord. Try transposing it to different keys and chords.

Example 16 uses the half tone/whole tone scale in a sequential pattern.

Ex. 16

Example 17 combines the scale pattern in example 11 with a pattern based on the half tone/whole tone scale.

Ex. 17

Example 18 shows the chromatic scale made up of half steps in a series.

*Continued*

Ex. 18

Example 19 is a pattern based on the chromatic scale.

Ex. 19

1 3 1 2 1     2 3 1 2 1 3 2 3 1          etc.

Example 20 makes use of chromatic movement over a C⁷ chord.

1 2 4 3 2 1 4 3 2 1 4 3 1 2

Example 21 shows a series of fourths played in chromatic ascending movement.

Ex. 21

Example 22 shows chromatic motion used in a series of grace notes.

Example 23 shows a chromatic run that jazz great Art Tatum used over a C chord.

262

As patterns increase in length they should have dramatic rises and falls to make them interesting. Example 24 shows a typical question and answer type pattern.

Arpeggiating harmonies is another way to create runs. Example 25 shows a C^maj7 chord arpeggiated in a pattern.

More interesting arpeggios involve jazz harmonies. Instead of playing a simple C7 in example 26, play a C7 with an eleventh and a thirteenth.

Example 26

The C7 with an eleventh and a thirteenth can also be formed into a scale passage, as in example 26a.

Example 26a

Example 27 shows another variation of the C7 harmony.

Example 27

Example 28

Example 28 shows a minor harmony.

*Continued*

Example 29 uses fourths.

Example 29

Here's some more information about using fourths. We began our $C^7$ arpeggio using fourths on the 6th of the chord. We could have also started on the 3rd, or the 2nd: E, A, D or D, G, C. Take a number of different chords and try playing three-note arpeggios built in fourths by starting on the 6th, 3rd, or 2nd of the chord. This can be a very beautiful color for your sound canvass. You may also want to try these arpeggios with major seventh chords.

Example 30 shows some variations on a $B^{b7}$ harmony.

Ex 30

Example 31 shows a harmony on a $D^7$ chord which rises and then falls. Experiment with different harmonies on different chords and create patterns using them.

Example 31

Example 32 is based on a $B^b$ major harmony. Practice this example very slowly. The whole hand shifts and then shifts again. Now try playing it descending and then play it both ascending and descending.

Example 32

Example 33 uses an alteration of two harmonies over the same chord: First a C harmony, then the harmony a tri-tone away (based on F#). Then back to the C and again to the F#. Harmonies based a tri-tone apart are often used as substitutes for each other in jazz playing.

Example 33

264

Example 34 was created by Charlie Parker and goes over a V-I progression; in the key of C this is a $G^7$ chord to a C chord.

Example 34

Example 35 was used by Art Tatum. This is an arpeggiated harmony.

Example 35

Example 36 uses the pentatonic scale which works well over the progression I-VI-II-V-I.

Example 36

Example 37 is a sequence that can be used over a $G^7$ chord.

The above patterns can be designed to fit over any chord progressions.

Example 37

Example 38 uses the cycle of fifths. Play it a few times until you are familiar with it and then get it up to speed.

Example 38

*Continued*

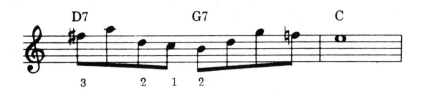

Example 39 is a sequence pattern built over a B⁷ chord. 39a is the same pattern built over a C chord. Take the time now to build this pattern over an F chord.

Example 39

Example 39a

Example 40 follows the cycle of fifths from a C⁷ chord to an F⁷ chord to a B♭ chord to an E♭ chord. At the end of each of the groupings the hand must be lifted up and placed down again. Practice this with prolonged separations between each of the groupings.

Example 40

Example 41 is the last sequence example. This pattern is based on repeating the same pattern on the 1, 3 and +5 of the chord. You must shift the entire hand for each grouping. The fourth finger is very important in this exercise.

Example 41

# CHORDAL RIFFS

Example 42 is a very simple chord riff.

Example 42

Example 43 is more difficult. When playing this riff allow the hand to move from side to side so that it remains relaxed. Play it slowly, concentrating on this motion. Example 43a is a variation of this riff.

Example 43

Example 43a

Play examples 44, 45 and 46 slowly until you are comfortable with them and can get them up to speed.

Example 44

Example 45

Example 46

Example 47 is played over an F⁷ chord. This pattern can also be arpeggiated or broken up.

Example 47

Example 48 can be played over a I-V-I chord progression.

Example 48

Practice example 49 which is another chord riff.

Example 49

As these runs become second nature to you, you'll be able to string them together into longer solos or insert them in your music whenever you feel you would like to. Practice these runs in every key until they become a part of your own style. And, of course, don't be afraid to try your own variations.

SI ♩

# Harmony at the Keyboard

## JAZZ IMPROVISATION

We asked jazz master Lou Stein, who has played piano with such musical luminaries as Benny Goodman, Percy Faith, and Bobby Hackett, to name just a few, to give us a sample of his style of improvisation on the children's favorite, "Mary Had A Little Lamb." (This little lamb is very hip, indeed.)

Notice how Lou keeps his improvisation in a limited area of keyboard by constantly changing direction of the jazz line. He never has more than four successive notes in one direction, ascending or descending. Most often he uses just two or three notes before changing direction of the line. This technique yields the nice "tight" solo for which he is famous.

Also notice that Lou ignores the tonic chord "C" as the opening chord, substituting instead the F# diminished. This substitution principle was explored in an article on the circle of fifths (January 1981), which explained how many substitutions are created by using a chord directly opposite the original chord in the circle.

Have fun playing this improvisation!

## Mary Had a Little Lamb

*Arranged by*
Lou Stein

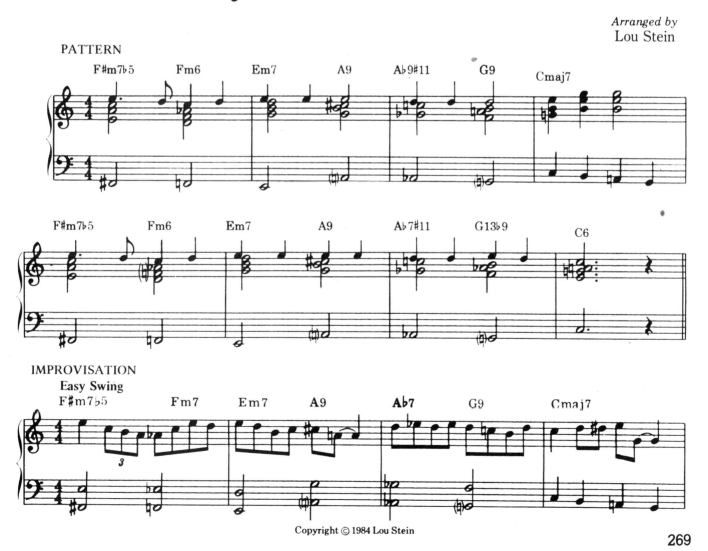

# Introducing LOU STEIN

Lou Stein began his piano study at the Settlement School in Philadelphia and acquired a thorough classical training under Gregory Ashman, accompanist to Ephraim Zimbalist. Early in his career he performed with the Glen Miller Band, Charlie "Bird" Parker, and went on to become an integral member of the Charlie Ventura group. That was just the beginning. Throughout the years his broad performance career has included playing with such notables as Percy Faith, Kostelanetz, Jackie Gleason, Bobby Hackett, Benny Goodman and Clark Terry. His recordings — too numerous to list here — appear on such labels as Epic, Decca and Capitol. Mr. Stein currently devotes his time to teaching, studying, touring and composing.

LS

# Technique

# How To Practice
## Part I

"If I don't practice for one day," said the great Ignacy Paderewski (1860-1941), "I know it; if I don't practice for two days, the critics know it; if I don't practice for three days, the audience knows it." Everyone has to practice at some time, but few pianists know how to make the most of their practice sessions.

Often, practice boils down to a hit-and-miss routine of dreaded finger exercises, a quick dose of some uninspiring "studies," and the painstaking work of learning to keep up with the tick-tick-tick of that cruel machine—the metronome—as you pound out the notes of a piece you once loved and now wonder why. There are pianists who read the morning newspaper while going through the scales. Others look for quick "tricks" to shorten the ordeal.

But if the thrill is gone, the practice session is not doing its job. Actually, practicing can be *fun!* It can be a time of discovery and relaxation. When Wanda Landowska, the famous harpsichordist, said, "I never practice; I always play," she meant that she gave her all every time she sat down at the keyboard—and that those moments were always filled with musical rewards and pleasures!

Somehow, the idea that practicing should feel bad got started in the nineteenth century. Pianists were even encouraged to inflict pain on themselves as part of a "healthy" regimen. In Germany, there was the vise, constructed to stretch the fourth finger into obedient submission.

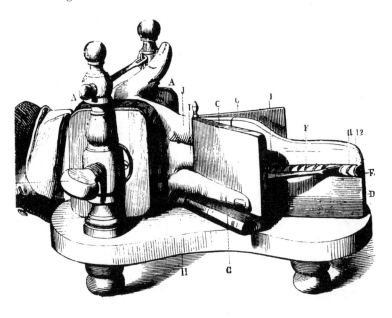

In America, we had the Atkins Finger-Supporting Device, to hold the fingers in "correct position." Springs overhanging the rings on each finger forced the wearer to use extra strength when depressing the keys. It was, indeed, a very depressing device!

**ATKINS' FINGER-SUPPORTING DEVICE.**

Today, most experts encourage their students to find a "natural" way of moving. And that is one of the first rules of good practice: *nothing should be forced.* That is not to say that discipline is unimportant. But if the approach to each aspect of the practice session is one of openness and discovery rather than rigidity, so much more will be accomplished!

For example, exercises enable the muscles of the hand to "memorize" a sequence. This learned behavior is needed. But a pianist who places too much effort on this "acquired reaction," and not enough on bringing out spontaneous, instinctive actions, will find himself in a rut. That's one of the reasons it is sometimes important to practice with your eyes closed!

Another rule of good practice is to *look at things from as many different angles as possible.* A pianist who is asked to play these two figures against each other might have a hard time:

With the right analysis, though, the solution could be easy as pie:

In future instalments, we'll look at some tested ideas on making your practice time productive, enjoyable, and eye-opening.

**AZ**

# How To Practice
## Part II

## "As Fast As Possible!"

One of the rules of practicing we all hear over and over is "Be sure to practice slowly." Often the result of this is a feeling of inhibition, which leads to tedium. Picture yourself filled with excitement and yearning in setting out to learn a new piece. Suddenly a voice from the darkness whispers: "Don't touch those keys! Sit erect, play slowly, stay strictly in time, watch that fingering. . . ." and your smile is gone. I'm beginning to feel a cramp just talking about it.

The fact is, a certain amount of slow practice and attention to small scale detail is absolutely necessary. But there is something lacking in the approach so many of us have taken; we set out to make *music,* and end up playing what amounts to no more than a series of sterile exercises.

How can we overcome this problem? First of all, it's important to remember that music comes to life through shading, dynamics, differences in touch, the shapes of its phrases, the rhythmic vitality that is so much a part of the right tempo. These qualities are all missing in a slow, rigid "practice" version of a piece. They are just as essential as correct fingering, and they don't come across without careful work.

So, perhaps we should change that rule from "Be sure to practice slowly" to "Practice as fast as possible." But wait! This requires some further discussion. The slow part of practice helps teach the fingers where to go, and makes it much easier to learn the work. But in order to learn how to create music—how to make the piece sing—we must practice it at a tempo that will help reveal musical relationships and subleties of form. Pianists must have the opportunity to experiment with touch and phrasing while practicing—and there is little chance of boredom when so many exciting elements are introduced to the practice session.

Ideally, then, *both* ways of practicing should be used! First, we should practice slowly enough to learn the notes and fingerings. Then, we should "practice as fast as possible"; that is, as fast as we can without losing control of the basics we learned in slow practice.

Here's how this would work. Take a short part of the piece; you might choose a four- or eight-measure phrase. Practice it slowly. When you feel comfortable with the music, increase the tempo. *Don't* wait until you've practiced the entire work slowly. In this way, at each sitting you'll get to learn a little section, bring it up to tempo, and feel into what is needed to bring it to life.

At the next sitting, work on the next four or eight measures. When you have that section brought up to tempo, combine it with the first section. Now, you will begin to understand how the phrases relate to each other. You can introduce the idea of dynamic shading and decide which lines to bring out at a given moment. In fact, you will be making real, exciting music—even before you've learned the whole piece!

As you go on in this way, you will probably change your mind about how to play the work as new sections are added. This is part of the process of discovery and experimentation. Concert artists are always re-interpreting, because they think about these elements all the time.

So play as slowly as you need to; but as fast as you are able! Next time, we'll talk about when to close your eyes.

AZ

*Above: A caricature of Paderewski that appeared on the cover of the World's Fair edition of* Puck *in 1893, in which he seems to be playing at super-human speed. The caption read: "A Peaceful Solution—at the next World's Fair Paderewski will play on all the pianos at once."*

# How To Practice
## Part III

## *Without Looking*

**G**ood pianists utilize much more than just their fingers and feet when they perform, and a discussion of physical movement in playing could fill volumes. Yet, many people practice with more parts of their bodies than are really necessary. For example, the shoulders are often lifted in an anxiety-ridden and painful pose that actually detracts from one's ability to control the sound of the instrument. Elbows can be a problem, too. And, how many of us (unconsciously) tighten up our diaphragms as a regular part of our playing habits, with the result that we breathe very little, and the music breathes even less?

There are many approaches to working with these physical problems, but we are only going to cover the first stage in this article: becoming aware of them. One way to become aware of what is going on in your body when you play is to ask a teacher or friend to watch you. But there is also a simple technique that can be incorporated into your practice sessions: playing with your eyes closed.

Closing your eyes at appropriate times can have several benefits. It can force you to learn the "geography" of the keyboard, so that you know where notes are without having to look. Once you have the feel of a piece—when you know exactly where your hands have to go without spending a lot of energy and attention on hitting the right notes—you can "let go," and allow your emotional interpretation full expression.

Another benefit of closing your eyes is that it helps you listen to the sound you are producing. Often we are so caught up with the act of playing that we don't really know what the end result really is.

Finally, closing our eyes allows us to give full value to our feeling sense as well as to our hearing sense. We can take a moment to explore where the tension is, where the physical force is being blocked, where we are uncomfortable. Most of the time, we don't bother to find out exactly where the discomfort lies, and we find all kinds of poor solutions to the problem—like compensating for one tension with another, instead of learning to relax the original problem area.

With our eyes closed, we can feel our fingers on the keys, and become aware of how much pressure we are using, how the keys are responding, and a dozen other aspects to playing. We can sense which part of our finger is striking the ivory, what our wrists are doing, and how our finger joints feel. Where are our thumbs when they are not being used? Are the fingers curved and tense, or flat and lifeless? Do we lift them before striking?

All of this can be helpful if we remember that the awareness can be used to draw conclusions about how to get the sound we want, and how to increase our ease in getting it. Practice should not feel like a wrestling match. Ideally, as we work on improving our playing ability, we should experience more and more that the solutions to technical problems generally involve *letting go* of something. By closing our eyes we can discover what it is that needs to be released, and where our physical equipment is not quite in balance.

So, try sitting at the keyboard with your eyes closed. Take a moment to sense yourself. Breathe. Check to see whether you are playing with your hands, or with some part that is foreign to good technique. Traditionally speaking, gall bladders just don't produce a beautiful piano tone.

**Next time: Memorizing.**

AZ

---

*Above: a nineteenth century illustration of Liszt at the piano. There's really no need to be so flamboyant, but it sometimes helps to play "without looking."*

# How To Practice
## Part IV

# *Without Music*

There was a time when the great pianists would not appear on stage without music in front of them. Clara Schumann seems to have been the first to perform from memory, and for this she was considered "insufferable," pretentious, and disrespectful toward the composers who wrote the works she played. Today, though, many consider memorization one of the most important aspects of piano playing.

Most books which discuss the how-to of memorizing stress the importance of understanding the intricacies of musical form. When you approach a piece you want to learn, the suggested practice is to break it down into various components, so you can see the exposition of a theme, the introduction of other themes, a development section, key relationships, modulatory passages, and so on. Of course, we can get even more complex about it. With the advent of home computers, it won't be long before every piano student is required to analyse all pitch series permutations and rhythmic stratifications on every page of an assigned piece!

I'm kidding, of course. But it is easy to get carried away with theoretical detail, and the dryness of an approach such as this can betray the initial thrill which brought us to the keyboard in the first place.

Don't get me wrong. I'm not against education. But it is important to avoid a kind of divorce which sometimes happens between the *experience* of music and the study of it.

In order to memorize a piece, it helps to analyse the music in a tactile, practical sort of way. Here's what I mean. Take a work you wish to memorize. Start with the opening phrase, and learn to play it without the music. Then, pause for a moment, to consider this: If you were the composer, how would you continue? You might, for example, repeat the original idea starting on a different pitch; or turn it upside down; or embellish it. There are, of course, countless possibilities.

Now take a look at what the composer of the piece actually did. Is what comes next very ordinary, or is it surprising? Note these first two phrases. Does the second answer the first? Are they short or long? Are they of equal size? Are there rhythmic ideas which repeat? Is there a natural rise and fall in the shape of the phrases, or do they leap and zigzag?

Let's also consider the physical demands this music is making. Is there a tricky fingering that comes up at a certain point? If so, play it over a few times, to remember the feeling. Are the hands playing together, or alternately? Are they moving in opposite directions? On which notes does the thumb go?

Each time you ask one of these questions, play those first phrases over before answering. Then, close the book.

You are ready to try playing without the book. When you hit your first blank moment (which might pop up right away), open the book and find the spot in the music you couldn't remember. Play through it a few times. At the beginning, you might have to play for a while just to memorize the notes. Later, there will be just a spot here and there that will cause problems. In those cases, you might want to imagine a picture which you can associate with each section of the music. It can be anything at all, like ocean waves for arpeggios, or raindrops for a staccato passage. Then, close the book again.

You can repeat this process over and over until you are sure of the music. Then, you'll want to move on to the next part of the work, thinking again about how the composer decided to continue, what the shape is, and what configurations you will find your fingers in.

Each time you hit a blind spot, you should refer to the printed page. If you hit the same blind spot over and over, it's important to "analyse" it in the context of the phrases which come before and after (including, for example, how your "ocean" becomes a "storm," and so on). By repeatedly closing the book, you are forced to confront any part of the music which is not completely clear to you. Each time you forget, you are actually getting an opportunity to deepen your understanding of the piece!

When the entire work is memorized, it will be necessary to test your ability to play it every so often, because some memorization is only *short term* — and it is only through constant questioning and evaluating that a deeper kind of learning takes place.

The advantages to following this routine are many. Not only will the music unfold in new ways — think of all the money you'll save on a home computer.

**AZ**

# How To Practice
## Part V

## "Perfectly?"

Recently, I was interviewed for a National Public Radio Show in connection with this series on how to practice. The first question was, "Does practice make perfect?" It was the kind of question that sends me right to the chiropractor!

The problem is with that word, "perfect." We began this series with a look at some of the strange devices nineteenth-century pianists used to achieve better-than-human technique (even the editor of *The Etude* endorsed the practice of cutting finger tendons for superior freedom). Today, many of us still think that with enough work we might eliminate all human frailties, and take on the qualities of a finely honed machine.

When people try to play "perfectly," they usually set themselves up against some ideal: a great performer, their teacher, or perhaps a talented cousin who lives down the street. (Seldom do they imagine perfection as being the best expression of their own musical personalities.)

Yet, we all know that each of us has a set of fingerprints which is ours alone. We celebrate the fact that every snowflake is different from all the others. When it comes to piano playing, the same attitude should apply.

After all, outer standards for pianistic "perfection" are always changing. Lately, recordings have created an expectation for note-perfect performance. Most musicians would agree, however, that having all the right notes in place hardly constitutes musical perfection. The great pianists didn't worry about such things. They saw their jobs as bringing out the music hidden beneath the notes!

"How," you may ask, "can we practice to achieve this?" Simply by making sure that our practice time is free of *empty gestures.* For example, when we play a passage without feeling—in a very personal way—exactly how we want it to sound, we are simply "going along for the ride." Pianists who play scales for hours in an attempt to perfect their technique are wasting time. If instead they were to play a scale for just a few moments, while listening to each note—investing all of their concentration—so much more would be accomplished!

Practicing in this deliberate way will not, of course, prevent accidents. But, the fact is, the very *imperfection* of each person is what adds the richness of personality to performance. I don't mean to say that we should be ill prepared. There is no point in playing a work if you aren't sure of the notes, if your fingers can't negotiate its technical hurdles, and if you haven't given a great deal of thought to how it should be played. I am saying that if we work to rid ourselves of empty gestures at the keyboard, *instead of focusing on the attainment of some kind of technical perfection,* the result will be musical and satisfying.

Suppose you are learning a new piece and you want to practice it in the light of this attitude. You might try a variety of touches. If you should choose, for musical reasons, to play a fast passage with a very legato touch, it might be technically more difficult than if you were to use staccato. Somehow, the individual notes might become swallowed up in the sweep of the phrase. The articulation might be seen as less than perfect. But if the musical gesture is a result of your own inner conviction, the idea of perfection hardly matters.

If you practice in this way, each movement and musical thought will take on more importance. The aim will be to make every note and every moment count. And the fullest musical expression of *your* personality will become the goal to attain. Remember: if it were perfect, it wouldn't be you.

**AZ**

# How To Practice
## Part VI

## *With Space Invaders*

**O**ne of the big controversies now mushrooming across the nation centers on the obsession many young people have for video arcade games. For some reason, these kids seem less interested in practicing the piano or in doing homework, than in alternately dodging and chasing after an insatiably carnivorous light beam. Wherever one stands on the issue, there is something to be said for learning to practice *Space Invaders Piano*.

What is *Space Invaders Piano?* It is a way of incorporating the best aspects of the man versus machine game into your practice sessions.

One of the fun aspects of those electronic gadgets is the way they intensify each moment. Every bit of action on the screen demands an immediate reaction on the part of the player. After all, when little spaceships are about to descend on your head, you can't take time to think about that wool blazer you've been dying to buy, or to consider deep questions like "Who shot J.R.?"

In the video game setting, cause and effect follow each other with an immediacy that is often missing in everyday life. Primitive man, of course, had the excitement of chasing and dodging dinosaurs. But, unless you are a taxi driver in New York City, that kind of spine-tingling existence is long gone.

Practicing the piano seldom provides the kind of emotional satisfaction we're discussing. Many people regard practice as an unappealing means to the pleasure we can derive from a finished performance. From that point of view, hours and days of toil are seen as merely the sacrifice necessary for a much-delayed reward.

It doesn't have to be that way. The real problem is that practicing the piano does not often carry with it the immediacy of results that we might find playing a video game (or any other high-pressure activity, like tennis). Consequently, it is easy for one's attention to wane. If a few notes are missed, or if the rhythm isn't exactly right, well...maybe next time it will sound better. There is a kind of half-heartedness that sets in; if you think about it, you'll probably be able to come up with examples of this kind of cheating in your own practice sessions.

It may be a cliche that the more we give to something, the more we get out of it—but it is also absolutely true. So, the result of these little moments of cheating in practice is a high degree of dissatisfaction and restlessness.

How can we bring some of the excitement of *Space Invaders* into the session? By making each moment absolutely thrilling. Suppose you want to practice a piece you are learning. Set your metronome to a reasonable tempo. Begin playing the piece in time. Is there a point at which you stumble? BOOM! Your ship has been disintegrated! But don't stop....The time is still clicking away, and you'll want to continue on. Of course, you must concentrate intently (and the tempo should not be too fast or too slow).

Let's take another example. You want to play some scales. Again, you may set the metronome to any tempo, preferably a slow one. Begin playing the scale, but listen carefully. Is the rhythm absolutely smooth? Is the sound a polished legato? Is the dynamic level from one note to the next completely even?

Picture those scale notes as little figures walking a tightrope. As soon as a note sounds uneven compared to the others, OOPS! It falls off the tightrope into the waiting mouths of musical Pac-Men. Too bad, but don't stop....You want your final score to be as high as possible.

You might want to make up your own games; I'd love to hear what they are. The more you invest in each moment, the more fun you'll have, regardless of what you are doing. ■

**AZ**

# *Mozart Did It With His Nose*

S. Fica

# How To Practice
## Part VII

There is a story about Mozart in which he gives one of his pieces for harpsichord to Haydn, with a challenge to the old master: "You'll never be able to play it."

Not one to take such a claim standing up, Haydn quickly sat at the keyboard and began to play. About halfway through, however, he met a passage in which there were chords in the high treble and low bass, with a single note in the middle register! Haydn decided it was impossible to execute, at which point Mozart demonstrated the solution. He played the chords with his right and left hands, and used his nose for the single note. "With *your* nose," said Haydn, "it looks easy."

Mozart was making use of a concept important to any artist, athlete, or businessperson who wants to succeed: he was simply taking advantage of a natural endowment. Part of learning to practice well involves recognizing your *own* particular strengths and weaknesses, and working with them.

This may seem obvious, but teachers and students often adopt very rigid approaches to practice time: fif-teen minutes of scales, ten minutes of the left hand of that Bach invention, and so on. The fact is, each pianist is unique and requires a very particular program of study.

Take scale playing. Some pianists need to work with scales in order to improve finger dexterity and control. Others have "well-oiled" digits, but need to work on piano tone. Still others play perfectly well, but lack a certain amount of emotional connection to the music. It would be a mistake to assign the same practice routine to everyone.

For developing control, there is nothing like working at a slow tempo with a metronome. Developing an even tone, however, is another matter: it requires listening with intense concentration, which is not compatible with the constant clicking of a mechanical time keeper. For developing emotional expressiveness, another kind of practice may be needed altogether.

Perhaps the most difficult thing about designing a practice session just right for yourself is determining what you really need. Of course, if you can't play a particular passage you have been working on, it's clear that some energy must be devoted to overcoming that particular problem. But what about more subtle aspects of playing that also require attention?

For example, some pianists suffer from a harsh piano tone. If you were to recognize this as one of your weaknesses, you would want to schedule practice time to work on this problem. But how? Often a harsh sound results from not enough concentration on the *physical* connection between the hands and the keyboard. This can be helped by actively "listening" with your fingers to the movement of the keys; imagining the impulse that sends your fingers into the ivory moving through your hands, beyond the keys, and into the strings. Try it.

On the other hand, some pianists have a wonderful, pearly tone and good emotional command of the music, but lack control. Others have a firm grasp of things, but have difficulty in "letting go," and allowing the music to soar.

In each case, there are techniques that can be used to work on these very individual problems. Remember, everyone has both strengths and weaknesses. The more you learn about yours, the more easily you will be able to accomplish your goals.

The psychologist Carl Jung created an interesting chart which describes different personality traits and the ways in which they influence activities like playing the piano. In our next column, we'll present a sort of checklist to help you see where you might fit in. After discovering what your tendencies are, you'll be able to choose the techniques that will be most constructive during your practice session.

In the meantime, there is one time-tested way to rid yourself of the tedium of the same old practice routine. It's called playing with your nose!

**AZ**

# How To Practice
## Part VIII

## *Find Your Piano Personality*

Last issue, we mentioned that the psychologist Carl Jung developed a school of psychology based on the idea that our different personal characteristics fall into a number of common "types." As promised, this column will present a little checklist so you can decide which ones come closest to your own personality. Next time we'll look at how to use this information in your own practice sessions!

We'll start with the two main categories into which all the others fall. Ready? Get out your pencils!

*1) The weather is cold, and you are going out. What do you do?* a) Put on a coat. b) Challenge the elements by going out without one.
*2) Something happens a certain way one thousand times in a row. On the thousand and first time, you:*
a) assume it will happen again. b) doubt the outcome.
*3) You're writing an essay. How do you go about it?*
a) Gather all the research you can. b) Think about your own reactions to the subject.

Jung called the two main types the *introvert* and the *extravert*. Of course, these terms are used fairly often in everyday speech, but Jung used them in a very specific way. If you forego the coat and doubt the outcome on that thousand and first event, you're probably an introvert.

According to Jung, extraverts count a lot on what goes on outside themselves, rather than on subjective thoughts. They are comfortable with facts and with traditions. When they create, it is by constructing new combinations out of the materials at hand.

Introverts are more abstract. Their thinking often seems arbitrary. Their creations seem to spring up from nowhere. It's not so easy for them to explain themselves to others.

Which are you?

*4) Someone asks you what your favorite film is. You answer:* a) an obscure foreign production about the relationship between the building of the Parthenon and the life cycle of the fruit fly. b) *Love Story.*
*5) You want to explain why you love Bach's music so much. The reason is:* a) his exquisite sense of form and complete mastery of counterpoint. b) the man was burning with passion.

Within the two broad categories, there are four more types: thinking, feeling, sensation, and intuition. Although we are all of these in varying degrees, we do tend more toward one or two.

Thinking types don't rely much on their feelings. In fact, they hold them in check. Rather than letting passions take over, they prefer living by rules and formulas, "oughts" and "musts."

Feeling types, on the other hand, may consider thinking a boring, lifeless activity. For them, feelings are the lifeblood of experience. Of course, everyone uses both thinking and feeling. The difference is one of emphasis.

Do you tend to emote a lot, or do you consider strong feelings a distraction?

*6) You are enjoying a fine French meal, and order mousse for dessert. When it arrives you:* a) delight over its texture in your mouth, and savor the delicate flavor which runs over your tongue and palate. b) notice the creamy topping, and its shape reminds you of the swirling clouds which danced across the sky earlier that afternoon.

Sensation types are very tied to concrete sense impressions. They take great pleasure in the texture, color, mood, temperature, and taste of things. They enjoy the interaction of their bodies with other objects.

Intuition types are not all that concerned with such physical effects. They are caught up in less tangible aspects, not in tasting an object but in envisioning its possibilities, or in experiencing dreamlike images around it, which may spring up from deep, unconscious sources.

It's tough on the basis of such cursory descriptions to find oneself in the maze of character types. But try an experiment. As you go through your day, notice your "style" in relation to the world around you. If you know people who act very differently from you (perhaps they drive you crazy), see if they fit any of the descriptions above. You might have the opposite tendencies. Or, you might have the same ones, but like to think of yourself as being different.

Only you can decide. When you do, think about how your piano playing may reflect your character. Next time, we'll explore how this personality checklist can come in handy at practice time.■

AZ

# How To Practice
## Part IX

# With A Difference!

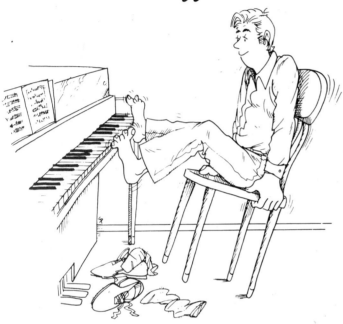

Last issue we explored the idea of personality types, and gave you the opportunity to decide what kind of character *you* are. It's easy to imagine that someone who is geared toward tactile sensation will play the piano very differently from someone who tends toward a more philosophical bent. But how can this be of use in a practice session?

If we think about the qualities we would like to bring out in "ideal" playing, we'll probably come up with a list that is fairly balanced between depth of emotional content and thoughtful control of the musical elements. We'll want to produce creative interpretations, but we won't want to neglect the tone or technique through which we express them.

So, our job is to fill the missing gaps in our own approaches. *Feeling* types will tend to play with a lot of emotion. That can be a strength. But, there is also a weakness inherent in such an attitude. They will tend to emphasize unrestrained "feeling" more and more, and at a certain point discipline is sorely needed.

*Thinking* types may learn to play with an exquisite sense of form and a clarity of direction. But here,

again, there could be something missing in their playing that leaves an audience dissatisfied. For them, the injection of a less controlled emotional strain might be healthy.

Using the questionnaire from the last column, decide which categories—feeling, thinking, sensation, intuition—you most strongly fit into. Then begin to practice developing the *opposite* traits!

If you are a *feeling* type, try analyzing the music and sticking to an interpretive plan, regardless of how carried away you may feel while playing. Practice with a metronome to be sure you are playing with a reasonable adherence to the work's tempo indication. Practice scales and exercises more carefully!

If you are a *thinking* type, try turning off the metronome. Put your handbook of style away, and approach whatever piece you are working on as though the different voices were characters in a Gothic novel. Think of your neighbor, whose dog keeps digging up your carrots, and use the music to tell him a thing or two.

If you are a *sensation* type, you love the feeling of your fingers on the keys, the movement of the muscles and joints while you play. You may want to blur your focus somewhat, to concentrate less on the physical end of practice and more on what your im-

---

## "Try doing things opposite to the way you normally do them."

---

agination can do with the material at hand. Try to let the music speak to you as if it had a life all its own, apart from the individual sounds which result from depressing the keys. If you were playing in a dream, how would things be different?

As an *intuition* type, you need some of that concrete, down-to-earth orientation that sensation types have. Become very conscious of the movement of your fingers on the keys; practice scales more often. Study the fingering in your pieces; make note of the physical requirements for a technically polished rendition.

The more you resist the idea of doing any of these exercises, the more you need them! In fact, one clue for determining which applies to you is to decide which disgusts you the most.

Next time, we'll get back to some more traditional subject matter: practicing rhythms that involve three notes in one hand against four in another. ■

**AZ**

# How To Practice
## Part X

The rain in Spain...

# "Sound Advice"

According to the old song, rhythm is "fascinatin'," but for many pianists, a more accurate description might be "frustratin'." Practicing complicated rhythmic figures can be a difficult chore. Unless they are aproached in the right way, the piano's keys won't be the only things that get depressed!

One device that pianists have used to get a grip on triplets and syncopations is the chanting of common words or phrases that sound like the correct rhythm. For example, sixteenth notes might be represented by the word "Alabama." Triplets sound like "Sym-phon-y."

According to that brilliant musician and writer Nicolas Slonimsky, many classical themes have been turned into doggerel by irreverent musicians.* He claims that students at the St. Petersburg Conservatory used to render the difficult 11/4 rhythm in Rimsky-Korsakov's opera *Sadko* by repeating the Russian words, Rimsky-Korsakov Sovsem Sumasoshol," which means "Rimsky-Korsakov is altogether mad." The main theme of the Mendelssohn *Violin Concerto*, says Slonimsky, has been turned into "Oh, Moyshe, oh, Moyshe, the business isn't good."

The thing to consider when using this approach is how to get the "sound" of the rhythm in your ears. Once the notes on the page are turned into a recognizable sound, the battle is almost won.

Sometimes, this means carefully figuring out the *resultant* sound of the different rhythms taking place at the same time. For example, suppose you wanted to play the Mendelssohn *Song Without Words*, Op. 53, No. 2.

Figuring out the mathematical relations between the right- and left-hand rhythms is a simple matter of finding a common denominator between them: two and three both fit nicely into a count of six.

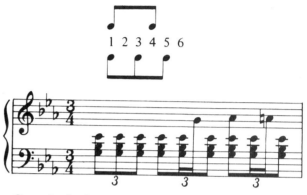

Once the final sound is realized, playing the piece at the proper tempo is not difficult at all.

Three notes against four can be figured out by taking the common denominator of twelve.

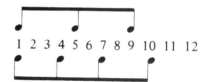

This tricky rhythm can be found in Chopin's posthumous etude.

You can try practicing the resultant rhythm at a very slow tempo, and then, *keeping the sound of the figure in mind,* bring it up to performance level. In cases where the two hands are playing very complex and different figures, the best way to practice is to memorize the sound of each hand separately. Once you are sure of the individual sound pictures the composer wanted, everything will fall into place when these sounds are brought together.

If you find the right words to fit a tricky passage, feel free to use them, no matter how silly. Nicolas Slonimsky points to a setting used for the tune of Dvorak's *Humoresque:* "Passengers will please refrain from flushing toilet while the train is standing in the station, I love you." Which is as good a way as I can think of to keep keyboard practice from becoming "depressing."

**AZ**

*A Thing Or Two About Music* (Westport: Greenwood Press, 1972).

# How To Practice
## Part XI

Confidence

In 1951, Oscar Hammerstein penned the immortal lyrics that changed the facial cast of a generation of music lovers: "Whenever I feel afraid, I hold my head erect, And whistle a happy tune, So no one will suspect I'm afraid." It's good advice for walking down dark country roads, but concert performers have to find another way to combat the fright of coming face to face with an audience.

Stage fright can be paralyzing to an amateur, and even professionals have their share of its effects. The experience can range from just plain nervousness to memory loss and debilitating problems. Sometimes it just causes an occasional wrong note. For example, most of us have had the experience of thinking about a difficult passage before reaching it, or of sighing relief after getting through it; how many times have performances gone wrong during "easy" parts because we were busy concentrating on something other than what we were playing at the moment?

Less obvious effects of a chronic lack of confidence include cold, mechanical playing, or playing filled with empty gestures, or even over-dramatization! These are symptoms of trying to maintain complete control over a scary situation; unfortunately, there's no way to become poised, spontaneous, relaxed, and secure through sheer willfulness.

To understand what's behind the phenomenon, think back to the first time you went to school. The environment was strange, and the people were new. Undoubtedly, at some point you were rejected or hurt by a classmate. How did you react? Some people cut off their feelings, and pretend it doesn't matter. Others may exaggerate feelings, to overpower the situation.

Stepping up on stage puts us on a similar footing. All the disappointments of life conspire to "prove" to us that the audience is a potential enemy, to be conquered; so, we try to make sure everything will go exactly the way we want. Just as in our school days example, we can pretend it doesn't matter, or try to control the performance through strictly worked-out interpretations, or through exaggerated gestures. We can try to win acceptance through powerhouse theatrics, or through a gentler kind of seduction.

But none of these are real solutions. Underneath it all, a fearful insecurity still lurks; and it takes its toll.

How is it possible to practice gaining confidence? One way is to become very aware of the irrational thoughts that often remain unconscious, or just below the surface. We can do this even when we're playing alone.

For example, when practicing a difficult passage, is there a little voice inside that says: "I'll never make this passage with people watching"? Or, does it say, "This will knock their socks off!"? Either way, the desire to please or to prove a point is coming between you and the music.

Become fully aware of this kind of inner dialogue. Think about it during your practice session. You may discover that these extramusical aspects are even influencing your choice of repertoire. You can lighten the weight of these thoughts by bringing them into your playing: if you feel afraid, or angry, or boastful, bring out these characteristics through the way you are playing. This will at the least help prevent a deadness from setting in.

The next step is to question what you really want out of the performance. Why is it so important? What would happen if you didn't get it?

This is not easy. Most of us really believe that if we make mistakes, if we don't gain the admiration of our audience, or teacher, or parent, it will be a terrible disaster. It is helpful to consider a worst-case scenerio. Imagine the greatest performance catastrophe of your career actually taking place. Would it really be a fate worse than death? The discrepancy between our real needs and what we (often subsconsciously) *believe we need* is amazing. After all, what really counts is the sense of musical pleasure that brought you to the piano in the first place.

Of course, gaining emotional confidence is a gradual process. You can't simply force your feelings to behave—that would be another pseudo-solution. But you can work on it. Ask friends over, and play for them, taking note of that "inner dialogue." Share what you find with people you trust, and you'll discover the world isn't so dangerous. The more aware you are of the feelings beneath the surface, the less out of control you'll be.

Use physical exercise to release the energy your body generates in its "fight or flight" reaction to fearful situations. Be sure to master the music through practice of the piece itself; there's no way to gain confidence if you don't know the notes you are going to play.

Most important of all, keep in mind that you are aiming at *growth* rather than instant *perfection*. When you allow yourself the freedom to grow and change, that spontaneous, poised attitude essential to music making can emerge. As the poet Virgil wrote, "Let us sing on our journey as far as we go; the way will be less tedious." ■

**AZ**

# How To Practice
## Part XII

## *Making Music*

## *"This is a way of creating variety from the inside-out!"*

"No matter how scrupulously a piece of music may be notated," wrote composer Igor Stravinsky, "it always contains hidden elements that defy definition." Perhaps that is why so many great artists have turned to poetic imagery for help in interpreting the written music.

That strange and wonderful French composer Erik Satie used to give directions in his music such as "Like a nightingale with a toothache," and "Don't light it yet; you still have time." He is a rather severe example, but listen to Wagner describing the pauses he conducted in Beethoven's *Fifth Symphony:* "I arrest the waves of the ocean, and the depth must be visible; or I stem the clouds, disperse the mist, and show the pure blue ether and the radiant eye of the sun."

Such dreamy romanticism is not always well suited to the music at hand, but one thing is *always* essential: there must be a real involvement in every piece. Stravinsky offered a simple rule to anyone performing one of his works: he demanded from the interpreter "a loving care." That care involves finding ways to bring the music to life.

One helpful device for finding and bringing forth the musical "personality" in a piece, other than through imagery, is to isolate, and experiment with, all the different elements: phrasing, dynamics, articulation and more. Each subtle aspect of your playing can be combined in many ways; the result, in the best moments, will be like the flavor of a rare wine: pleasureable, surprising, harmoniously complex.

When I was younger, my friends and I used to "dissect" great music by listening to recordings in the following way: The first time through, we would focus on just the bass. Then, we would listen again to just the melody. Next, we would listen for the harmonies. It was a lot of fun and rewarding, too.

You can do something similar in your practice sessions. Take any piece of music, and look first at the melody, or the bass, or the inner voices. Play that one part alone, and consider how phrasing can help express it. Next, consider the dynamics that should be applied: gradual changes in volume can help create a breath of flow; contrasts will either bring out different parts of a phrase or uncover hidden melodies. Then, try legato and staccato techniques. Explore how *silence* works in conjunction with the notes you play: it is just as important as the *sounds* you produce!

Once you have applied these practice ideas to establish the character of your bass lines, try the same thing with the melody line. Then, combine the two. Suddenly, you have an interaction taking place between two musical "personalities." Here is an opportunity to formulate a poetic image! How do the lines interact? How do they work for or against each other?

Now you can add the next part of the music on the page. In this way, you'll end up juggling all the parts that go into producing the musical work, and have the chance to change the colors and flavors of each line. What's more, you can breathe new life into the piece at any time, simply by changing the "personality" of one of the parts. This is a way of creating variety from the inside-out!

Try practicing more than just the notes on a page. You might end up sounding "like a nightingale with a toothache." Then again, maybe you won't. ∎

**AZ**

# TECHNIQUE
# Playing Scales

## "If you pay attention to these points, you will acquire a great technique in just a few weeks."

*Walter Gieseking was one of the most brilliant pianists of his generation (1895-1956), known particularly for his interpretations of Debussy. Together with his teacher, Karl Leimer, he wrote a number of essays on technique and pedagogy; the following first appeared in 1932, in a publication called* The Shortest Way To Pianistic Perfection.

I am not absolutely opposed to finger exercises, scales, and arpeggios, nor do I reject the study of etudes; but I am of the opinion that these means for developing technique are, as a rule, used too much. To sit at the piano and practice scales and exercises for hours and hours, generally without concentration, is a very roundabout way of obtaining results.

If this intensive work is done by the help of strong concentration, it is possible for technique to improve so rapidly that marvelous results will be sometimes obtained. Almost always, however, brain work is left out, and the pupil is obliged to spend many years of practicing daily, and for hours at a time, in order to acquire a somewhat serviceable technique.

To a certain extent, of course, the practicing of finger exercises and scales cannot be avoided, and it is well therefore to make a few further remarks, which I think will be advantageous when studying.

Scales are played with a view to training the fingers, so that they do their work evenly and smoothly. Every tone of a scale must be struck with a certain vigor, and the ear must be carefully trained to hear the exact volume of sound required. We must have an accurate knowledge of the notes appearing in the scale, in order to be able to play it from memory; and we must further acquaint ourselves with the fingering, that is, the use of the thumbs and the third and fourth fingers. Not before the notes and the fingering are familiar to the pupil should he begin playing.

As the ear must pass judgment on the correct volume of sound, it is the first condition, when playing scales, for each hand to practice alone. If this is not done, the left hand is drowned by the right hand, or *vice versa,* for it becomes almost impossible to find out the grade of strength of the different tones with the two hands playing together.

In the scale of C major, for instance, **C** in the left hand is played with the fifth finger, in the right hand with the thumb; **D** in the left hand with the fourth finger, in the right hand with the second finger; and so forth. As the fingers are unequal in strength, they cannot at first be expected to touch the keys evenly. It is almost impossible for the beginner to hear these dissimilarities if both hands are played together.

The most important thing when training the fingers (the control of which we call technique) is to be able to judge correctly the dynamic value of the tones, by means of the ear. One must, therefore, bear in mind that the tones of a scale must be played with equality of strength. For the thumb there must be an extra pressure; for the second and third fingers there will be a certain amount of restraint; and then again for the fourth and fifth fingers there will be an added strength of stroke.

Strange to say, it is little known that in many cases the thumb touches the keys too feebly, a sure sign of how imperfectly the ear is generally trained. The movement which comes naturally to the thumb is to bend it under the other fingers, whereas the striking of a key from above downward necessitates practice. Its position, by reason of its being somewhat closer to the keys than the other fingers, encourages a weaker playing. For the same reason the thumb very often strikes too feebly when bent under the fingers, or else too vigorously, either through want of relaxation or through clumsiness.

After the thumb has been bent under, attention must be given to the secnd finger and, in descending, to the third and fourth fingers. Only by playing very slowly can we assure ourselves of the dynamic value of each tone, which is necessary in order to discover and to correct inaccuracies of equality in power. The best and quickest way to do this is to play short passages of the scale, and to practice five tones ascending and descending. The most careful attention must be given to the rhythm and touch of every tone.

Having taken note of the volume and the rhythmical value of tone, attention must be given to movement of the muscles. The feeling for absolute relaxation must become second nature to the pupil, and it must be continuously felt when playing scales. If the player gives constant attention to these points, keeping watch over both hands, and practicing a short time every day, in a few weeks he will have acquired so great a technique that he will be able to play scales in a much better manner than many pupils who have been studying for years and have practiced scales one hour or more a day. If the pupil follows these rules, his playing will become smooth and rippling. Then the hands may be occasionally practiced together, in order to accustom the ear to the precise striking together of the tones of the two hands.

A great difficulty when playing scales is the passing over and under of the fingers. We must think ceaselessly of relaxation. I advise the passing under of the fingers to be practiced principally by rolling of the lower arm; this is usually done by a side movement of the hand over the keyboard. It is quite easy to relax the muscles when using a rolling of the lower arm, and this is difficult when the hand is bent sideways.

Without relaxation it is quite impossible to play a pearly scale. After having touched a black key, it is comparatively easy to pass the finger under; but this is not so after having touched a white key. For this reason, the scale in C major is the most difficult to play smoothly. It is therefore advisable not to commence with the C major scale.

I do not consider it necessary to play scales in all their variations of sixths, thirds, contrary motions, and so on, as too much valuable time is wasted thereby. Scales, or parts of scales, however, as they constantly appear in compositions, should be carefully studied, so that in time their rendering will, with the help of relaxation, become more and more perfect.

**WG & KL**

# Major Scale Manual

C

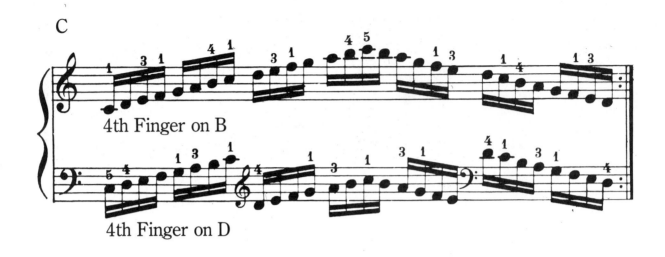

4th Finger on B

4th Finger on D

G

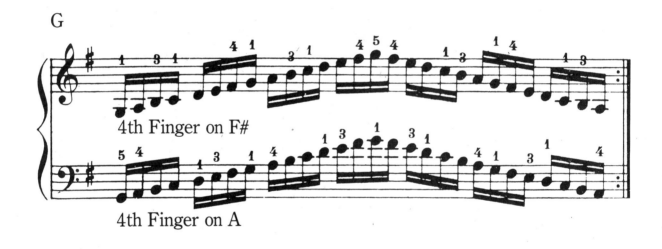

4th Finger on F#

4th Finger on A

D

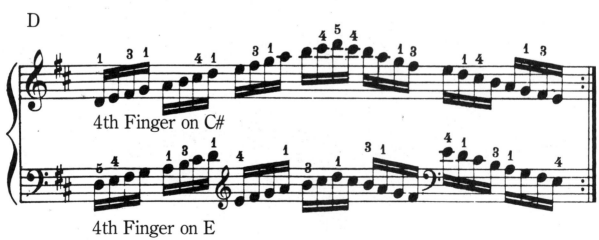

4th Finger on C#

4th Finger on E

A

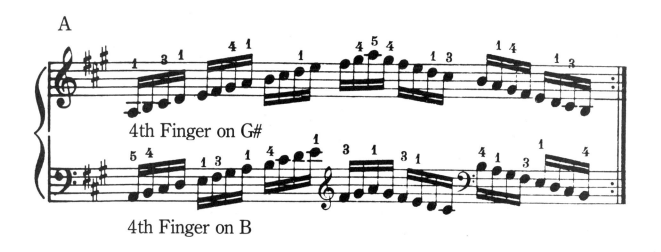

4th Finger on G#

4th Finger on B

E

4th Finger on D#

4th Finger on F#

B

4th Finger on A#

4th Finger on F# and on the initial note

287

**F#**

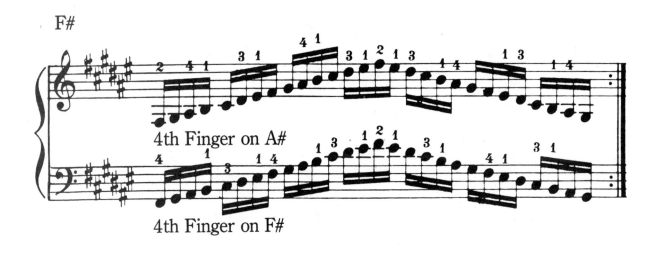

4th Finger on A#

4th Finger on F#

**C#**

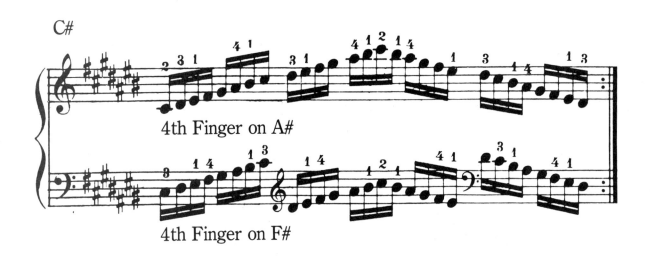

4th Finger on A#

4th Finger on F#

**A♭**

4th Finger on B♭

4th Finger on D♭

288

**E♭**

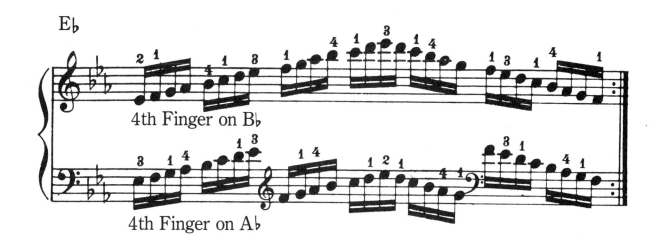

4th Finger on B♭

4th Finger on A♭

**B♭**

4th Finger on B♭

4th Finger on E♭

**F**

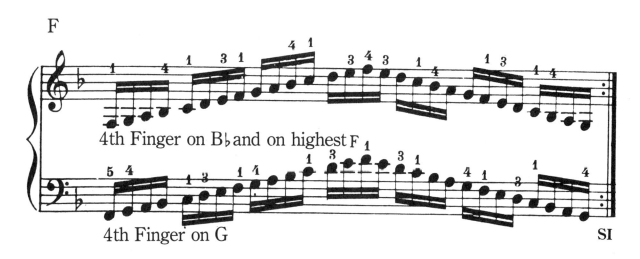

4th Finger on B♭ and on highest F

4th Finger on G

SI

# TECHNIQUE

# Make Waves

*"Many pianists risk learning a 'lockjaw of the wrist.'"*

When pianists talk of scales, they often ask, "How can I make my scales smoother (faster), without getting tight?" Scales are five-finger passages repeated when the hand shifts sideways. Stiffness may occur when we have a poor finger sequence, or our thumb passage is rough, or an unbalanced arm weight makes the shift too heavy.

Hanon's exercises still rate the best for smoothing the finger sequence in a five-finger position. Moreover, that great invention of his—skipping one small note on the way "out" from the thumb—guarantees that the hand moves step by step *through* a scale, reshaping itself to changing "handfuls" as the music continues.

Variations on Hanon's patterns will get your hands "splashing" from the start:

Often, problems come about in the action of the thumb-wrist. I hyphenate here because one *depends* upon the other. Since the hinge of the thumb—and pivot of its free movement—lies *deep* inside that swamp of bone chips we call the wrist, it cannot move when the wrist is locked; neither can the wrist move when the thumb is tight.

Try flapping your hand from a loose wrist, as if you were waving good-bye with a large handkerchief to someone in a disappearing train. As you continue to flap your hand up and down, draw your thumb slowly *under* the hand. What happens at the wrist? Keep on bobbing the hand and sense the various ways by which the arm substitutes for the stiffening wrist: first by forearm movement (from the elbow); gradually, by upper-arm action (from the shoulder).

You risk learning this "lockjaw of the wrist" if you take seriously the frequent injunction to "put the thumb under the hand, ready for the next position." That term "position," in this case, conveys a fixed, rather than a dynamic, idea of how we move as we play.

It is far better to use the thumb, in its natural way, by simply dropping onto it at the start of short slurred groups, up and down an octave of the C scale:

Drop your hand weight onto the thumb and let it roll easily through the fall of four succeeding fingers, as naturally as water poured from a glass sprays into droplets. Notice, too, how your hand lightens as it rolls, in a naturally rising slant up toward the little finger. It is this basic "geometry" of keyboard movement—curves to make a (scale) line—that leads to *wave-form scales.*

The most positive way to (1) activate the thumb playing alongside *each* finger in turn, and (2) keep the wrist flexibly ready for the small undulations of the fingers is, I have found, to apply to scales little wavelike figures, then to vary those "waves," just as composers do when they play with scales in their pieces.

It is usual to find scales in musical works swirling or eddying, like this:

Or even cycloning like this:

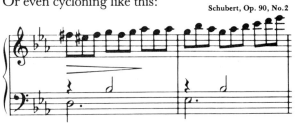

Schubert, Op. 90, No. 2

All composers know that such figures beguile the ear.

Many an old étude embodies the secret of even scales, like this one by Czerny *The School of Velocity,* op. 299, no. 18:

But look out! Without spaced stress points, which allow your nerves a "breather" and your mind to "preset" its next thought, you will tighten before the end of page one and cramp well before the finish line! Earlier applications of pure work ethic: "Just play it slower, and keep on playing it" simply do not help us soon enough. One needs spaced stresses.

First, sound out a scale like this.

*Use regular scale fingering* for the waves and feel a single octave-long phrase:

Next, loosen that wrist thumb with "white caps," bouncing your hand with two light beats before "diving forward" with the upbeat triplet to the next downbeat:

Finally, you will need a brisker pace for the "breakers," which "backlash" your hands from the "rock" (see *).

Continue to work one-octave scales in *every* key, up then down, at a moderate tempo, trying for musically animated shapes. It is *shape*—not speed—that catches and holds the ear. "Wave-form" scale practice will help lubricate your fingers too, however, for the reward of evenness with lightness is speed.

**RD**

*Robert Dumm was named Dean of the Boston Conservatory when he was only twenty-five, and became a critic for* The Christian Science Monitor *a year later. He served fifteen years as head of graduate Piano Pedagogy at The Catholic University before retiring in 1979. Mr. Dumm is active as a teacher, contest judge, and writer on musical subjects.*

# TECHNIQUE
# Yoke It Up!

*"There's something about 'yoking' the hands that balances, lightens, and guides their movements."*

Here is a practice method that works! We've often heard the saying "Many hands make light labor," to which I would add, "especially when they're *yours*." There's something about having your two hands play the same passage together that balances, lightens, and guides hand and finger movements.

"Yoking" (as in yoking two oxen or harnessing two horses) seems to act somehow the way a gyroscope does in guiding the steering of a boat. By doubling the bass part with the right hand, and transposing it an octave higher for clearer sound, many advantages can be obtained for the performance of bass figures, skips, and passages that require endurance. The following are some concrete examples.

**For wavelike figures in the bass.**

*Chopin, Fantasy-Impromptu*

Doubling the left hand with the right here will put its lighter fingers, 3, 4, and 5, over the topmost notes, where a contoured shape is needed. Moving along with the left hand, the right will lend its lighter action around those top notes, melting them and shaping them with hand weight as it rolls. Thus, the right lends, or "teaches," the left its feeling of swirling around the bend, helping the left to carry *around* its thumb, which, heavy in itself, will stick if you "poke" an accent with it.

### In Alberti Bass passages.

*Beethoven, Rondo, Op. 51 No. 1*

First, double the left part with the right hand. Then, practice the figure *two* ways: (1) exactly *as is* in both hands, then (2) with the right hand playing *an inversion* of the left, in symmetrical action.

### Two-handed guidance system for wide skips (or better, shifts).

Two pianist-composers gave us clues as to how to handle shifts accurately.

*Schumann, Fantasy*

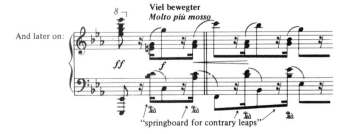

*Chopin, Sonata, Op. 35*

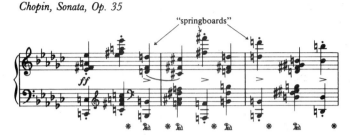

In each case, the composer provided the performer with a "launching pad," or strong note, *from which* to "spring" his leap. It is not the note you leap *to* that matters as much as the note you leap *from.* Put your weight emphasis there. For giant skips such as these, both composers have you play in a *symmetrical* motion of the two arms.

### Yoking for oxlike endurance.

There are hundreds of examples where the composer wisely yokes his two "animals" for the long haul. Take this one from Beethoven's "Waldstein" Sonata, C Major, Opus 53, first movement.

The contrary motion of both hands synchronizes their action, distributing even power to the fingers. Perhaps most importantly, it *places* rotary accents at the outside of both hands, which allows for endurance through an economical use of energy.

*Beethoven, "Waldstein" Sonata, Op. 53*

I apply "yoking" daily to concerto passages where one or the other thumb is stiff. The passage above, and countless others in Beethoven's concerti, "work" because the motion is symmetrical. Symmetrical action is a rhythmic action that both liberates and harmonizes all the performer's powers: physical, emotional, and spiritual—and that is no "yoke"! ■ **RD**

*Robert Dumm was named Dean of the Boston Conservatory when he was only twenty-five, and became a critic for* The Christian Science Monitor *a year later. He served fifteen years as head of graduate Piano Pedagogy at The Catholic University before retiring in 1979. Mr. Dumm is active as a teacher, contest judge and writer on musical subjects.*

# TECHNIQUE

## *"Splay It Again, Sam!"*

### "A pianist's hand should shape the tones of a chord, just as a sculptor leaves his fingerprints on warm clay."

Often the poorest sounds that otherwise good pianists produce are chords, particularly full chords. They often hook their hands stiffly and bring them down like a cookie-cutter, with predictable results. This is because they confuse ends (volume) with means (slam), forgetting that even a solid chord sound is an impression that several fingers, each of different weight and strength, make by directing hand weight to certain keys.

For example, take this Beethoven theme:

**Beethoven, Sonata in F Minor, Op. 2 No. 1**

For the spontaneous splurge of sound in measure 3, the hand must *open into* the chord, particularly in the higher, thin register of the piano. This may be why Beethoven asked us to roll it. But rolled or not, the hands must not maintain a rigidly fixed position! Remember, the keys move downward as your fingers move *into* them.

Moreover, the wider the chord, the farther the fourth and fifth fingers seem to have to move. The resulting tension leads many pianists to think, "How can I increase my stretch?"—as if their hands were yardsticks with unfolding extensions. But such thoughts will result in an unpleasant, brittle rendition.

One new student of mine, clutching his rumpled copy of Chopin's *Polonaise* in A flat major Opus 53,

proudly declared: "I can play the first chord!" And he then did so, with an unsettling bang. It's important to keep in mind that composers intend their "big" chords as a sound that is full and vital, booming out important musical "news." It may mean good "news," such as:

**Bach, Toccata in G Major, BWV 912**

294

# "Hand weight, dropping with the thumb, splashes like droplets through the fingers."

Or bad, dire "news":

**Beethoven, Sonata in C Minor, Op. 13 (Pathetique)**

The problem in capturing the right sound results from trying to play a chord that is both sudden *and* full. This usually leads the hand to grab. The solution is to open your palm and "fan out" the hand weight. Picture your hand reaching for a ripe bunch of grapes a little out of reach. This is a *dynamic* gesture. A fully *live* piano hand not only opens over, but moves through the tones of a chord, shaping them as it goes, just as a sculptor leaves his finger-prints on warm and yielding clay.

The quicker the roll of a broken chord, the more dynamic is the hand's innermost impulse, like a charge set off in the center of the palm. Once placed, the hand itself must seem to "explode" into the chord, just as a falling kitten's four legs instantly splay flat out from its underbelly.

Is this just a fanciful suggestion? Wouldn't it lead to skidding off the key and playing wrong notes? What about control? Consider the *Etude* Chopin designed for large, rolled chords:

**Chopin, Etude in E Flat Major, Op. 10 No. 11**

Chopin begins his right-hand chords from the heavier thumb, the natural position to place the hand's weight. But hand weight, dropping with the thumb, splashes like droplets through the remaining fingers as the hand rises. (It is no different in the left; the low bass makes the initial sound, and the left hand roll-to-thumb simply "tops" that bass sound.) The chord tones are literally "shaken out of the hand." A rolled chord lets you pivot on and past the thumb in a sort of drop-swivel. For a solid chord, it is the *same* gesture, though instantaneous.

This action is not passive, though. The lifted hand aims, then *sends* its weight into the first note of each chord. The stopped fall rebounds at that point and electrifies each succeeding finger in turn.

Here is a practice routine that will "splay" your hands free, and "spatter" rebounded hand weight in repercussive ripples through the fingers:

**RD**

*Robert Dumm was named Dean of the Boston Conservatory when he was only twenty-five, and became a critic for* The Christian Science Monitor *a year later. He served fifteen years as head of graduate Piano Pedagogy at The Catholic University before retiring in 1979. Mr. Dumm is active as a teacher, contest judge and writer on musical subjects.*

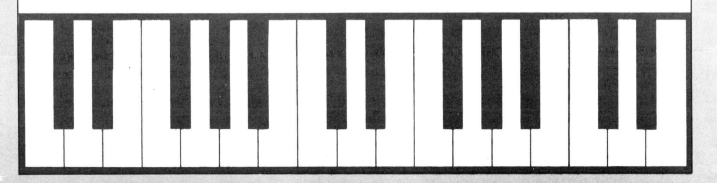

# TECHNIQUE

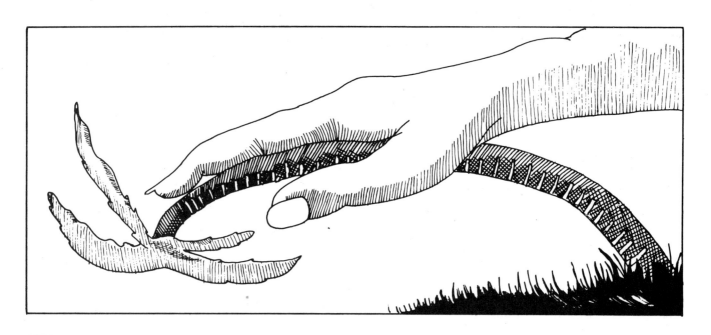

# "Palm Springs"

## "A ringing tone quality depends upon the invisible spring action of the palm."

ichelangelo, who was as much a sculptor as a painter, often spoke of "the hand that obeys the intellect." For a pianist, too, it is the vital animated hand that portrays his musical ideas. We have all heard chords crashed or thumped from the keys with what, I am sure, the pianist *thought* to be an impressive sound. Chances are, however, the player was aiming a fixed hand at those chords—what I call a "cookie-cutter" hand.

It is the touch of an *active* pliant hand—with "springs" deep inside its palm—that rings the strings clear as a bell, and produces the grand sound we expect of a piano.

To assure this quick flex inside the hand at the instant it touches the keys, we must (1) remain supple at the wrist, and (2) sense everything we play, from chords to single

tones, as "springing" from deep inside our palms. This spring of the hand's action lies in its "hinges," the small muscles underneath the hand knuckles. The need for minute, almost instantaneous action of the hinge is what kept your patient childhood teacher telling you to "raise your arch" and "curve your fingers" (they jiggle more easily when hanging freely from the hand knuckle).

To locate and feel the action of your hand hinge, place both hands flat down on a tabletop. Then flex your palms without moving your flattened fingers, mentally saying "open," then "close," as if an overturned turtle was lying there, gasping for air. But *your* "turtle" is right side up, ready to crawl. Slowly *draw* your fingertips toward the centers of your palms, letting your flattened fingers skid across the surface. Keep skidding until your hand-knuckle rises high enough to show "snow on the mountains"—the

# "We have all heard chords crashed or thumped from the keys with what the pianist *thought* to be an impressive sound."

cartilage of those knuckles showing white under the skin.

This daily exercise will give your hands a more lasting flexibility:

And the next exercise serves the same purpose for smaller hands:

For more advanced players, you can preserve flexibility during wider expansions of the hand with:

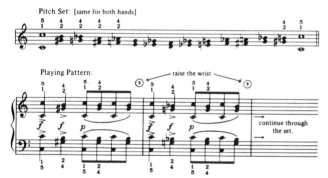

The alternation between the repeated, unchanging octave, with slowly shifting inner notes (the "windshield wiper") effectively massages the hand free of its tension. BUT! Be SURE to lift the wrist high at the end of each measure, just before you drop into each stressed octave, so that the falling arm weight will naturally "dip" your wrist down-and-up, like a young girl's quick curtsy before the queen. The lift-off lets the wrist "breathe" before again "diving" into the keys.

Next, this exercise has your arms reaching from center to both ends of the keyboard. Let their weight, dropping into each octave, cause the wrist to dip-rise more noticeably, like two rubber shock absorbers.

Never think of hand- and finger-action apart from the arms and body. When the body is poised and ready, the shoulders, elbows, wrists, should *all* jiggle like a line of "shock absorbers" at the impact of fingers on the keybeds, or there will be no spring-rebound from that point. In fact, the whole body, sitting tall and poised, often comes into piano play. The impulse for the following FF chords comes from thighs and abdomen: it is similar to the feeling a good jockey gets as he urges his horse over a fence:

Chopin: *Prelude,* C minor, Opus 28, no. 20:

Bodily poise includes letting the arms hang loosely down from the shoulder. "Elbows like lead, wrist like feather," said the late Ludwig Deppe to his students. Tall, lanky pianists (apart from sitting far enough back to make their arms a gently slanting "bridge" to the keys) may just want to "open their wings"—a slight, outward elbow flexion at the thought of the sound.

While the power of these chords comes from weight and energy, their ringing tone quality depends upon the invisible spring action of the palm hinges *at the instant of contact with the keys.* Those "hand springs" are the last, the final tuning of multiple energies rolling down the arm.

Carl Philipp Emmanuel Bach reports that his father, Johann Sebastian, would place his hands ready on the keys, fingertips in a line:

"The impulse thus given the keys, or the quantity of pressure, must be maintained in equal strength, and that in such a manner that the finger be not raised perpendicularly from the key, but that it glide off the forepart of the key, by gradually drawing back the tip of the finger towards the palm of the hand."

Was Bach—nearly three hundred years ago—not inviting us to "palm springs"? ∎

**RD**

*Robert Dumm was named Dean of the Boston Conservatory when he was only twenty-five, and became a critic for* The Christian Science Monitor *a year later. He served fifteen years as head of graduate Piano Pedagogy at The Catholic University before retiring in 1979. In 1983, Mr. Dumm was awarded the highest certification—Master Teacher—by The Music Teachers National Association.*

# TECHNIQUE
## "Good Vibes"
### *Vibrato* Touch In Piano Playing

**"Picture yourself standing on the brink of a high, slanting cliff. Now drop a rock and watch it go bounding to the bottom. That's *vibrato!*"**

In his wise and pithy book, *Liberation and Deliberation in Piano Technique* (Schroeder & Gunther, 1941; reprint ed., 1982), Carl Roeder defines the *vibrato* touch as "the playing of two or more notes by a single impulse from the arm."

"This touch," he explains, "is used in wrist or arm work with fixed (set) fingers. The hand rebounds on a free but elastic wrist, the impetus coming from the forearm in short or light groups, and from the shoulders in extended or more vigorous passages."

What does this mean in plain terms? Take a basketball player. He is using *vibrato* when he "dribbles" the ball. Or, picture yourself standing on the brink of a high, slanting cliff; you drop a rock and watch it go bounding to the bottom. That is, again, *vibrato:* a single impulse producing numerous repercussions.

Nearly all *"finale chords"* call for the *vibrato* touch:

*Mozart, Piano Concerto in A Major, K 414*

Here, a single impulse of energy, quick as an electric shock, generates the hand reflex that plays the next chord. Even if, in a more forceful chord, you use the forearm instead of the hand, your impulse is *single,* not double—a sort of shudder.

Rapid two-note slurs are a good place to feel *vibrato* in your touch, such as here:

*Beethoven, Sonata in D minor, Op. 31 No. 2*

Chopin clearly shows us his own *slow* vibration of a repeated sound (an "after-touch"), by the stress, slurring, and fingering of the right hand here:

*Chopin, Prelude in B minor, Op. 28 No. 6*

Carefully play his stress, then lightly substitute the fourth for the fifth finger. You will then draw the fourth over and just behind the receding fifth, sealing the sound in its own faint vibration.

By definition, *vibrato* is usually found at a faster tempo, as in this other Chopin *Prélude* (Opus 28, no. 12, in G# Minor):

*Chopin, Prelude in G Sharp minor, Op. 28 No. 12*

Play this passage with *both* hands and mark the left-hand part. Drop the right hand freely onto each slur, then instantly "let go," resting on the keys. By first poising above and then dropping vertically into the *first* note of each slur, your hand weight, stopped by the keybed, jiggles just enough to "catch" the second note on its light rebound. Say the word "Ditto," and you've got it; it feels like a shudder down your spine.

As you experiment, direct your thought to the nub of the key action, the escapement point, which occurs partly down into the key descent. I call it the "tone-spot," and you will sense it as a slight resistance to your touch. It is precisely at this tone-spot that *vibrato* touch conveys energy to the hammer.

Another good way to develop your *vibrato* touch is to play accented patterns *in octaves*. Since when the hand is opened wide for an octave, *nothing but* the wrist can move, the patterns must be formed from wrist vibrations tiny as electrons:

*Mozart, Sonata in A Major, K 331 (Theme put into octaves.)*

Now that your hand — a large member — is vibrating freely, its tremors will carry into your finger action. Try this exercise, the light right-hand finger sequence of 4,3,2,1, against octaves in the left.

*Dumm Exercise*

At the downbeat, drop *both* hands, but *favor the left mf* (as compared to *p* in the right). This will shunt weight *away from* the vibrating hand (I call it the "lightning-rod" effect), leaving the right to shiver out its spate of notes. Repeat this spattering figure down each step of the C Major scale. Then reverse roles for "spatter-fingers" in the left hand. Remember, let gravity do the work. The smaller our movements, the better our technique. ■

*Robert Dumm was named Dean of the Boston Conservatory when he was only twenty-five, and became a critic for* The Christian Science Monitor *a year later. He served fifteen years as head of graduate Piano Pedagogy at The Catholic University before retiring in 1979. Mr. Dumm is active as a teacher, contest judge and writer on musical subjects.*

**RD**

# Finger Painting
## *How To Bring More Color To Your Playing*

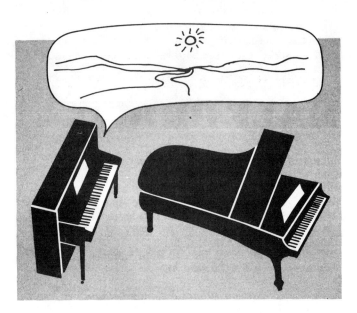

"Every pianist has a palette of touches, like the brush strokes of a good painter."

The brush stroke of a good painter is swift and sure. As you watch him work, this dot, that line, that smudge of color first hints at, then gradually clarifies, the whole picture — the big, detailed vision the artist has been holding before his "mind's eye."

A good pianist is guided in the same way by the "mind's ear." Experience and emotion both add "colors" to plain pitches. Personal chemistry continually produces new mixes of those colors, and drives the pianist to seek technical gestures that can "paint" them into the piano. His palette of touches often allows his playing, even on records, to be uniquely identified.

### Preparing to Paint

In order to shape the quality of sound we produce, we must become conscious of the exact spot where the piano tone is produced. That point in the key action lies nearly halfway into its descent. Officially, it's called the *escapement* (after the little jack that "kicks" the hammer inside). I call it the *tone-spot*. You can find it quickly on a grand piano. Just press one key down slowly till you meet a slight resistance midway. Think of your finger as actually touching the hammer there, and "pop" it toward the string.

That small nudge conveys immediate energy to (A), the leathered knuckle under the long end of the hammer shank. Increasing finger pressure causes the jack underneath that knuckle to send the hammer the rest of its way up toward the string. The action is like bunting a baseball from the bat.

So immediate is this energy contact, that *the speed and timing of the hammer blow matter much more than force.* A hammer popped quickly produces a louder, brighter sound, while a more deliberate pressure at the tone-spot gives a mellow, large, carrying sound. The tone-spot is the pianist's "bow," and the hammer is his "arrow."

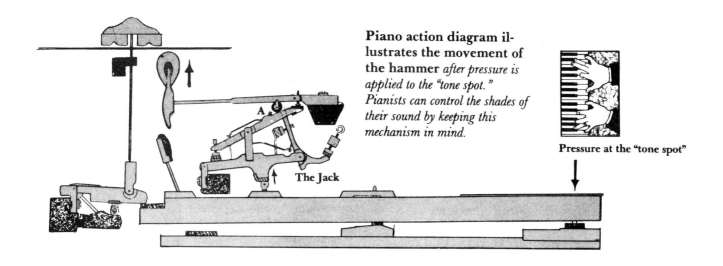

Piano action diagram illustrates the movement of the hammer *after pressure is applied to the "tone spot." Pianists can control the shades of their sound by keeping this mechanism in mind.*

The Jack

Pressure at the "tone spot"

---

# "*Legato* is an illusion, but it's the trademark of a pianist's success."

### Legato Touch: Sound Melting into Sound

Let's begin our survey of "brush strokes" with *legato*, a smooth connection of tones. Though *legato* is an illusion, made possible by cleverly minimizing hammer strokes in favor of string sounds, it is both the Holy Grail and trademark of a pianist's success. In Paris (1978) I questioned Lionel de Pachmann about how his legendary father, Vladimir (1848-1933), had gotten his marvelous melting of tones that still sings under the sizzle of historical recordings. In answer, Lionel sat down, at age ninety-two, and playd this exerpt from Chopin's *Nocturne,* in E Flat, op. 9 no. 2:

Chopin, *Nocturne* in E♭ Op. 9 no. 2

There it was, the famous melting merger of tones *"sans marteaux"* (without hammers)! He held the keys deep, and repeated or connected without letting them up. There was some changing of fingers for repetitions. There was certainly a *full* tone for each note, and a sense that it grew from, and replaced the previous one. (Note his dynamics!)

Part of the illusion consists of that full, warm tone that overlays (and disguises) the initial hammer-blow of the next tone. And part lies in riding the key low in the saddle, so that no hammer has far to travel toward its strings. Try this exercise with a light surge toward the *second* note of each two-note slur; minute

dynamic gradients allow the ear to "seal" the gaps from note to note.

To sustain the illusion, one must also watch tapering intensities, especially the marked decay of a *long* tone. Match the hammer-blow of the new tone with what is left of the long one:

Schubert, *Sonata* Op. 120

In the example below, the high register demands extra intensities to maintain any sense of line:

Beethoven, *Sonata* Op. 13

Since touch, like taste and sight, can be stimulated by its opposite, light, *staccato* taps will seem like a "smoothing" of your brush before its next lush stroke.

## Staccato

Return now to the "tone-spot"—the pressure point where a minute impulse of the finger tip "pops" the hammer to the string. Though the hammer rebounds immediately from its blow onto the string (which allows you to repeat that tone without raising the key), the depressed key still holds up the damper (or the sound could not continue).

To cut off the sound, you need only raise the key from the tone-spot up to the point where the sinking damper snuffs the vibrating strings. This is an *infinitesimal* rise of the key. This basic *staccato,* in which you consciously decide where the sound stops, I call a "contact staccato." It is what you will see Ashkenazy, Brendel, Horowitz and others doing on TV.
As with *legato* touch, minimizing energy and movement at the tone-spot will consciously refine the point where you cut off the sound and let in the silence. Try allowing one part sound to one part silence, like this:

at (A), "pop" the key right *at* the tone-spot;

at (B), *let* the key rebound naturally, but *only* to the point where the damper snuffs the sound.

Incidentally, did you notice that the damper did not stop the string sound immediately but by gradually "shading" its vibrations? Each alteration of the vibratory pattern will change its tone color and awaken some harmonics of the string. This is a rich color resource for slow fadeouts.

The following chart will help you to place some common touches on a legato-staccato continuum.

Remember, you are a picture painter, not a house painter. You do not "apply" a touch to a piece, like whitewash. You must first *imagine* a color-organ of sounds—each note pulsing in vivid, changing colors. Then, you *play* them.

Simply combining these basic touches produces an endless variety of color, and of changing intensities. An artist's best practice is largely absorbed in the discovery and projection of such color mixes.

*Robert Dumm was named Dean of the Boston Conservatory when he was only twenty-five, and became a critic for* The Christian Science Monitor *a year later. He served fifteen years as head of graduate Piano Pedagogy at The Catholic University before retiring in 1979. Mr. Dumm is active as a teacher, contest judge and writer on musical subjects.*

# CHART OF PIANO

Extra holding "melts" one tone into another:

Mozart, *Fantasy* in D minor K.397

By not lifting each tone, Brahms arrives at a total "overlap":

Brahms, *Intermezzo* in B minor, Op. 119 no. 1

### Normal Legato

Legato uses a warm tone to conceal the hammer blow of the tone which follows.

### Slurred Legato

One tone is stressed, the other is noticeably lighter.

Schubert, *Moment Musicale* in A Flat Op. 96 no. 6

In a rapid tempo the stress stands out.

Beethoven, *Sonata* Op. 13 (Pathétique)

# TOUCHES

## Non Legato (Only Slightly Disconnected)

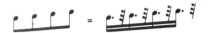

Bach, *Menuet* from French Suite III

## Portato (Similar To Portamento For The Voice)

Drop-hand, and "hang loose," balancing on the "tone-spot"

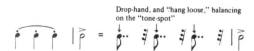

The hand weight is "dragged" from note to note; the sound leans toward *legato,* but with a heavier, expressive touch.

Grieg, *Arietta* Op. 12 no. 1

## Staccato-Tenuto (Long Staccato)

The sound lingers past the midbeat, and is played without hand weight.

Chopin's bass staccato dots (as below) often mean this touch, without an accent.

Chopin, *Nocturne* in G minor Op. 15 no. 3

## Normal Staccato

Mozart uses notation to convey normal staccato in the example below.

Mozart, *Concerto* in C Major K.467

## Short Staccato

Beethoven, *Sonata* in F minor Op. 2 no. 1

## Staccatissimo (The Shortest Staccato; Often Louder)

The shorter the sound, the brighter the "pop" of the hammer. Debussy's "quasi guitarra" draws on a whole rainbow of plucked sounds.

Debussy, *La sérénade interrompue* from Preludes, book I

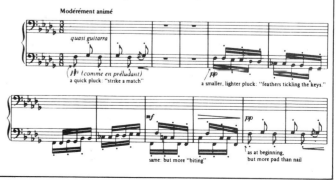

**RD**

303

# TECHNIQUE

# Finger Painting

"Squeeze the juice from every key. Then try the 'Pelican Plunge.'"

*Part II*

Last issue, we looked at a variety of piano "touches" that create contrasting colors. Before moving on to a new subject, I'd like to share some of the images I use to help animate the hand as it "paints" those tonal shades and landscapes.

### On The Legato Side

For warm, legato sounds, "squeeze the juice from every key"; or "press your fingerprint" onto the ivory.

For an active hand-shaping of a small group of notes, "lean into the wind as you go."

Mozart, *Fantasy* K.475

*Focusing A Tone*

The ear can be drawn to a single sounding tone by elimination. A full, pedaled sonority is "sheered away" by levels of pedal and hand weight until only one tone still sounds, which seems to crescendo.

Chopin, *First Ballade*

*Put An Ear-Ring Into Your Ornament*

Bring out the sound of the main note (the starting note) of a trill, or turn, or mordent. It's the continuing vibration of the initial tone that "ornaments" or adds luster to the melody.

*Glistening Glissandos*

Begin your glissando rather slowly, then *trail* your arm weight in a single sweeping stroke as you speed up.

Debussy, *Prelude* from *Pour le Piano*

## On The Staccato Side

"Salt and pepper" or "perforated line" staccato is achieved through legato fingering, lightly "flicked" to the tone-spot.

Bach, *Two Part Invention No. 13*

"Needlepoint" staccato "pricks" the "skin" of the keys, swiftly, like the prick of a doctor's blood test.

Kabalevsky, *A Little Joke*

"The Pelican Plunge" touch, for concerto chords, produces those short but dramatically loud chords that end big pieces and leave the hall ringing. Bring the whole arm and upper body into the tone, just as a pelican swoops to pluck a fish from the water without interrupting the dip-rise of its full flight.

Beethoven, *"Waldstein" Sonata*

Equally suggestive as images are those of other instruments of the orchestra. I was able to convert some pianistic chatter the other day with this orchestral scenario:

**RD**

*Robert Dumm was named Dean of the Boston Conservatory when he was only twenty-five, and became a critic for* The Christian Science Monitor *a year later. He served fifteen years as head of graduate Piano Pedagogy at The Catholic University before retiring in 1979. Mr. Dumm is active as a teacher, contest judge and writer on musical subjects.*

# TECHNIQUE
# A Sight-Reading
# Workshop
## *Part I*

## "The three guardian monkeys–see no evil, hear no evil, and speak no evil–remind us of the three elements of good sight-reading."

Almost everyone is familiar with the three guardian monkeys—see no evil, hear no evil, and speak no evil. They remind me of the three elements of good sight-reading, which combine sight, hearing, and touch. If you don't want to just monkey around at the keyboard, keep in mind that a good sight-reader is guided by what he or she *sees* (on the printed page), *hears* (either before, or after a note is struck), and *feels* (on the keyboard).

Hearing is important; ideally, your inner hearing guides your hand and fingers, keeping them on track. However, the average pianist will perform a little trial and error before finding the right notes; this is often true even for a familiar piece. Take, for example, the melody of *Beautiful Dreamer:*

When you arrive at the * and play a C or an E instead of the correct note, something tells you it's not right. You may try again, and play a B natural or E flat. You flush a little, try them all until the right note is sounded, and by this time you've lost your place on the page!

How can this be avoided? Music reading requires the harmonious cooperation of all three elements: you see, you touch, and you hear together. This cooperation can be strengthened through practice, so that you will see and hear recurrent patterns, and your touch will become in turn more accurate.

### Touch

Chances are, your sense of touch is weaker than your sense of sight. "Reading" the keyboard is similar to reading Braille, the sequence of tiny bumps that spells letters and words for blind people. A good sight-reader feels his way through a piece, not note-for-note, but handful-by-handful.

# "You flush a little, try again, and by this time you've lost your place on the page!"

Many adults have a quick comprehension of the printed page—of what it "signals"—but are helpless with the keys. They endure considerable frustration in trying to find a key to press for *each* individual signal. The eyes do a jiggle from page to hand, and rhythm, musical shape, and continuity disappear in the hunting and hesitation. They are spelling their musical "words" letter by letter!

So we must begin improvement with *keyboard feel.* The answer is scales! Behind every melody or chord there lives a scale, and the *feel* of that scale is your tactile "slide-rule" for measuring the correct movements of your fingers.

First, feel the major scales in five-finger "slices" up and down the keyboard:

Then, derive the major chords (triads) by first playing the five-note scale, and leaving out the passing notes between chord tones:

Work through the same patterns in all keys, in this order: C, G, F, D, A, E, B, D-Flat, A-Flat, E-Flat, B-Flat and finally G-Flat. Try to find the notes of each scale by "ear" first; if that doesn't work, you can then fall back on this formula:

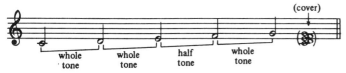

Be patient with yourself. In most everyday activities, whether you are handing someone a pencil or turning a page, your four fingers work *against* your thumb. Scales, on the other hand, ask you to open the hand partly, then keep it half-open while each finger in turn lightly squeezes down its key, then lets go. You may feel a little "thick" at first, simply because you are getting brain signals through to unexplored places!

The next step in familiarizing yourself with the feel of keyboard patterns is to play other types of scales and intervals.

Next time, we'll continue our survey of scale-type figures, and discover how they can lead us into an awareness of chord inversions. Then, we'll move on to reading the map of "musical constellations" found on the pages of our printed materials.

**R D**

*Robert Dumm was named Dean of the Boston Conservatory when he was only twenty-five, and became a critic for* The Christian Science Monitor *a year later. He served fifteen years as head of graduate Piano Pedagogy at The Catholic University before retiring in 1979. In 1983, Mr. Dumm was awarded the highest certification—Master Teacher—by The Music Teachers National Association.*

# TECHNIQUE
# A Sight-Reading
# Workshop
## *Part II*

RACHEL GORDON

---

"One important aspect of good sight-reading is an infallible sense of 'touch.' Here are helpful exercises to develop that sense. No peeking!"

---

Let's continue to develop the sense of "touch" necessary for good sight-reading, with some of Hanon's five-finger exercises. Hanon, whom one of my old teachers, Maurice Dumesnil, remembered at the Paris Conservatoire as the bent and wizened gnome of *La Mecanique*, invented the "escalator clause" in music. His five-finger scales "leave out a note, but *not* a finger," which allows the action of the fingers, moving in sequence, to slowly spiral the hand forward on the keys.

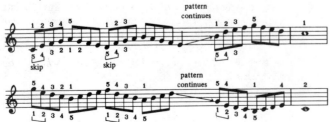

One octave is enough, then turn back, working that octave toward the starting point. As soon as you can, play this with eyes shut — no peeking — which, especially in scales with black keys, will improve your touch to the point that you will have "eyes in your fingers."

Next, try what I call "Hanon On Wheels," in triplets. They keep your wrist flexing ("breathing"), as you play.

Hanon's exercises can be helpful in getting the feel of triad inversions, which account for more keyboard chords than the root position triads we built last time. When you structure Hanon No. 1 by accenting fingers 1, 2, and 5 in the right hand, you have the first inversion of an A minor chord.

Notice how often first-inversion chords appear in pieces and arrangements you play:

You can tell them by their "gap" — the wider spacing (of a fourth) between the upper two tones:

The upper note of that "gap" is the root, or *name* of the chord. "Meet me at the top of the gap," I say to my students, recalling to them the *spelling* of the chord they are seeking.

Second inversion chords have their "gap" between the *lower* two notes:

Here is a way to work all triads, in all three positions, into your hands. This will "program" a large part of piano music into your "memory bank":

Be patient with yourself. Work slowly, making good tones, and try each of these studies with just one hand first, then with both, moving in *parallel* and *contrary* patterns.

**Seeing**

Now that we have worked through several exercises to teach your fingertips to feel, and your hand to cover standard shapes and anticipate changing forms, let's begin to examine how printed notes signal your movement on the keyboard.

# "This is a way to 'program' a large part of piano music into your memory bank!"

Each C on the keyboard begins and *names* an octave. Here are those names:

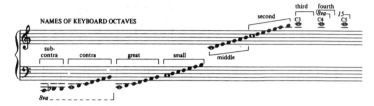

Since the "Grand Staff" roughly corresponds to the full piano keyboard, you should become familiar with *any* location it charts. Look out for those *Ottava* and *Ottava bassa* signs ("Play one octave up," or "Play one octave down"), with their light dotted lines, which are hard to see. You should also be aware of the little word *"loco"* which appears after one of these signs; it means return "in place" to play the notes *as shown*.

Next time, we'll explore "star maps" of the musical galaxy; lines and spaces in musical phrases; and "anchor tones," which cue your fingers to the position of the next note! ∎

**RD**

*Robert Dumm was named Dean of the Boston Conservatory when he was only twenty-five, and became a critic for* The Christian Science Monitor *a year later. He served fifteen years as head of graduate Piano Pedagogy at The Catholic University before retiring in 1979. In 1983, Mr. Dumm was awarded the highest certification—Master Teacher—by The Music Teachers National Association.*

# TECHNIQUE
# A Sight-Reading
# Workshop
## Part III

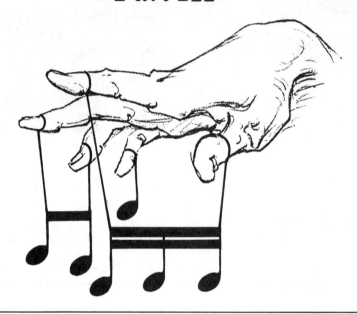

## "Here's a way to combine the *sight* aspect of reading with the *feel* of the notes beneath your fingers."

In our last installment we looked at a chart of the full keyboard and named each of the octaves it covers. The "Grand Staff" corresponds roughly to the range of most piano music, so it is important to become at ease with any location on it. I give my students this "Star Map" of the musical galaxy, and ask them to practice reading and playing notes in its various regions.

Practice writing down and playing in random order little "star treks" out and back from the landmark notes in the example above.

Such experiments help you to read steps and skips of a single, horizontal melody line accurately. Pianists,

however, are two-handed players, and we'll want to practice reading and feeling all intervals which lie under the five-finger position. We can group intervals on the staff as "likes" (line-to-line) or "unlikes (line-to-space).

The feeling aspect of this exercise is most important. It is a good idea to play through little progressions such as the following one, without ever breaking touch with the keys. Hold the common-tones, which I call "anchors," even if you must substitute another finger to hold a note as you move your hand into position for the next interval.

Mistakes are due either to mis-readings (something not seen or forgotten — such as a key signature), or to *mis-feelings*. In order to cultivate the ability to feel your way around the keyboard, it is necessary to "program" each key securely into your fingers. The note groupings and hand shapes in a piece will likely reflect the scales and chords of the key it is in.

In F Major, for instance, there is a B Flat in the signature. B Natural does not exist in that scale. So you'll want to "program" the B Flat into your playing mechanism before approaching a piece in F. Work the scale through by slices, in five-finger positions.

KEEP YOUR EYES CLOSED if you can. Now you have experienced most of the "handfuls" a composer will present to you in a piece in F Major. The piece will be yet another "program" of patterns placed on top of these basic scale-chord patterns.

The next step is to work on chord inversions. (You will meet them more often than chords in root-position!) Again, develop a sense of touch, using the following "feelies."

Now you are ready for a practical application of the points we've been discussing. Work through the G Major chords of Purcell's little *Prelude* before you "sight-read" it like a pro.

Last time we worked on spotting the "gap" in each chord. Here, you have begun to combine this *sight* aspect of reading with the *feel* of the notes beneath your fingers!

Next time, we'll look at *accidentals,* and alert you to some troublesome obstructions to good sight-reading. ■

**RD**

# TECHNIQUE
# A Sight-Reading
# Workshop
## *Part IV*

RACHEL GORDON

## "Keep these elements in mind and you won't be afraid to face the notes on a new page of music."

In this conclusion to our sight-reading series, we will look at various pitfalls that should be kept in mind when reading a piece.

**"Accidentals"** are the sharps (♯), flats (♭), and natural signs (♮) which alter any regular scale tone, however briefly. Sharps "push" a note to the right; finding a flat beside a note signals a move to the left. In a way, these signs function as turning lights on the musical roadway. Everybody knows they remain in force for only the bar in which they appear and are then cancelled by the barline, but hardly anyone remembers this in sight-reading.

For example, in Bach's "Little Prelude" No.1 in C Major first sharps appear in the left hand, then flats in the right hand of the next measure. (See example 1.)

(See example 1.)

"Pulls" toward F major

**Example 1**

"Leans" toward A minor

These alterations — I call them "Promissory Notes" — forecast a new scale or key to come, and may or may not be "paid." They inject variety and expectation. (If you notice the *same* sharp or flat inserted again and again, a new key is being asserted by the composer.)

In order to play these correctly, try to analyze and keep in mind what is taking place in terms of possible key changes. In the Bach example above, the sharped notes direct the music toward A minor; the flatted notes create a pull toward F Major. Making sense of those accidentals make then easier to read.

Here are some other obstructions to good sight reading.

**Repeated Notes:** Busy eyes are likely to see them as moving up or down instead of staying in one place. You can mark them with a straight arrow as a reminder.

**Tied Notes:** That second black note-head is very likely to signal your muscle to twitch and play the same note again. A good cure is to *lightly* press the held key at the new beat.

**Breaks:** At the end of lines, look ahead to "cue" the next notes in the continuation of the music.

**Skips:** "Choreograph" your hand movements in relation to each other (with black-key groups as sensors).

**"Road Closed" Signs:** Watch for these nearly always tiny warnings of immediate key changes, signaled by miniature key signatures often hidden at the ends of lines.

**Register Changes:** *Ottava, Ottava bassa, 8va, col 8,* indicate changes of register; the word *loco* restores play to the notes as printed.

You will go a long way toward removing these pitfalls to accurate reading by:

1) Surveying The Scene (before you play), especially the key signature — the most overlooked of all signals!

2) "Pawing Out" The Music, that is, laying it out and experiencing it by handfuls. This has a lot to do with finding the fingering natural to your hands. Try to feel the "handfuls" in the music — the way your hands naturally fall over the keys — so that you will come to form automatically the physical posture needed for smooth playing. (See example 2.)

3) Playing Freely, with the confidence allowed by "feeling ahead."

4) Listening To Yourself. Taste each note-group as a "tune," and savor the continuing sound of each chord.

5) Above all, Taking Your Time. Probe with your fingers, approving each probe with your ear.

Keep these elements in mind, and you won't ever again be afraid to face the notes on a new page of music. Sight-reading can be fun, and these few steps should help to smooth the way to many rewarding moments at your piano. Happy sight-reading! ■

**RD**

*Robert Dumm was named Dean of the Boston Conservatory when he was only twenty-five, and became a critic for* The Christian Science Monitor *a year later. He served fifteen years as head of graduate Piano Pedagogy at The Catholic University before retiring in 1979. In 1983, Mr. Dumm was awarded the highest certification—Master Teacher—by The Music Teachers National Association.*

## Example 2

1. Play "handful"    2. "Squash" it gently

# ETUDES

*Etudes is a department which features technical exercises composed by masters throughout history.*

*Johann Friedrich Burgmuller lived from 1806 to 1874. After settling in Paris, he adopted a light style which satisfied the Parisian public, and garnered him a considerable reputation in the world of salon music. His several albums of piano studies have become standard works.*

*The etude below focuses on playing repeating notes with alternating fingers. It is a good idea to play slowly at first; the hand should be relaxed at all times, so that the fingers may exchange places without stress or strain. Make sure your shoulders are uninvolved in this process. Try to achieve an eveness of tone.*

## CHATTERBOX

JOHANN FRIEDRICH BURGMÜLLER

# ETUDES

*Etudes is a department which features technical exercises composed by masters throughout history.*

Clara Schumann (wife of composer Robert) was considered one of the greatest pianists of her day. At the age of eight she was playing Mozart concertos, and later championed the music of Beethoven and Brahms, shocking the public by playing their works from memory! George Bernard Shaw called her a ''nobly beautiful and poetic player.'' ''An artist of that sort,'' he wrote, ''is the Grail of the critic's quest.''

Clara's early training was with her father, Friedrich Wieck. She and her sister, Marie, were drilled with Wieck's studies, two of which are shown below. They are to be played with "the utmost tranquillity and softness of touch, but must continue to be so played until extreme velocity is attained," according to Marie.

Both of these etudes involve tricky finger changes. We found them to be challenging, but fun. ■

# TWO ETUDES

FRIEDRICH WIECK
(1785-1873)

*Etudes is a department which features technical exercises composed by masters throughout history.*

# ETUDES

Carl Czerny, the Austrian pianist, composer, and pedagogue, is famous for his technique studies. The two studies below may be used in conjunction with Robert Dumm's advice on bringing out "bell tones."

# Rhythm

# pop piano

## Pop Rhythms Unravelled!

Pop rhythms are easy enough to remember and perform once you have the sound in your ears. But often the sheet music for these bouncy syncopations look impossibly complicated, like a roadmap to somewhere you don't want to visit. So, here is a three-step procedure for figuring out how to play what's on the page, without coming down with a migraine headache.

1) *Look for the shortest note value in the melody, and think of the whole phrase in terms of that note value.* For example, in a tune like Burt Bacharach's *Always Something There To Remind Me*, there are many phrases that mix eighth notes with quarter notes — sometimes in offbeat combinations:

It becomes easier to count out the rhythms of these phrases by seeing the dotted quarter notes as a quarter tied to an eighth, and by converting the quarter notes which appear on the second half of a beat into two tied eighth notes. In other words, we can see these phrases as being based on an eighth note count:

2) Now that everything is clearly based on the shortest note value we have to count, the next step is to *remove the ties*. Now the rhythms aren't complicated at all! You can practice all of this at a slow tempo, to help make things crystal clear.

3) After practicing the phrases without any ties, look at the tied version once more. Play the phrases with an accent on the first note of each tied group, and hum the second tied note instead of playing it.

After you've run through this routine, you can bring the whole thing up to tempo. Voila! That back roads map has gotten you to the right place after all.

♩ SI

# Rhythm Workshop

## Why 3/4 isn't 6/8

In one of the showstoppers in Leonard Bernstein's *West Side Story*, the girls sing and dance a scintillating number called "America" ("I want to be in A-mer-i-ca. . ."). The driving rhythm of the piece is generated by the subtle difference between constantly alternating bars of 6/8 and 3/4:

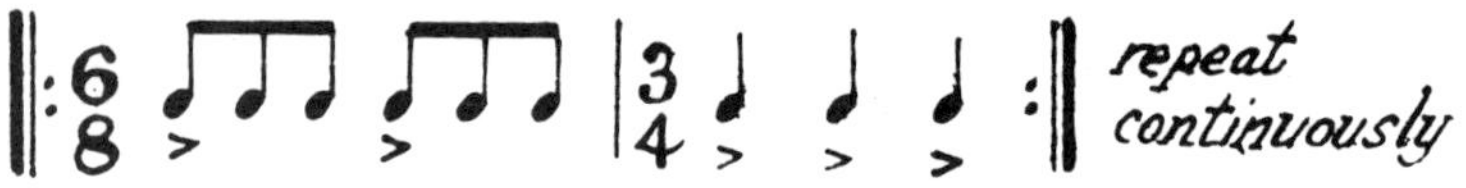

But, considering that both meters contain six 8th-notes, or their equivalent, in every bar. . .

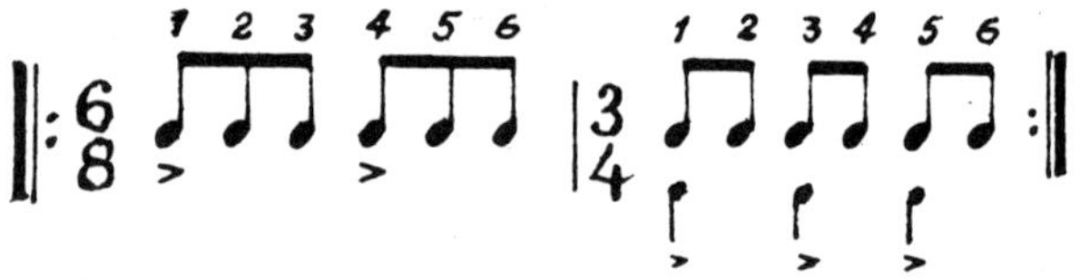

. . .what is the real difference between the two?

The answer lies in the *fundamental pulse pattern* of each meter: that is, in their basic beat, and the way the 8th-notes are grouped.

3/4 is a *three*-beat meter; 6/8 is a *two*-beat meter. This essential difference is clear if we set down, one under the other, the *grouping* of the six 8th-notes in each meter:

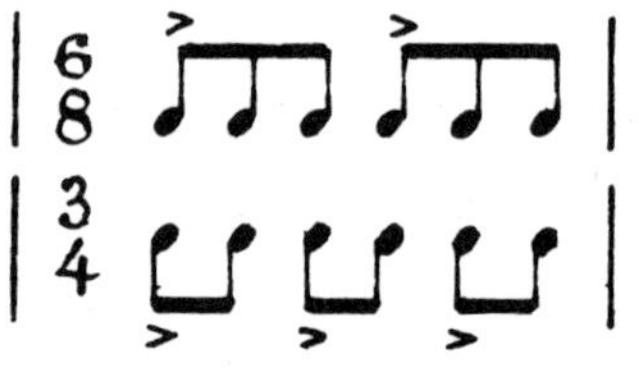

Note that the 8ths in 6/8 are written and felt in *three's*. . .

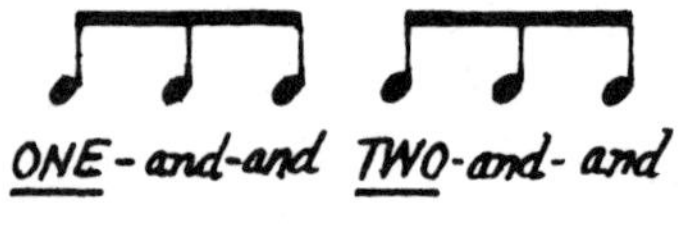

ONE-and-and TWO-and-and

. . .but the 8ths in 3/4 are written and felt in *two's*:

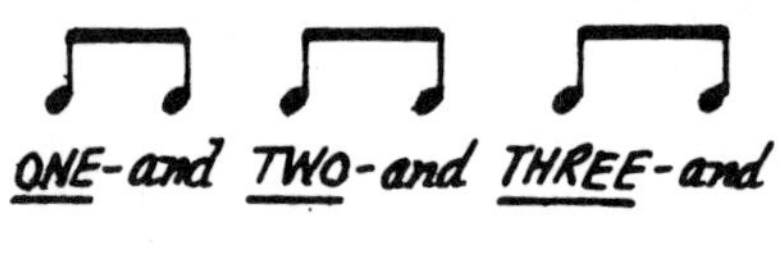

ONE-and TWO-and THREE-and

This difference between a pulse in *two* and a pulse in *three* becomes even clearer when we move from 8th-notes to the next higher note value in each meter. In 6/8, the next higher note value is a *dotted quarter note;* in 314, the next higher note value is a *quarter* note:

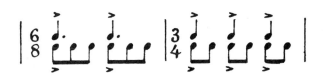

Therefore, when Bernstein alternated between 6/8 and 3/4, he was delivering to the listener's ear a persistent shift of beat emphasis, like this:

*ONE*-and-and *TWO*-and-and    *ONE*-and *TWO*-and *THREE*-and    (*repeat*)

You will sense the difference immediately if you read this line aloud, exaggerating each capitalized word, while holding on to an absolutely steady pulse. If necessary, regulate the pulse by speaking the line in exact time with a metronome — one word for each metronome tick, with no speeding up or slowing down:

| *tick* | *tick* | *tick* | *tick* | *tick* | *tick* | | *tick* | *tick* | *tick* | *tick* | *tick* | *tick* | |
|--------|--------|--------|--------|--------|--------|---|--------|--------|--------|--------|--------|--------|---|
| *ONE* - | and | - and | *TWO* - | and | - and | | *ONE* - | and | *TWO* - | and | *THREE* - | and | (*repeat*) |

The adventurous reader can take this exercise a step further by practicing the following pattern that involves foot-tapping, finger-tapping, and voice. Go slowly at first, keeping the basic foot taps absolutely steady and regular. Help yourself with a metronome, then work toward doing it all on your own. And don't give up!

RH ♩

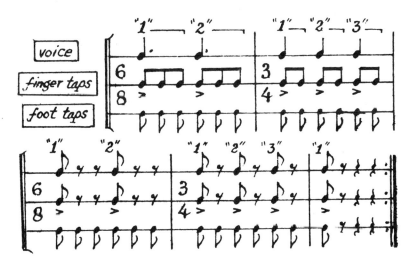

# Rhythm Workshop

## The Songwriter's Guide to Rhythmic Notation Part 1

### Why bother about rhythmic notation?

Countless rehearsals and recording sessions have ground to a dead stop because the composer or arranger did not bother to give the player the best possible notation of this or that rhythm pattern. What happens? The player reads the part, plays it wrong, stops the rehearsal, scratches his head, talks to the leader, questions the composer/arrangers, gets things straight, pencils in the correction . . . and *then* resumes the session.

Not many sessions escape this typical scene, even among professionals who ought to know better. But among amateur songwriters, arrangers, copyists, and players, this stop-start scenario is played out again and again, until the rehearsal amounts to little more than an expensive, time-consuming, exhausting, and unproductive editing-and-correction session.

This recurrent problem is completely avoidable if someone (you? your arranger? a copyist?) pays scrupulous attention to the way each rhythm pattern is communicated to the player on the written page. This is not a hit-or-miss operation: good rhythmic notation follows exact guidelines.

### A basic principle of good notation

For accurate performance, write each rhythm pattern so that *its beat structure within the meter* is instantly clear. This means that the *visual* appearance of the notated rhythm should neither hide nor confuse the basic structure of the meter of your music.

### Meter and time signature

*Meter* is the way beats are grouped to form a measure. We speak of a "2-beat" meter, a "3-beat" meter, a "5-beat" meter, and so on.

A *time signature* is a number formula that describes a particular kind of beat grouping. Thus a "2-beat" meter may be numerically described by the formula "2/2" or "2/8"; a "5-beat" meter, by "5/4" or "5/16," and so on:

### Metric structure: "primary" and "secondary" accents

Every meter has its own basic structure, built on two elements.

Its first element is the *primary accent*, or "downbeat": that is, the initial beat ("ONE") of the measure.

Its second element is the *secondary accent* within the measure. Whereas *all* downbeats are in the same place, regardless of which meter you are working with, the placement of the secondary accent *varies according to each different meter.*

## The secondary accent in a balanced meter

"A "balanced" meter is any beat grouping with an *even* number of beats per measure (2, 4, 6, 8, 10, 12, etc.). Thus, such meters as *2/8, 4/4, 4/2, 6/8, 8/8, 10/16, 12/8*, etc., are all balanced beat groupings. In other words, they are divisible into two equal halves.

Whereas the primary accent kicks off the first half of a balanced measure, the secondary accent begins the second half:

## The secondary accent in an unbalanced meter

An "unbalanced" meter is any beat grouping with an *uneven* number of beats per measure (3, 5, 7, 9, 11, etc.). Thus, such meters as *3/4, 5/8, 7/16, 9/2, 11/4*, etc., are all *un*balanced beat groupings. In other words, they are divisible only into *un*equal parts. Moreover, the unequal parts will vary according to the composer's whim, based on the pulsation of the music.

A very common example of variety within an unbalanced measure is the following setup of a 5/8 measure: In (a), the five beats are divided 3 + 2; in (b), 2 + 3; in (c), 4 + 1:

In even larger beat groupings — such as 7/8, below — there is still greater variety in placing the secondary accents:

[2 + 2 + 3]      [2 + 3 + 2]      [3 + 2 + 2]      [3 + 3 + 1]

But keep in mind that these metric divisions are not arrived at mechanically, as a mathematical exercise! These are rhythmic pulsations, notated to match the flow of the music. Some of the most effective applications of unbalanced meters, with their varying secondary accents, are found in **Dave Brubeck's** album, *Take Five* — a classic, pioneering adventure in jazz experimentation that breaks away from the traditional 4/4 format.

## Exceptional secondary accents in a balanced meter

Although a balanced meter, such as 8/8, traditionally builds each measure in equal halves (4 + 4), it is possible to deliberately *un*balance the even number of beats if the music stresses an irregular pulsation:

[3 + 3 + 2]      [2 + 3 + 3]

The 3 + 3 + 2 construction of the 8/8 meter, by the way, is not confined to jazz experimentation, and is certainly not new in music literature. This subdivision lends enormous vitality and rhythmic excitement to any number of driving folk dances of Bulgaria, Rumania, and Hungary — an irregularity equally embraced by such "serious" composers as Béla Bartók and Zoltán Kodály.

## Summary of Part 1

The concepts of balanced and unbalanced meters, and of traditional and experimental divisions and subdivisions of beat groupings, are fundamental to our understanding of how rhythm patterns should be notated for clarity and ease of performance.

Everything we do in this mini-series, in future studies, will be based on the simple, basic principles we've covered in Part 1. In fact, your easy grasp of our later work will come out of these preliminary steps, and will be made that much easier if you take the time to review this introduction and relate these ideas to the music you read and play every day.

RH ♩

# Rhythm Workshop

# The Songwriter's Guide to Rhythmic Notation
# Part 2: Misadventures in 4/4

*This is the second article in a new mini-series concerned with accurate, professionally competent rhythmic notation. The first article appeared in the Feb. 83 issue.*

The first chapter of this Guide stated the single, fundamental rule of good rhythmic notation: that a rhythm pattern — no matter how simple or complicated — should be written *so that it clearly reflects the basic beat structure of the meter* of your piece of music.

If your music is in 4/4, for example, and you want to write a string of 8th notes to fill one bar, then the clearest notation of this pattern is either

Because 4/4 is a *balanced* meter — that is, because it can be divided into equal halves (2 + 2) — then its "secondary" accent falls on Beat 3:

(The "primary" accent of the bar is always on Beat 1, the downbeat; the "secondary" accent in a balanced meter is on the beat that begins the second half of the bar.)

Keeping that structure in mind — strong beat on 1, stress on 3 — you can see that *both* notations of the 8th-note pattern are good: notation A shows all four beats; notation B reflects the equal halves of the balanced meter (four 8ths + four 8ths).

By contrast, it is inaccurate and confusing to notate the same string of 8ths as

or, worse, as

In both examples, the beams (the broad connecting line) confuse the balanced beat structure by *hiding* the secondary accent (Beat 3) in odd places.

Following the same reasoning, the written pattern

also hides the secondary accent. Where is

Beat 3? Obviously *somewhere* near that central quarter note! Beside confusing the balanced beat structure of 4/4, that particular notation adds an extra complication by presenting the performer with two note groups that *look* like triplets but are not.

324

The clearest notation for that pattern avoids the "lost" Beat 3 simply by showing it:

The *sound* of the two notations is exactly the same . . . but the first will stop a rehearsal while the

player figures out what the composer *really* intended!

And how would like to meet *this* notation in the middle of a long rehearsal?. . .

. . .a classic example of the hidden (in fact, buried) secondary accent on Beat 3. Compared to either

or

— two solutions that sound exactly the same as the terror above — there is no question that now the composer is at least giving the player a fighting chance to play the part accurately. Both solutions

clearly reflect the balanced bar, and are therefore equally acceptable. The first good notation is very common; the second has the added advantage of showing Beat 2 (the tied quarter) as well as Beat 3.

An even fancier, and more frightening, pattern turns up again and again in beginners manuscripts, looking something like this:

This time we can find only the *downbeat!* Where is Beat 2? Beat 3? Beat 4? They are all there, of course, but totally confused by careless beaming.

Why suffer with it, when

(the identical sound) makes immediate sense?

If this concept is clear, try out your solutions to the following rhythm patterns. Our solutions will appear in the next installment of this series.

RH ♩

325

# Rhythm Workshop

## The Songwriter's Guide to Rhythmic Notation Part 3: Solutions

*This is the third article in our mini-series on professionally accurate and effective rhythmic notation. Earlier articles appeared in our Jan. and Feb. 83 issues.*

Last month's cliffhanger ended with three rhythm patterns that were deliberately misnotated to create reading confusion and — if they ever showed up in a rehearsal — a costly, time wasting interruption.

Problem 1, written this way . . .

. . . should be rewritten as:

The poor notation makes only one mistake, but a crucial one: The quarter rest, placed at the exact rhythmic center of the bar, completely hides the secondary accent of the 4/4 meter — that is, Beat 3 of the four-beat bar . . . the beat that begins the second half of this balanced meter.

*The solution is simply to break the quarter rest into* two 8th rests. This division immediately shows the player that the bar consists of two equal halves. (The dotted barline should not of course appear in your score. Its sole purpose here is to emphasize the rhythmic separation of the two halves of the bar.) The correct notation shows all four beats of this common pattern.

Problem 2 . . .

. . . can be solved several ways:

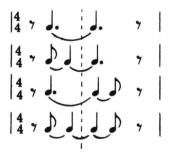

Although the four solutions use different note combinations, they have one feature in common: *Each one divides the dotted half note into tied notes* in order to reveal the hidden secondary accent (Beat 3).

Solution (a) is the simplest of the lot, slicing the dotted half note into two equal parts (two dotted quarters, tied). This creates a perfectly balanced visual picture of a bar divided into equal halves.

Solution (b) and (c) are alike in the way they break down half of the bar into still smaller parts. Solution (b) shows Beat *2*; Solution (c) shows Beat *4*.

Solution (d) has the advantage of revealing all four beats, but the disadvantage of cluttering the bar with an overload of notes and ties. Keep in mind that someone has to *read* your music, and that every added symbol (notes, rests, ties, and so on) means added reading time for the player. The best overall solution is invariably one that is both rhythmically clear and uncluttered.

Which one to choose? Solution (a) does the job efficiently, and is probably the best choice. But using the other solutions — all of them correct — is a matter of personal taste.

Problem 3, in this confusing notation. . .

... should be rewritten like this:

This time we are not concerned about a hidden secondary accent, since the equal division of the bar is entirely clear. The 8th-16th patterns occupy the first half of the bar, and the half note occupies the second half.

The confusion in this example centers around a hidden Beat *2*, caused by faulty beaming. At first glance, the incorrect notation *seems* to be reasonable because of the appearance of the familiar pattern

But this is deceptive *because the third note of the bar (the 8th) is actually part of Beat 1*. not Beat 2.

Compare the two notations to see how the beam correction immediately tells the player how the notes are grouped into beats. Once the beaming of Beat 1 is corrected, the notes belonging to Beat 2 can now be beamed together (eliminating that "leftover" 8th note just before the half note).

Why the concern for clear secondary accents and accurate beaming? Simply because the composer or arranger must take the time and trouble to give the player the best possible notation of every rhythm pattern in the score. Ignore this and you unnecessarily complicate a rehearsal, a reading, or a performance that should be devoted to making music, and *not* to decoding your rhythm patterns.

RH

# Rhythm Workshop

## The Songwriter's Guide to Rhythmic Notation
## Part 4:
## Silence in a Balanced Bar

Beginning songwriters tend to cram each bar full of notes, either in the voice part or in the piano accompaniment. If your next piece looks like this. . .

$$\frac{4}{4}\ \,\downarrow\ \downarrow\ \downarrow\ \downarrow\ |\ \downarrow\ \downarrow\ \downarrow\ \downarrow\ |\ \downarrow\ \downarrow\ \downarrow\ \downarrow\ |\ \text{etc.}$$

. . . experiment with a few carefully placed *silences,* to get away from nonstop singing or playing. The addition of rests adds rhythmic variety and bounce, and helps define the phrasing of a musical line by breaking down the line into smaller fragments. If your piece is in 4/4, for example (as in the pattern above), and your pattern contains notes of equal value (such as consecutive quarter notes), then a rest may take the place of any note:

$$|\frac{4}{4}\ \downarrow\ \downarrow\ \downarrow\ \xi\ |\ \xi\ \downarrow\ \downarrow\ \downarrow\ |\ \xi\ \downarrow\ \downarrow\ \xi\ |\ \text{etc.}$$

You may also introduce rests of greater value (longer duration) — provided that the rest notation *does not hide the secondary accent of the bar:*

$$|\frac{4}{4}\ \downarrow\ \downarrow\ \xi\ \xi\ |\ \xi\ \xi\ \downarrow\ \downarrow\ | \quad \text{becomes} \quad |\frac{4}{4}\ \downarrow\ \downarrow\ -\ |-\ \downarrow\ \downarrow\ |$$

In this example, the substitution of one half rest for two quarter rests does not interfere with the picture of the bar as a *balanced* pattern: both halves of the 4/4 bar stay *visually* clear.

If you want *two* consecutive beats of silence in the *middle* of a 4/4 bar, then write

$$|\downarrow\ \xi\ \xi\ \downarrow\ | \quad -\,not \quad |\downarrow\ -\ \downarrow\ |$$

Although some writers use the half rest this way, it is not as clear as the two quarter rests. The half rest tends to fool the reader's eye, hiding the secondary accent (Beat 3) of the balanced bar; the two quarter rests show the beats in the clearest way.

If you want *three* consecutive beats of silence in a 4/4 bar, follow the same principle (show the eye the balanced bar) by writing either. . .

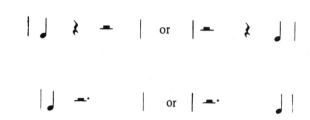

instead of

SHOW THE EYE THE BALANCED BAR! If you want silence in the *first* half of the bar, then

Rest notation in 6/8 — also a balanced meter (3+3) — follows exactly the same principle:

For silence in the *second* half of the bar,

If you want *two* consecutive 8th-note beats of silence in the *middle* of a 6/8 bar, then write

The "wrong" notation is tempting because we see it so often in *3/4* measures. But remember that 6/8 is a balanced meter (3♪ + 3♪), and should maintain a notation that shows those equal halves of the bar.

A bar of 3/4 is *un*balanced (2♪ + 2♪ + 2♪), and therefore needs a different notation. (We'll look at rests in an unbalanced meter in a future article).

If these few basic ideas are clear, try your hand at renotating the following bars. Each one is in a balanced meter. Therefore, each one should help the music reader by using the clearest possible rest notation. (Solutions will appear in the next installment.)

RH

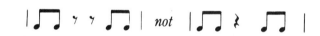

# Rhythm Workshop

# The Songwriter's Guide to Rhythmic Notation
## Part 5:
## Silence in an Unbalanced Bar

Before we launch into new matters, here are the solutions to the notational problems that appeared in our June/July issue. Remember that the best solution for each is a notation that clearly shows the reader *how the balanced bar is balanced!*

PROBLEM                                SOLUTION

(a) [musical notation in 4/8]  ........  [musical notation in 4/8]

(b) [musical notation in 4/2]  ........  [musical notation in 4/2]

(c) [musical notation in 4/16]  ........  [musical notation in 4/16]

(d) [musical notation in 6/16]  ........  [musical notation in 6/16]

(To check these and similar notations, you should be able to draw a dotted line through the *exact center* of each bar, with the *simplest possible* notation clearly visible on each side of that line.)

While a balanced bar divides cleanly in half, an *un*balanced bar does not. A bar of 3/4, for example, divides into three parts; a bar of 5/4 usually splits unevenly, as 3 + 2 or 2 + 3; a bar of 7/4 (rare in popular music, but commonplace in Eastern folk music and modern concert music) divides unevenly as 3 + 2 + 2, 2 + 3 + 2, and so on. The dotted lines, below, show these unbalanced divisions at a glance:

Music engravers do not of course fuss with dotted lines to point up the rhythmic stresses of an unbalanced bar! Those uneven splits are suggested in the music itself — either by the composer's phrase marks . . .

. . . by added accent marks . . .

. . . or by the placement of a left-hand chord:

In *8th*-note meters, however, the unbalanced divisions are far clearer, because of the presence of *beams:*

# Rhythm Workshop

---

Just as the various rests in a balanced bar followed the music's pattern of *balance*...

$\frac{4}{4}$ ♩  ♩  ┊ ▬ ┊

...the rests in an *un*balanced bar follow the pattern of *imbalance*:

$\frac{3}{4}$ ♩ ┊ 𝄽 ┊ 𝄽 ┊

The same applies to these 5/4 bars (divided 2+3)

$\frac{5}{4}$ ♩ ♩ ┊ ▬ ┊ 𝄽 ♩ ┊ ♩ 𝄽 𝄽 ┊ ▬ ┊ 𝄽 ♩ ┊
(>)

...and to these 7/4 bars (divided 3+2+2):

$\frac{7}{4}$ ♩ ♩ ♩ ┊ ▬ ┊ ▬ ┊ 𝄽 𝄽 ♩ ┊ ♩ 𝄽 ┊ 𝄽 ♩ ┊
(>)

In unbalanced *8th*-note meters, the rests again *follow the design of imbalance:*

$\frac{3}{8}$ ♪ ┊ 𝄾 ┊ 𝄾 | NOT | $\frac{3}{8}$ ♪ 𝄽 |    *(although some composers hang onto the second notation)*

[3 + 2] $\frac{5}{8}$ ♪ 𝄾 𝄾 ┊ 𝄽 | NOT | $\frac{5}{8}$ ♪ ▬ |    *(confusing! 3 + 2? 2 + 3?)*

[2 + 2 + 3] $\frac{7}{8}$ ♪ 𝄾 ┊ 𝄾 ♪ ┊ ♫♪ | NOT | $\frac{7}{8}$ ♪ 𝄽 ♫♫ |    *(appears to be 3 + 4)*

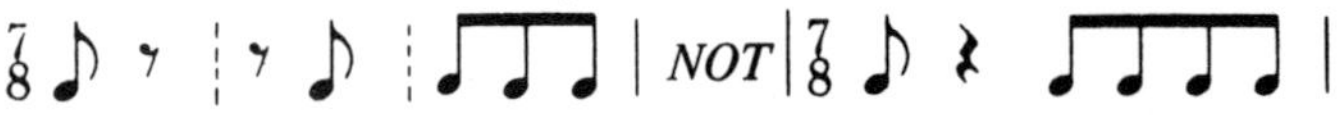

---

If these general principles seem clear, try your hand at some more cliff-hangers! (Solutions to the incorrect notations will appear in the next installment.)    **RH** ♩

(a) $\frac{3}{8}$ 𝄽  ♪ | ♪ 𝄾 ♪ 𝄾 𝄾 |

[2 + 3]

(b) $\frac{5}{8}$ ♪ 𝄽· ♪ | 𝄽 ♫♪ |

[2 + 3 + 2]

(c) $\frac{7}{8}$ 𝄽· 𝄽 ♩ | ♫♫ 𝄾 𝄾 𝄾 |

# Rhythm Workshop

# The Songwriter's Guide to Rhythmic Notation Part 6: Stem Up? Stem Down?

One of the oddities of the music writing business is the matter of which way a note should point. Should the stem—the vertical line attached to the note head—go up or down? Does it matter? Yes, it does if you want your manuscript to have a professonal look. It matters if you want a potential publisher of your song or original piano or organ piece to bother looking twice at what you have submitted. Remember that the average publisher receives *piles* of unsolicited manuscripts everyday. Because they are gone through quickly, you need every edge, every immediate advantage, you can get. Face the facts: A good-looking score gets more attention than a sloppy one. A well-written score reflects your caring attitude toward your music. If it is clear that *you* care, then the publisher might just care a bit more to read through your music.

The matter of stem directions is probably the most neglected item of music writing. Nobody talks about it. Only a handful of books touches on it, and it is rarely taught. This neglect is pointless because the basic rules of correct note-writing—following international engraving standards—are simple to learn and apply to your manuscript.

From here on, we're going to refer constantly to "the middle staff line." In the treble clef, this means the "B" line; in the bass clef, this means the "D" line. Keep in mind that these rules apply to *all* clefs: The "middle staff line" is in the middle, no matter what clef you use!

**Rule 1:** *Stem directions for single notes*
For a single note *below* the middle staff line, draw the stem going *up*. For a single note *on* the middle staff line *or above*, draw the stem going *down*.

**Rule 2:** *The length of a stem for a single note*
A stem for a single note should be at least *one octave* long:

**Rule 3:** *Stem directions for beamed notes*
(A *beam* is the thick line or lines connecting the stems of eighths, sixteenths, thirty-seconds, etc.)
For two or more beamed notes, the note *farthest* *from the middle staff line* dictates *all* stem directions within the beamed group. If, for example, you want to write these two notes

as a pair of eighths, then think this way:

(a) "Which note is farthest from the middle staff line?" (Answer: The first note.)

(b) "If that first note were by itself, which way would I draw its stem?" (Answer: The stem would go *up*.)

(c) "Then *both* stems must go up."

The same rule applies no matter how many notes are in the beamed group, and no matter how fast the rhythm is. For instance, if you want to write these four notes as a group of sixteenths, think:

(a) "Which note is farthest from the middle staff line?" (Answer: The third note.)

(b) "If that third note were by itself, which way would I draw its stem?" (Answer: The stem would go *down*.)

(c) "Then all four stems must go down."

*(If the farthest notes are* equidistant *from the middle staff line, all stems in the beamed group go* DOWN.*)*

**Rule 1**: *The slant of the beams*

In the old days of metal engraving, all music symbols were either cut or die-punched into a metal plate. This laborious process produced elegant scores but created a basic inking problem. When the finished plate was ink-rolled for the printing press, the liquid would naturally collect in tiny pools wherever two lines crossed each other. One of the messiest pools occurred when a thick beam intersected a thin staff line.

To minimize the problem, engravers established some guidelines:

(a) Don't allow a slanted beam to cross more than one staff line.

(b) Avoid extreme slants of the beam, even if this means that certain stems must be *longer* than an octave in length.

(c) Keeping the above rules in mind, gently slant the beam in the general direction of the note group: *up*, if the pitches ascend: *down*, if the pitches descend; *straight*, if the pitches ascend and descend more or less equally within the beamed group.

Following these guidelines, compare these right and wrong notations:

334

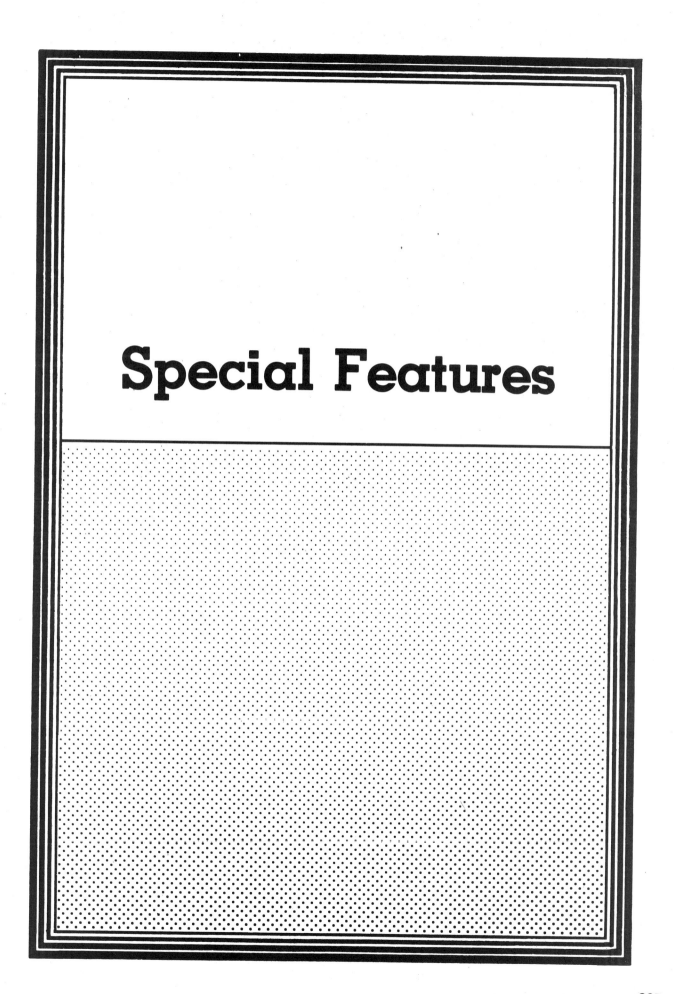

# Special Features

335

# MUSIC

## For a HEALTHY HEART

Have you ever wondered why it is that musical conductors, as a rule, outlive most of their contemporaries? Arturo Toscanini, for example, was active on the podium when he was ninety. Eugene Ormandy is now eighty-four. Arthur Fiedler, Ernest Ansermet, and Richard Strauss kept right on expending all that musical energy well into their eighties. Leopold Stokowski made it to ninety-six. Then there are Sir Adrian Boult (ninety-four), Franz Allers (seventy-eight), Walter Damrosch (seventy-eight), and the list goes on and on.

Is it the nature of music that makes them so happy to be alive that they just keep going? Or is it all that frantic waving of the arms? The answer is that it is probably a combination of both, with an emphasis on the latter. Concurrent theories regarding the involvement of the upper torso for meaningful cardiovascular benefits are popping up all over the place. The latest exercise craze called "Heavy Hands" is a prime example. Dr. Leonard Schwartz, in his book entitled *Heavy Hands*, prescribes and describes his method of upper torso involvement through the use of hand-held weights, which he has been practicing for more than seven years. He started when he was fifty, took his eighty pulse down to thirty-eight, and now no longer needs his blood pressure medication. He has, after a lifetime of trying, finally achieved a normal pressure through exercise, and looks to be in better shape than most thirty-year-olds you may know.

In a recent article for *Medical Tribune*, Dr. Hans Neumann of the New Haven

Health Department deals directly with the music angle. He explains the longevity of conductors as follows: "There is evidence that exercise of the upper extremities is more beneficial for the cardiovascular system than training and use of the lower half of the body. While the weight carried by the conductor is no heavier than a baton, and his work is not overly taxing in any short unit of time, the activity is protracted and does not allow one to give in to fatigue."

Does this mean that all you joggers have been wasting a lot of time? Not at all. It does mean, however, that you would derive more than twice the benefit if you got your arms involved. In fact, a brisk walk with a good, high arm swing is probably more beneficial than a simple jog. That is certainly Dr. Schwartz's contention.

Dr. Neumann, in further discussing the conducting theory, states that studies have shown that the heart and circulatory system gain a great deal more from this sort of conditioning than from leg exercises only. Part of it is also, he says, due to the fact that the conductor is involved with a *sustained* activity or exercise. It takes approximately forty minutes to conduct an average symphony from one end to the other, to say nothing of all the practicing at home and the rehearsals with the orchestra. He points out that continued use of large muscle groups, as is required for conducting, tends to lessen the anxiety and depression that often come with added age. (Therein probably lies the answer to Dr. Schwartz's reduction in blood pressure. Not only do you open up the arteries with this type of exercise, you can "conduct" away all those festering anxieties too!)

So the trick is: get those arms involved. To that end we are giving you a quickie course in how to conduct a march, a waltz, and a piece in common (4/4) time. Find yourself a Sousa record, or one by Strauss, and start getting into the *swing*. In fact, the energy required to conduct marches, waltzes, and some good big-band "swing" pieces is probably just what these doctors ordered! ■

E S

1. 2. 3. 4. 5. 6.

NELSON

# CONDUCTING PATTERNS

*Use both hands to conduct.* Notice that they move in opposite directions, and that there is a curving or looping motion used most of the time.

## Pattern 1
### *Two-beat. (March, polka, cut-time, etc.)*

This pattern begins with both hands in front of the chest (six or eight inches from the body), approximately three inches apart. Hands and arms out to the side on the first beat, back in together for the second beat to eye level. *A curve out, a curve back in.*

Preparation     Beat 1     Beat 2

## Pattern 2
### *Three-beat. (Waltz)*

Again, begin this pattern at the same position as Pattern 1. Always maintain the six-to-eight-inch distance from the body throughout each beat, for all **patterns**. The first beat is straight down to belly-button level, with a slight bounce; the second beat curves outward and slightly up to chest level; and the final beat brings both hands back in together at eye level, ready to repeat the pattern for the next measure.

Preparation     Beat 1     Beat 2     Beat 3

## Pattern 3
### *Four-beat. (Common Time)*

Hands should be spread apart at the starting position. They are at shoulder height and descend straight down for the first beat (about twelve inches). The second beat brings hands in toward the center, curving up to chest height. Beat three has both hands curving up and out to shoulder height, and beat four brings them together at eye level.

Preparation     Beat 1     Beat 2     Beat 3     Beat 4

Remember to keep all these patterns fluid and curvy by using a looping motion. Add your own variations (as all conductors do) when you have mastered the basic patterns.

One last bit of advice: always use a record or tape, rather than conducting music that is in your head. Also, change your selections periodically to keep up the interest. You'll be amazed how quickly a half-hour of exercise can go by!

**ES**

# Getting Your Music
# Published
## *A Game Plan For Today*

You say you're a brilliant young composer struggling with your latest opus in a small shack in the Florida marshlands, or in a garret (do they still have garrets?) on Manhattan's Upper West Side. You have glorious visions of your work being published and distributed internationally to orchestras and individual musicians who immediately sing its praises in performances throughout the world?

Well, get ready for the sharp slap across the face. As the golden mists clear, we're back to reality. Music publishers, composers, and professional organizations all agree that publishing is not only secondary to a composing career, but that it is practically impossible for an unknown to achieve print without an established history of performance.

There have been many changes in the music publishing industry over the past twenty or thirty years, and the emphasis on performance is understandable. A publishing house can no longer merely print and distribute sheet music. According to established composers Ned Rorem and Eric Salzman, a good publisher must also act as a composer's agent, helping actively to promote his or her works. "Today," Salzman says, "it would be sheer vanity to pay fifty percent of your earnings to a publishing house for the prestige of having them make copies of your score."

Rorem feels music publishing as we've known it might not exist in another fifteen years or so. "Soon it will all be

*"The real publishing of music today is recording. You've got to get your notes down on disc."*
Eric Salzman

computerized. There'll be no pretty covers, no binding. You'll just punch up the score you want and out it will come."

Publishing, though, has not yet become an obsolete enterprise. "Semiobsolete" Salzman calls it. "The real publishing of music today is recording. Once, publishing was the only available means of distribution; everyone read music and everyone had a piano in their living room. Today you've got to get your notes down on disc instead of on paper."

ASCAP, the American Society of Composers, Authors and Publishers, which represents over 6,000 music

publishers, collects and disburses royalty payments for performances. Surprisingly, the society offers little information on classical publishing, although it provides an extensive booklet of hints for the pop music sector. Margaret Jory, Director of the Symphonic and Concert Department of ASCAP, was firm in agreeing that performance should be a young composer's first priority. "Publishing is not the be-all and end-all of composing; performance is. You shouldn't begin to approach a publisher until you have established a performance career. Those days when a young composer, music manuscript under his arm, could

*"If you want to get your music published write specifically to a publisher's needs."*

Ned Rorem

approach a publisher and gain acceptance are gone—if they ever existed at all. Even with established composers, it's impossible to get more than one piece at a time handled by a publisher."

She does suggest a course of action, however. "Keep performing, or having your music performed. Save all your clips. Above all, keep people interested in your work; build up a good mailing list. From this, amass a substantial portfolio. Then do some research. Check out publishers catalogs and see what kind of material they seem to want. Your best bet is a small press with special interests. If you find a house that specializes in flute or marimba music, say, and you can write that, your odds of success are increased."

Appealing to a specialized market within a larger publishing house's province will also increase your odds. Composer Rorem suggests you "write very specifically to a publisher's needs. Generally, they accept easy choral pieces with one, two, three or four parts, with or without piano accompaniment. They'll also look at band music (for educational facilities like high schools and colleges) and easy piano pieces (also in the educational sector)."

A spokesman for the National Music Publishers Association, an organization devoted to copyright protection of its membership, suggests arming yourself with knowledge about a publishing company's specific needs "Shawnee Press, for instance, favors choral works. In general, choral and piano music are the most in demand. Often, a special interest house will look to expand its catalog, or will need something on a specific level of performance difficulty. Dramatic music for performance—whether it be opera, ballet, or concert—is an extremely limited market in the U.S. A young composer in these areas might consider approaching a foreign publisher through a representative here, or might even go directly to Europe."

Now that you've been properly warned, you may still wonder what the chances are for getting into print. Bruce MacCombie, Vice-President and Director of Publications of G. Schirmer, offers some dismaying statistics. "Schirmer publishes in three main areas: the professional market, the educational market, and the amateur market. We get many works submitted to us, some 2,000 annually. We publish about 150 pieces each year. Most works we actually publish are solicited by us. Thirty percent of our output is serious music for professional performance. This is produced solely by the fifteen or twenty composers under contract to us—Gian Carlo Menotti, Gunther Schuller, Lenny Bernstein and John Corigliano among them. Sixty-five percent of Schirmer's published work is educational material for college conservatories: choral pieces, piano methods, or literature for teaching. Most of this comes from established composers whom we use regularly but who are not contracted to us. The last five percent is the amateur and leisure market.

"We do look at everything that comes in to us, but we prefer to have some indication of a new composer's performance or recording credits instead of simply receiving a manuscript cold. Our policy is to examine all submissions and judge them by a number of factors: instrumentation, length of piece, difficulty level, production costs, and our catalog needs at the time. It's not always an aesthetic judgment. We accept or reject pieces without explanation; otherwise we'd be spending enormous amounts of time on explanatory letters."

*"Out of 2,000 works submitted annually we accept about 150. It's not always an aesthetic judgment."*
Bruce MacCombie

Stewart Pope, Chairman of Boosey & Hawkes, Inc., was a bit less liberal in the area of unsolicited manuscripts. "Do *not* send your music; we will send it straight back, unexamined. There have been incidents in which publishing houses have become involved in plagiarism suits. It's best to write a letter first, describing your music and style. We'd like to know whether you're re-writing Chopin or Henry Cowell," he jests. "Send us a résumé, tell us what you have had performed or recorded. Then wait for a response; any good publisher always responds."

Boosey & Hawkes' statistics are even more depressing than Schirmer's. The firm prints about 200 pieces a year; this covers *both* the United States and Europe. B&H prefers to handle all the music of a handful of composers instead of the odds and ends of a great many. There are a mere twelve composers on retainer with the house. "We choose to help establish the careers of a very few composers. We are a serious music house. We do have a series

of band music publications, but for that we solicit only composers we know."

Ned Rorem feels lucky to be one of Boosey & Hawkes' blessed dozen. He has had an exclusive contract with B&H for twenty years, and has had hundreds of his works published. "If I wrote something for seven bass flutes and

*"Do not send your music. Write a letter first. We'd like to know whether you're re-writing Chopin or Henry Cowell."*
Stewart Pope

twenty harpsichords, they'd publish it. They feel even my unsaleable works may have some future value. I was lucky. I didn't paper my room with rejection slips when I started. I had my first work, three songs on a religious text, published in 1945 when I was twenty-one. David Diamond gave them to Associated Music Publishers and they were published immediately on his recommendation." Stewart Pope and Bruce MacCombie both agree that an established composer's recommendation will strongly influence their decision.

One last route out of the Florida swamps and into publication is competition. The NMPA spokesman suggests you get your works involved in competitions like those sponsored by ASCAP and BMI. Seek out other organizations responsible for competitions. He claims publishers will look more closely at award-winning works. Then, besides submitting awards, recording, and performance information along with a manuscript, include a tape as well. "Most publishers want both," he states.

Even if you follow all these astute suggestions, you may not turn up an instant winner in the publishing game, it will almost certainly take time. Eric Salzman's *Civilization and Its Discontents*, which he describes as a "music-theater comedy," was first performed in 1977, and was recorded about two years later by National Public Radio and then by Nonesuch. The work won the Prixe Italia, and has been broadcast to a large portion of the English-speaking world, achieving much critical acclaim. Salzman signed a publishing contract for the work in 1979 or 1980, and despite all the accolades, the piece is first scheduled to be published as a piano and vocal score this year. Salzman also claims to have had difficulties earlier in his career; some years back, another firm reneged on publishing his works in spite of an exclusive contract to do so.

A young composer can avoid these headaches and heartaches by exploring alternate sources of distribution, or by starting his or her own publishing company. Rorem points to three successful composers—Harry Partch, Donald Martino, and Alan Hovhaness—who did so out of sheer desperation. Salzman joins Rorem in touting self-publication, adding that "modern print reproduction methods like the Xerox machine make it easy and cheap for a composer to copy and distribute his own scores." The two composers independently praise the American Composers Alliance, an organization that makes unpublished music available to performers.

So, all you composers up there in those dusty garrets or marshy shacks—maintain your glorious vision: just change the emphasis. You still have a chance. ∎

**PW**

# Piano Doctor

## "Have you ever wondered what to do about those sticking keys?"

Have you ever wondered what you can do about those sticking keys, or notes that sustain long after you release them, or the "bubbling" that results from a hammer striking multiple times with just one blow? How about those squeaks and rattles, or a "touch" that is too sluggish, or too "light"?

Many piano problems require the services of a competent technician, but there *are* things you can learn to do in your home, between visits from your "piano doctor." These columns will help you to better understand how your instrument works, and what the causes are of the most common problems. We would like to invite you to send your questions in, too; they'll be addressed once we've covered the general principles involved in diagnosing and adjusting modern pianos.

To begin, it is important to understand that a piano's sound is created by a number of separate, but interdependent, components. This may sound obvious, but I often have to explain to customers that tuning a piano won't automatically fix broken notes, make the action more responsive, eliminate buzzes, or change the quality of sound. So to begin, here are the main components of all pianos.

**The soundboard,** usually made of spruce, amplifies the vibrations of the strings; it can be seen directly underneath the strings and iron plate. The strings vibrations are carried to the soundboard via the bridges, which are usually made of hard maple. These are glued to the soundboard, running from the bottom in the bass to the top in the treble. On the back of the soundboard (underneath in the grand piano) are the *ribs,* usually running diagonally (perpendicular to the grain of the soundboard), which support the soundboard and maintain its crowned shape. A "cracked" soundboard (not as disastrous a situation as many people have been led to believe) is usually a symptom of separation from the ribs, and often causes noises and rattles. We will talk about this in future columns.

**The plate,** or frame, is found directly over the soundboard; it's usually made of cast-iron. Its function is to rigidly support the structure of the piano, so it can withstand the pull of the strings. A cracked or broken plate pretty much spells curtains for a piano and is fortunately rare.

**The strings** are secured at the back end to the plate's hitch pins, and at the front end to threaded tuning pins, which are embedded in the *pin block* or *wrest-plank.* The *copper-wound bass strings* are usually cross-strung over the *steel strings,* an arrangement that allows for maximum string length. The bass strings start out at one-per-note, then become two-per-note (sometimes three); the steel tenor and treble strings are all three-per-note (except in some small vertical pianos), with one length of wire looping over the hitch pin to make up two strings. (Note that one wire can thus serve two different notes vibrating at different pitches, a fact that surprises many people.) Strings occasionally break in playing, but more frequently during tuning—especially if they are rusty and the pitch needs to be raised a lot.

**The keyboard and the action** constitute the entire mechanism (removable from the piano) by which the motion of the key is transmitted to the motion of the *felt hammer* which strikes the string. When this happens the *damper* (the soft felt resting on top of the string when the action is at rest) is lifted so the string is free to vibrate. Also to be generally included in the action are the *pedals,* the most important being the sustain pedal. Most good grands have an "una corda" (soft) pedal and a sostenuto pedal; uprights have a soft pedal (different from the grand) and sometimes a bass sustain pedal (of limited usefulness).

All problems concerning the general "feel" and responsiveness of the piano, and most malfunctions of individual notes can be traced to the action and keys. Grand and upright actions work very differently (the grand being inherently superior in design), and some of our future columns will deal with the variety of action parts and their functions.

**ME**

# Piano Doctor

## "Keys may stick for several reasons. Here are four, and what to do about them."

In this column we will talk about the problem of sticky or sluggish notes; that is, when the note plays but returns slowly or only partway so that repetition is poor. Often this problem is most noticeable when the sustain pedal is depressed, but this is not because there is something wrong with the pedal or the dampers. It is simply that the weight, or spring action, of the damper aids in the return of a key, so that when the dampers are held up by the use of the sustain pedal sluggishness in a key becomes more apparent.

There are many possible causes of this problem, and like good diagnosis in any field, common sense and deductive reasoning are essential to find the source. Before getting into specific things that might be wrong, let's consider it from a general point of view. Keys can stick because: a) something is rubbing against something else it shouldn't be touching, thus getting "hung up"; b) a point of rotation or contact between a stationary and a moving part is too tight or somehow bound up or impeded, hindering free movement of that action part; c) a spring that is necesary to the return of a moving action part is broken or weak; d) a piece of action felt or buckskin has become pitted or worn in such a way that the part that rides against it gets caught up. These four points don't include all possibilities, but they certainly cover a lot of territory.

Let's look at these general areas more specifically. What parts could be rubbing? If the offending note or notes are naturals (white notes) check to see that the front of the key isn't making contact against the key slip (the long piece of wood that goes along the front of the piano directly in front of the white keys). Sometimes key slips warp, causing rubbing against keys in a section or even along its whole length.

If there is rubbing here, the slip can be shimmied out away from the keys. First note the area of contact. Find the front-most screws underneath the key bed that secure the slip and remove them. (In some cases the slip is not screwed in but can be gently pried up; in some other pianos it is held down by the cheek blocks at either end next to the highest and lowest notes and these must be removed first.)

Having removed the slip, glue a thin (approximately ½" wide) strip of veneer or cardboard along the bottom of the slip at the offending area. Some trial and error might be necessary to determine the thickness of the shim required to hold the slip away from the rubbing keys; once this is done, screw it back in and the problem should be solved.

Other rubbing parts could be the hammers themselves. Open up the top lid if the piano is an upright; if it is a grand, remove the music desk and peer down between the strings. Is one hammer touching an adjacent hammer when the note is played? If so, is it because thay have shifted too closely together, or is it because one hammer is twisted so that it is not parallel to its neighbor?

If the hammer is twisted, it can be corrected by the application of heat to the shank (the shaft the hammer is glued to) while twisting in a counterdirection, but I don't advise a beginner to try this for fear of setting fire to their action! If the offending hammer is straight but has shifted sideways it is usually possible to correct this by moving the hammer flange (connected directly to the shank in a grand, and to the hammer butt in an upright) in the necessary direction.

In a grand this will require removing the action, which I will discuss in a later column. In an upright it is only necessary to remove the front board. (There are many ways front boards are fastened; simple observation should reveal how to remove it.) Shine a good light in the action and determine if the butts are attached to flanges that are screwed in at the front, in back of the jacks. If they are secured to a brass rail with no flange, you will not be able to adjust the hammer alignment by this method.

If there is a screwed-in flange, carefully work a thin-bladed screwdriver past the jack into the slot of the screw. You will have to exert a little side pressure against the jack, so be gentle. Loosen the flange screw a little so that there is side-to-side play in the hammer. Align the culprit hammer so that it is centered to the strings, then tighten the screw. *Voilà!* The hammer should no longer rub.

**ME**

# Piano Doctor

## Swollen Parts

S.Pica

This column will continue with some of the causes of sticking and sluggish notes. As mentioned last issue, one general cause of sluggishness is excessive tightness where there is a moving part. Almost all moving parts in pianos have some kind of felt bushing, and this felt (or the wood surrounding it) can swell or get gummed up, impeding free movement. This impedence can be either in the key itself or in an action center (one of a number of rotation points for each note in the action).

Each key has two guide pins around which it moves. ("Key" properly refers to the key lever only, not to the entire action-string mechanism.) One, called the *balance pin,* is at the fulcrum, or pivot point, of the key and comes through a felted piece of wood glued on top of the key called the *button.* The other key pin, called the *front pin,* comes through the bottom of the key in front and also passes through a felt bushing.

If the felt around either or both of these pins is too tight, the note will tend to stick. To test if this is the cause of stickiness, try two things: first, lift up the key slightly (about ¼ ") higher than its natural point of rest and see if it drops back easily. (It may be necessary to remove the name board and sometimes the key cove rail, both of which go across the width of the keyboard and limit the upward travel of the keys. Doing this is usually a simple matter of observing how they are screwed in.) Second, depress the suspect key and try to wiggle it from side to side to determine if there is any movement. If there is absolutely no play, grasp the key firmly and wiggle it side to side fairly forcefully to try to compress the felt a bit. (With the white notes, this is better done with the key slip removed, as described in the last issue, so that the key can be grasped firmly between thumb and forefinger on top and bottom.) If the tightness is not too bad, this procedure might free up the key, but if the problem is more severe, you will probably have to ask your technician to ease the keys with special pliers.

If the key didn't drop down easily in the first test but did have a little play in front, chances are the tightness is in the key button. Remove the front and name boards so that you have access to and can see the balance pins coming through the center of each key. (It is not necessary to take the action out in a grand to do this, but a good light could be helpful.)

Put a finger on the key button of the suspect key and wiggle it to see if there is some play. Again, if there is no play at all, a little firm pressure pushing the key from side to side at the button while slowly depressing and releasing it might ease things up sufficiently. Don't go overboard, however, because key buttons break quite easily. The whole problem of tight key bushings is most common in new pianos, or when the keys have been recently re-bushed, or in humid areas (especially if the piano is not played often).

If the problem is not in the key itself, it's probably in the action. Most commonly it would be in the flange or bushing upon which the hammer shank swivels. In an upright, when a hammer is pushed by hand to the strings, it should drop right back when released. If it drifts back to the rail slowly, there is a problem. First make sure that the butt spring, which is the spring behind each hammer shank (on the string side in front of the dampers), is intact and in position. If it has slipped out of position, it is possible to push it back into place without any special tools.

Shine a light overhead, observing how the other springs are inserted in grooves in back of the hammer butts, and gently reposition the slipped-out one with a single finger. If the spring is O.K., odds are good that the flange is tight. There are various concoctions to lubricate or shrink tight action centers, but for occasional use, WD-40 is a readily available and easy-to-use product. Insert the extender nozzle into the action getting as close as possible to the butt flange. (Again, good light is essential!) Squirt a shot of WD-40 to one side of the flange at the busing (toward the top), remove the nozzle, and reinsert it at the other side of the flange and spray again. Then place a finger on top of the hammer and, pushing with slight downward pressure, work it up and back, to and from the strings. This should ease a moderately tight action center; in severe cases, your technician might have to ream out and repin the tight centers.

In a grand piano, the same principle applies, but it will be necessary to remove the action, which I will describe in this column next month. ∎

**ME**

# Piano Doctor

## *Removing Your Insides*

As promised last month, I will describe how to remove a grand action. This is not a very difficult procedure, but certain precautions are necessary to avoid damage.

First, make sure you have enough clearance around the piano so that once you begin to lift the action out you can move with it without banging into walls, furniture, et cetera. Second, know where you are going to put the action once you have it out. A table covered with newspaper for protection is fine.

To remove the action you must first remove the two cheek blocks (directly adjacent to the highest and lowest notes respectively), the key slip (running directly in front of the white notes and cheek blocks across the width of the piano), and the name board (running the width of the piano directly behind and above the keys). The key slip is usually screwed in from underneath, but on some grands there are no screws and it can be simply pried up, which should be done carefully to avoid damage to the finish. (On some Japanese grands the slip is held down at either end by the cheek blocks and these must be removed first.)

The cheek blocks are also usually secured by screws from underneath the piano. They will be found at either end of the keyboard slightly in back of the screws that hold down the key slip. Since there can be other case screws under the piano, note the position of the blocks and draw an imaginary vertical line through the piano to make sure you are turning the screws that go into the blocks. If there are no cheek-block screws underneath, then chances are the blocks are secured by screws going down from above, behind the name board. (Sometimes there is a screw from both above and below.)

The name board is usually attached by simple hinges at either end that release when the fastening screws which protrude from the hinges are loosened. Again, there are variations: sometimes the name board is connected directly to the cheek blocks and must be removed in one piece with them. With sufficient patience and careful observation it shouldn't be too difficult to see how your case parts are attached.

At this point make sure there is nothing further holding down the action. On some grands there are additional pieces that go over the two guide pins or screws that emerge from the sides of the key frame, underneath where the cheek blocks formerly were. If there are, remove them and mark the fronts bass or treble so that you will put them back in the right place. On grands that don't have an *una corda* pedal, the action itself is sometimes screwed down with several screws at the very front; these must be removed also.

Once all these pieces are detached, the action is removable. Using the index fingers, grasp the sides of the key frame toward the front. Most important, keep all other fingers OFF THE KEYS! If a key is even slightly depressed when removing the action, the hammer will rise and there won't be sufficient clearance between it and the pin block, causing it to break off when pulled forward.

Exerting firm pressure against the sides of the key frame, begin to wiggle the action out, pulling first from one side and then the other. There might be some resistance at first, especially if there is a lot of dirt underneath the key frame, but you should feel it begin to move progressively more easily. Make sure you keep the action approximately straight as you pull it out unless directions printed on the action specifically contradict this.

After the hammers are well under the pin block and the front of the action is overhanging the piano a good six inches, you may grasp it from underneath and pull it out so that the hammers are completely exposed. Push your seat back a bit to make clearance and tilt the action down toward your lap as you continue to pull it out. When the front end is fully on your lap (make sure the back end is still resting securely in the piano!), you may wish to have someone's assistance to carry one side from underneath while you shift over to carry the other side. If no one is available, cradle the front of the action against your stomach, stretch out your arms, and grasp the action from underneath at both sides at about the center point. Making sure there are no obstacles, lift and stand up with the action and carry it to your table. Actions from large grands can be fairly heavy, so a two-man carry makes for less risk.

Putting the action back in involves simply reversing these steps. Push the action back, keeping fingers off the keys, until it returns to its original position. As a precaution, step on the sustain pedal while pushing it all the way back in case there is insufficient clearance between the backs of the keys and the damper mechanisms, although this should not be the case. It may be possible to push the action slightly past its original position, but the cheek blocks (or the hardware underneath them) should be factory adjusted so that when screwed down properly the action must be re-aligned to its original position.

**ME**

# Piano Doctor

## *Minor Surgery*

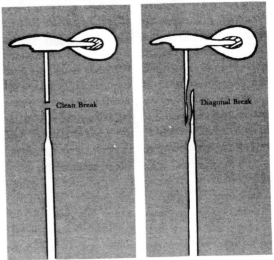

S.Pica

## "A gross malfunction, like a note suddenly not working, usually has a very obvious cause."

**M**any of the problems that affect pianos are subtle and take experience to diagnose properly. On the other hand, a gross malfunction like a note suddenly not working at all usually has a very obvious cause. We will talk about two of these gross malfunctions in this issue.

Many people react to the sudden loss of a note by assuming that they broke a string. Since only the very lowest notes have only one string, this would not usually be the case for a higher note (unless there was already a broken string for that note). If there is a broken string observe whether it is a plain steel wire or a wound string. A plain wire can be replaced by your technician with wire of the same diameter. A wound string replacement can be made up from a universal set, or, as is preferable (but requires a wait), an exact replacement can be ordered. If the string broke at the tuning pin rather than lower down, it is usually possible to repair the original string by making a splice. Although some technicians may disagree with me on this, I usually prefer to make a splice on a broken bass string because it will not change the tone the

way a new string will, and it will also have more tuning stability than a new string.

Assuming the strings are okay, the next thing to look for if a note suddenly breaks is a broken hammer shank. If you have a shank that is broken at the very top right next to where it enters the hammer head, it cannot be fixed effectively by simply trying to glue the parts together; the shank should be replaced. On the other hand, if there is a jagged or diagonal break so that the two broken edges mate together easily, you should be able to make the repair yourself. On an upright it is not necessary to remove the action. Obtain a plastic drinking straw that slips easily over, yet fits snugly around, the exposed piece of broken shank. (The most common-size straw is usually right for the standard 7/32" diameter shank.) Cut off a length of the straw sufficient to cover the area of the break; at least two inches is safe. Spread a good-quality

**A clean break is not repairable.**

Clean Break          Diagonal Break

**A diagonal break can be fixed.**

white or yellow wood glue over both surfaces of the break; then slip the straw over the part of the shank that remains connected to the butt so that half the straw's length overhangs the broken end. Then simply slip the other part of the shank down into the straw, making sure it goes all the way down so the glued surfaces mate properly (wood glue is *not* a filler). Check the angle and height of the repaired hammer against its neighbors. Give the glue ample time to set before playing the note.

On a grand, remove the action as described last issue. Grand shanks are usually a different diameter than uprights, so rather than use a straw it is better to hold the pieces together with thread. Unscrew the remaining part of the broken shank from the action to make it safe and easy to work with. Place glue on the broken surfaces, align the pieces carefully, and wrap the thread tightly around and around the whole area of the break until the pieces are held firmly together (use a little glue to keep the loose end of the thread from unravelling). Replace the rejoined unit, slip the action back in, and you should have yourself a permanently repaired hammer shank. ■

**ME**

# Piano Doctor

## Squeaks And Groans!

Nothing is more grating on the nerves of a pianist than a squeaking or creaking sustain pedal. There you are trying to execute delicately the pianissimo section of a Chopin *Nocturne* and every time you step on the pedal it sounds like you're opening the front door of Dracula's castle! When my customers have this complaint they often ask me to "oil the pedals," envisioning something akin to a lube job on a car. However, the source of the problem is generally not in the pedal itself, and the trick is to be a good detective and careful listener to deduce where the noise is coming from.

On an upright, take off both the top and bottom boards. Step on the sustain pedal and listen; is the noise coming from the top part of the piano where the action is, or the bottom where the pedals are? If coming from the bottom, first tighten down all the screws securing the pedals and trapwork (the wooden pieces the pedals pull on that connect upward to the action via wooden rods) to the floor of the piano. Do not tighten the nut that secures the threaded rod coming from the back of the pedal to the trapwork; this is only done to adjust the free play of the pedal.

If there is a leaf spring applying pressure directly under the pedal, push it away from the pedal by hand and then work the pedal. Does this eliminate the squeak? If so, remove the spring (simply attached by two screws), apply some graphite grease or solid lubricant to the tip where it comes in contact with the pedal, and put it back in.

Perhaps the pins coming from the back of the pedal are squeaking as they rotate in their securing brackets. A little spray of WD-40 or a few drops of graphite in liquid suspension right into the bracket holes through which the pins go should eliminate this. Sometimes in an upright a noisy pedal comes from the floor board starting to loosen up and move a little when subjected to downward pressure. (This would be indicated if all the pedals make the same noise.) Ideally in this case the piano should be put on its back and have its floor board tightened, but a good temporary solution is to wedge books, pieces of wood, etc., under the piano until they are tight enough against the bottom to prevent the floor board from moving.

If the squeaking comes from the top of the piano, it is coming from the dampers themselves. Gently pull back each damper by hand away from the strings; do any of them squeak? If so, the noise is most likely coming from where the damper flange spring pushes against the front of the damper (facing you). Shine a good light into the action and you will see each damper lever has its spring cradled in a notch padded by felt directly below where the damper wire enters the top of the damper lever. (On many modern uprights there is no felt, but a Teflon-like surface which rarely squeaks.) Place the extender nozzle of your WD-40 directly pointing to this notch on the squeaking damper and give it a very short spray.

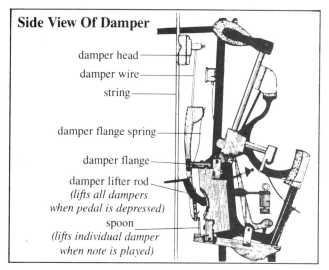

**Side View Of Damper**

damper head —
damper wire —
string —

damper flange spring —

damper flange —

damper lifter rod —
*(lifts all dampers
when pedal is depressed)*

spoon —
*(lifts individual damper
when note is played)*

## "The trick is to be a good detective. Here's how to find out where the squeak is coming from."

There *is* some possible risk using WD-40 close to the pinblock — some technicians prefer graphiting each slot — so if you can't see what you are aiming for or don't have a steady hand, do not attempt this. (And make sure the extender is inserted firmly in the nozzle!) Many uprights have a "dummy" damper lever with no head and an extrastrong spring to exert pressure against the damper lifter rod. This very often is the source of the squeak, so look to see if your piano has one and treat similarly. In some cases it is the coil of the spring, not the head, which is squeaking, but this is harder to get to.

It is possible that it is the metal damper lifter rod located in the back of the action which makes noise as it pushes the dampers away from the strings. (This rod runs the length of the action and moves out, thereby lifting all the dampers at once, when the wood rod coming from the pedal trapwork below moves up.) If this is the case you will want your technician to remove the action in order to correct the problem.

Next time we will talk about grand pedals. ∎

**ME**

# Piano Doctor

## Grand Pedal Problems

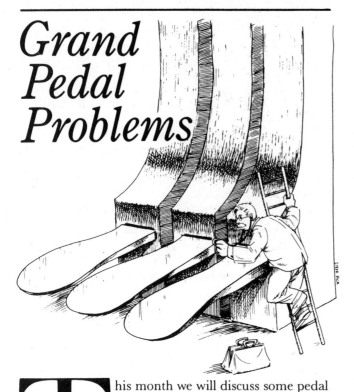

This month we will discuss some pedal problems that occur on grand pianos.

Grand pedals are attached to the pedal lyre which is suspended from the bottom of the piano. The lyre doesn't touch the floor, so the weight of the lyre plus the constant downward force of pedaling must be borne by the screws or bolts that hold it in. There are also wood or brass braces which come up diagonally from the back of the lyre and help keep it motionless while pedaling.

The first and easiest thing to check if there is noise when pedaling is that the lyre and braces are attached firmly. Go underneath the piano and tighten the screws or bolts that attach the lyre to the piano and the screws that attach the braces at either end. Wood braces do not screw in but are simply held in sockets at both ends. These wood braces should be tight to support the lyre. If there is up-and-back play, the holes they fit into should be shimmed out sufficiently to hold them securely (you can use cardboard, veneer, etc.). This requires removing the lyre, which is described below. You should also tighten all screws that connect the trapwork and springs to the underside of the piano, but do not tighten any screws that are for adjustment; if in doubt, leave it alone.

If the lyre screws are stripped and don't tighten up, or if parts of the lyre are becoming unglued (as revealed by wobble or play when shaken), the lyre will have to be removed to repair it. Two other problems requiring removal of the lyre are if a pedal itself is wobbling from side to side, or if the bottom board of the lyre, directly underneath the pedals above the floor, has worked loose.

Removal of the lyre is simply a matter of taking out the screws that hold it in. On some good-quality grands the lyre is also secured with a kind of locking plate which releases when the lyre is slid forward toward the front of the piano; if it is tight, a few taps with a rubber mallet should release it. As a precaution when removing the lyre, number the brass rods that travel up the lyre from the pedals to the trapwork; they are often different heights and must be kept in the same order.

If the lyre is becoming unglued, it must be repaired like any furniture: the loose parts must be separated and cleaned of the old glue; a good-quality wood glue must be applied; and then the parts must be clamped. (Look for a "squeeze-out" of the glue to indicate that clamping pressure has been applied correctly.) If the problem is that the screws holding the lyre are stripping, plug up the screw holes with dowels and re-drill the holes. Slightly longer screws may be used provided they are not so long as to come up through the keybed on which the action rests. If the bottom board of the lyre has worked loose because of loose screws, repair the screw holes similarly. If a pedal (or pedals) is wobbling side to side, remove the bottom board of the lyre to see how the pedals are attached. Since different makers attach pedals differently there is no single repair method, but observation and common sense should suggest a solution.

If there is a squeak when pressing the sustain pedal, it can usually be found in the trapwork or lyre below the piano, not in the individual damper levers (grand dampers, being gravity-returned, do not require heavy return springs which can develop squeaks the way upright dampers do). If the squeak also occurs when individual notes are played without pedaling, the damper levers themselves, or the damper wires coming up between the strings, are the noise source. Squeaks underneath the piano can be pinpointed by careful listening; having an assistant step on the offending pedal while you are under the piano is helpful. Look especially where a leaf spring presses against the trapwork, or where the brass pedal rods come in contact with the trapwork above or the pedals below, or where they are guided through felt-bushed holes toward the top of the lyre. Pedal and trapwork mechanisms vary in style, so you will have to observe how yours work. Once you have located the squeak, the preferred lubricant is powdered graphite, available at any hardware store as a lock lubricant. If a liquid application is desirable, the graphite may be dissolved in alcohol and applied as a solution which will evaporate, leaving the graphite behind.

**ME**

# Piano Doctor

# Ready For Action!

Up until now we have not dealt with how the mechanical structure of the piano, this is, the action, actually works. The degree to which a piano has an even, responsive and comfortable touch with good repetition and a minimum of mechanical noise has to do with the condition of the action parts and how well they are adjusted. All adjustments of the action can be loosely included under the general term "regulation."

If certain parts of an action are severely worn, brittle, dried out, or otherwise in bad condition, they may need to be replaced prior to regulation. This kind of work, depending on its extensiveness and completeness, can be labeled action rebuilding or restoration.

Modern piano actions are of two basic types—grand and vertical. The latter has two varieties, direct-blow and spinet-type drop action. All pianos of the same type pretty much work the same way with relatively minor differences. Therefore, even an inexpensive instrument can be made to have a relatively good touch if regulated properly.

Most regulation requires specialized tools. I am not suggesting that all piano owners purchase their own regulating tools, but I do think it is beneficial for the pianist to have a general understanding of the mechanics of their instrument and what the adjustment procedures are. I will first discuss vertical actions, which are somewhat simpler than grands.

Study the diagram of the direct-blow vertical action and the names of the main parts. When the key (1) is depressed, guided by the front pin (2) and balance pin (3), it raises at the back so that the capstan screw (5) pushes against the sticker (6), causing the whippen (7) to rise. (Smaller modern direct-blow verticals have no stickers and the capstan is in direct contact with the whippen.) The jack (8) which is connected to the whippen pushes against the hammer butt (10), causing it to swivel forward, thus moving the hammer toward the string. As the whippen continues to move up, the spoon (15) contacts the damper lever (22) causing the damper (14) to swing away from the string so the note can resonate while the key is depressed. Just before the hammer reaches the string, the heel of the jack (the bottom part which juts out) contacts the let-off button (26), causing the jack to swivel out from under the butt. The hammer is for this brief instant "on its own"; it carries by its own inertia the remaining distance to the string. This latter process is essential to all piano actions; it is called "escapement" or "let-off." The hammer then rebounds off the string but does not return to its original position; the catcher (11) is caught by the backcheck (9) and held until the key is released.

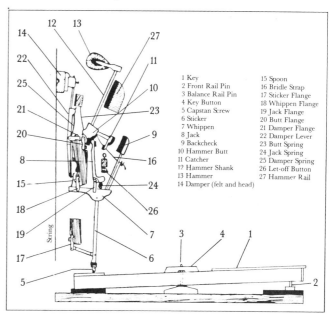

| | |
|---|---|
| 1 Key | 15 Spoon |
| 2 Front Rail Pin | 16 Bridle Strap |
| 3 Balance Rail Pin | 17 Sticker Flange |
| 4 Key Button | 18 Whippen Flange |
| 5 Capstan Screw | 19 Jack Flange |
| 6 Sticker | 20 Butt Flange |
| 7 Whippen | 21 Damper Flange |
| 8 Jack | 22 Damper Lever |
| 9 Backcheck | 23 Butt Spring |
| 10 Hammer Butt | 24 Jack Spring |
| 11 Catcher | 25 Damper Spring |
| 12 Hammer Shank | 26 Let-off Button |
| 13 Hammer | 27 Hammer Rail |
| 14 Damper (felt and head) | |

## Direct-Blow Vertical Action

When the key is released the whippen lowers, releasing the catcher. The hammer, pushed by the butt spring (23) and pulled by gravity aided by a tug from the bridle strap (16), returns to the hammer rail (27). The damper is released from the spoon and is pushed by its spring (25) to the string; similiarly the jack is pushed by its spring (24) back under the butt so the note is ready to play again.

The spinet drop action works very similiarly to the regular vertical action except instead of having the back of the key push directly up on the sticker and/or whippen above, it pulls up on a lifter wire or inverted sticker which drops down to and transmits the upward motion to the whippen below. Most spinets have an elbow which links the lifter wire to the whippen; this is a notorious point of breakage in many older spinets that used plastic elbows.

Next issue we will discuss the grand action, before moving on to the special problems and procedures involved in piano regulation. ∎

**ME**

# Piano Doctor

## *The Grand Action*

The grand action is really one of the marvels of nineteenth-century technology; it has remained essentially unchanged since Steinway introduced the basic design in 1884. Although it shares many features in common with upright actions, it is more efficient and faster repeating. Part of the reason for this is that the hammers, traveling up in a vertical direction toward the strings, are returned by gravity (and the rebound off the string) and do not need any help from a spring or a bridle strap as the horizontally traveling upright hammer does. Even more significant is the double-escapement principle in the grand action, in which an additional part on the whippen, called the *repetition lever,* allows notes to be repeated before the key returns to its original position.

Study the diagram and let us see what happens when a grand piano key is played. When the key (1) is pushed down, the capstan screw (2) pushes against the whippen (3), which causes it to rise. The jack (4) rises with the whippen, pushing against the knuckle (5), which is part of the hammer shank assembly (6), to which the hammer (10) is attached. Thus the hammer rises toward the strings. As the key continues to travel, its felted back end comes in contact with the damper lever (7) causing the damper (8) to lift off the strings, allowing them to resonate. When the heel of the jack (the front part jutting out) hits the let-off button (9), the jack swivels out from under the knuckle, allowing the hammer to "escape" or "let-off" from the string. The hammer then carries, by its own momentum, the remaining slight distance to the strings.

So far what we have described is very similar to what we discussed last issue for the vertical action, except that the jack is moving against the knuckle instead of the underside of the upright hammer butt, and the means of lifting the damper lever is different. Here the similarity breaks down because of the action of the repetition lever (11). The repetition lever is also lifting up the knuckle along with the jack as the whippen rises, so it too must "escape." This is accomplished by the front end of the lever coming in contact with the drop screw (12), which is part of the hammer flange (13). This causes the repetition lever to be pushed down away from the knuckle so that it is, for a moment, free of both the lever and the jack.

When the hammer bounces off the string (with the key still down all the way), the knuckle rebounds back to the "dropped" repetition lever. (The jack is still clear of the knuckle because its heel is still held against the let-off button.) The force of the hammer's return overcomes the resistance of the repetition lever spring (14), causing the lever to be pushed down still further by the knuckle until the tail of the hammer (its bottom end) is caught by the back check (15), which is at the back of the key.

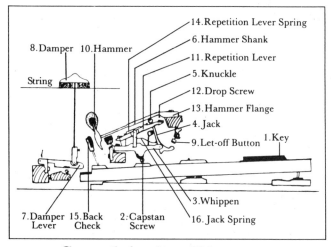

**Grand Action Diagram**

At this point the repetition lever is exerting an upward force against the knuckle, but the back check prevents it from moving. When the key is released the hammer is freed from the back check, and the upward push of the repetition lever allows the hammer to be supported so that the jack, pulled by its own spring (16), can get back under the knuckle before the key returns to its resting position. This allows the note to be re-struck very quickly. As the key returns the damper lever is also released, and the damper is pulled by gravity (aided by a spring in some grands) back to the string.

One can surmise from the descriptions of the grand and vertical actions that for either one to work at maximum efficiency each step in these sequences of events (which take place faster than the eye can see in normal playing) must be adjusted very precisely so that everything happens in the right order, at the right time, at the right distance, with the right force, etc. This is the essence of regulation. Next issue we will begin to discuss the procedures involved and some of the problems that occur when a piano is not regulated properly. ■

**ME**

# Piano Doctor

## "Bad" Action

The many procedures involved in fine-regulating a piano are interdependent; one cannot properly make one adjustment without making others, since all the operations of the action should work together for maximum efficiency and responsiveness. It is beyond the province of this column to attempt to teach complete action regulation, because this requires specialized tools as well as considerable experience. However, it is often possible to dramatically improve a "bad" action by relatively simple adjustments that most piano owners can do themselves.

One of the most basic action adjustments is setting the capstan screws, located at the back end of the keys (see the grand and upright action diagrams from the last two issues). This accomplishes slightly different ends in these two basic kinds of actions, but the underlying principles are the same. In uprights, the hammer shanks rest on the hammer rail so that the distance from the resting hammers to the strings is "set." Theoretically, just as soon as one touches the key the jack comes in contact with the hammer butt so that the hammer starts moving toward the string almost immediately. However, due to compression and wear of the felts under the whippens and under the key ends, and of the buckskin on the underside of the butts, a distance is created between the top of the jack and the butt. When this occurs there is excessive "lost motion" in the key; that is, the key must be partially depressed before the hammer begins to move. By turning the capstan screw up one can remove this lost motion, since the whippen will rise and bring the jack into closer contact with the butt.

In the grand the situation is slightly different. The hammer shanks are not meant to rest on the hammer rail in the grand (the rail is only there for the shanks to bounce off of on a short hard blow). The whippen should be in contact with the knuckle of the shank at rest; thus, there should not be any lost motion at all. (In the upright there should be a very slight amount of lost motion.) When the capstan is raised, therefore, the hammer is immediately raised by the rising whippen so that the distance between the resting hammer and the strings—referred to as the hammer-blow distance—is reduced. In a well-worn unregulated grand the shanks are often resting on the hammer rail and the capstans have to be turned a while before the hammers begin to move.

## "You cannot make one adjustment without making others."

A quick look at the physics of the piano action will explain the importance of the lost motion and/or hammer-blow distance adjustment. A properly regulated key will have a total up and down travel (key dip) of 3/8 inch or slightly more, depending on the piano. That motion of the key must be sufficient to bring the hammer to the strings —actually, to the point of escapement from the strings, which should be 1/16 inch to 1/8 inch from the strings, again depending on the piano. Once the hammers are past the point of escapement, there must be a little motion in the key "left over." This extra distance of key travel, called *aftertouch,* is essential to the proper feel and workings of the action. Without it the hammers will not check (be caught bouncing off the strings) properly, and will often bobble or double-strike the strings. The pianist will feel that the action has no power, because there is no follow-through to his finger motion. (It is analogous to a baseball player stopping the motion of his bat just at the point of contact with the ball.) In addition, when there is excessive lost motion, the actual weight of the touch is too light because initially the finger must lift only the weight of the whippen, not the whippen and the hammer butt assembly together. You can feel this effect in most uprights by stepping on the soft pedal, which raises the hammers closer to the strings, thereby increasing the lost motion. (This has no effect on the aftertouch since the hammer will end up at the same place at the same point of the key travel.)

We can see that if the capstan is set too low so there is excessive lost motion or excessive hammer blow distance, the key cannot properly complete its task of bringing the hammer to the string. In other words, since part of the motion of the key is being wasted bringing the jack up to the butt (lost motion) or bringing the hammer from an excessive distance away (too much hammer blow distance), there is not enough "left over" for the aftertouch. One could create aftertouch by making the keys travel further down or by making the hammer escape at a further distance from the string, but obviously unless these adjustments were incorrectly set to begin with this would be a case of trying to have two wrongs make a right.

Next issue I will describe how you can determine if the capstans need adjusting in your piano, and if so, how you can make the adjustment yourselves.

**ME**

# Piano Doctor

# *Lost Motion*

This issue we are continuing our discussion of the adjustment of the capstans for lost motion regulation (in the upright) and setting hammer blow distance (in the grand).

It is important to restate that good action regulation depends on many interdependent adjustments, so this particular adjustment should often be accompanied by other procedures. For instance, adjusting the capstans can create excessive aftertouch (see last issue) if the point at which the hammers escape ("let-off") is too far from the strings, or if the key dip is too deep. (Both of these conditions are common in worn actions and, unfortunately, occur occasionally in new pianos as well.)

Conversely, one can remove all the lost motion from an upright and still have insufficient aftertouch if the key dip is too shallow or if the starting point of the hammer—i.e., the hammer blow distance—is too far from the strings. (Note that hammer blow distance in the upright is set for all the hammers at once by adjusting the position of the hammer rail against which the shanks lean. The lost motion is then adjusted to this preset posi-

tion. In the grand, however, the capstan adjustment individually sets each hammer's blow distance.)

For our purposes at this point we will be assuming that these adjustments are reasonably close. Correct let-off distance is 1/16″ to 1/8″ from the string (check by depressing the key very slowly and watching where the hammer drops back), and correct key dip is 3/8″ to 13/32″ (check by measuring a depressed white key against an adjacent key with a fine ruler).

To determine if an upright has excessive lost motion, press the key slowly and feel for movement of the key before the hammer begins to move. A good visual check is to watch the backcheck, which sticks out from the whippen, and the catcher, which sticks out from the hammer butt; these should begin to move almost simultaneously. Make sure when doing this that the hammer rail is all the way back and not locked in a "soft" position; this will create a great deal of lost motion.

Look at the backs of the keys and determine which style capstans you have. If they are brass screws with holes in them, or dowels connected to wires stuck into the backs of the keys, you can turn them with an improvised tool such as a pointed awl, ice pick, or even a nail that fits into the hole and exerts sufficient leverage to turn the capstans. (One caution: wood dowel capstans on old pianos are sometimes fragile.) If the capstan is of the square-shouldered type with no hole, you may wish to buy a capstan wrench—quite inexpensive—since a regular open-end wrench, even if you can find one thin enough and of the right diameter, is not off-set, making it difficult to use. In any case, turn the capstans counterclockwise until the hammers begin to move almost immediately when the key is touched; a tiny amount of lost motion is necessary for good repetition. To be sure you haven't overadjusted the capstans, push the backs of the keys down gently. If any hammers move slightly it means they are being held off the rail because the capstan is too high.

Lost-motion regulation in spinet drop actions, where a wire comes up from the action through a cut-out in each key, is quite simple. Here there is no capstan; a button or grommet through which the wire is threaded can be turned by hand to remove the lost motion.

In grands, as you will recall from the previous issue, the hammers are meant to be off the hammer rail in rest position. Assuming the hammer rail is adjusted correctly (check the tightness of the nuts holding it down), a distance of 1/8″ between the hammer shanks and the felt of the rail is usually correct. Steinways and other makes which have no hammer rail, but pads of felt on the backs of each whippen underneath the shank, leave less room for doubt since there are no adjustment screws to work loose or be improperly set. The actual hammer blow distance varies from piano to piano, but a distance of 1-7/8″ from the tips of the hammers to the strings is usually in the ballpark. Use a ruler or make a simple gauge which can slip between the strings to measure this distance.

Even if the hammer blow is not set to exact precision in a grand, just getting the shanks "off the rail" can sometimes solve a host of problems, particularly when the keys are front-heavy, and the weight of the hammer is needed to return the key all the way back to rest position. Pianos with this condition, where the keys never come back all the way, typically have out-of-level keys, shallow dip, poor repetition, and bad dampening (because the damper levers are being pushed upward by the backs of the keys at rest). How gratifying it is to solve all these problems with one simple adjustment! ∎

**ME**

# Piano Doctor

## Keep It Clean!

One of the most common questions asked by owners of grand pianos is, "How can I clean the soundboard?" Many people keep the lids of their grands closed because they are embarrassed by the layer of dust that inevitably settles within. Cleaning a soundboard does take a little care and patience, but you *can* do it yourself.

The job can be done by one person, but two makes it easier. In any case, you will probably need an assistant for the first step, which is to remove the lid. With the lid fully closed and its front section folded back, pull out the two retaining pins from their hinges on the straight (bass) side of the piano. Lift the lid straight up and out, and place it down gently on a padded surface, being careful not to let the hinged front piece come slamming down. You may wish to remove the music desk as well to provide access to the front, where the tuning pins are. It will come out either by pulling it straight forward or by lifting it up and out through

notches in the bottom. (You may have to slide it up and back until you "find" the notches.) If you wish to remove dirt around the tuning pins, just use a dry brush and/or vacuum cleaner—no water or cleaners here!

Remove any foreign objects from the soundboard carefully with a tweezers or needle-nosed pliers (or, if appropriate, a small magnet). *Don't* force a tool between strings; be especially careful with the bass strings, because the copper windings are soft and can easily be damaged. If there is not enough clearance, use something like a popsicle stick or tongue depressor to push the object to a spot where you can get at it more easily. Next start to clean all the accessible areas of the soundboard and plate with a well wrung out damp cloth, rinsing it out frequently. There are a number of chemicals and preparations that are safe and effective for cleaning finished wood, but since you don't want to use anything that could conceivably leave an oily or soapy residue which could find its way into the bass string windings, simple water is the safest bet. Some technicians recommend using a very diluted solution of white vinegar (two tablespoons per gallon warm water). Although vinegar will soften hide glue (used in older pianos), such a weak solution poses no danger.

Cleaning the soundboard beneath the strings is, of course, the tricky part. Piano supply houses sell lengths of thin flexible steel (with a cut-out at one end to insert a rag) for this purpose, but you can make your own tool. Cut a heavy metal coat hanger where it is twisted together and unbend it into a straight wire. Wrap tape around it completely, so it won't scratch the wood or strings, then bend one end of it forming a small hook. Push the wire (hook end first) under the strings at the treble break (the point of sectional division where there is a larger space between the strings) until it comes out underneath the lowest bass string. Secure your rag well to the hook; don't use too big a rag, or it won't pass under the strings. If you have an assistant, tie a string to one corner of the rag and have your helper hold it at the bass end so you can work the rag back and forth between you from both sides of the piano. If you are working alone, just use the wire to manipulate the rag. Work slowly and carefully, rinsing and wringing the rag frequently.

Next work the rag the other way, toward the high treble end. To clean under the highest treble strings may require taking out the action to reach that small section of soundboard by hand directly from underneath. If you opt to do this (instructions for removing a grand action are in the March-April '83 issue), use this opportunity to vacuum or brush any dirt out of the now exposed key bed, being careful not to disturb the damper and sostenuto mechanisms at the rear.

If you wish to clean the damper heads (the wood pieces over the strings to which the damper felt is attached), it is best to go over them very lightly with a dry dust cloth; you don't want to risk bending the damper wires or getting the felt wet.

When you are all done, replace the lid the same way you took it out. It is sometimes difficult to line up both hinges together, so when you get one lined up, stick in the pin to hold it in position and then line up the other one. Finally, raise the lid, step back, and admire your clean soundboard!

**ME**